MEDIA
ENTERTAINMENT

ALLISON EDEN | NICHOLAS BOWMAN | MATTHEW GRIZZARD

Kendall Hunt
publishing company

Dedication

We would like to, as a team, dedicate this textbook to our graduate advisor, Dr. Ron Tamborini, Professor of Communication at Michigan State University. Without his guidance, insight, understanding, and great patience, this book would not have been possible. Thank you for all the Wednesdays and Fridays you spent with us, molding us into the scholars we are today.

CONTENTS

ACKNOWLEDGMENTS

We would like to acknowledge the following media entertainment scholars who have paved the way for us. These scholars have enriched our understanding of the place media entertainment holds in our lives. Their work has—and continues to—both delight and enlighten us.

Albert Bandura, Gary Bente, Frank Biocca, Jennings Bryant, Joanne Cantor, David Ewoldsen, Bradley Greenberg, Tilo Hartmann, Herta Herzog, Cindy Hoffner, Silvia Knobloch-Westerwick, Annie Lang, Marie-Louise Mares, Harold Mendelsohn, Robin Nabi, Mary Beth Oliver, Art Raney, Meghan Sanders, John Sherry , Ron Tamborini, Peter Vorderer, Dolf Zillmann

We would like to thank the students of MSU COM 375, who served as the beta-readers for the first draft of these chapters: Madalena Benson, Caroline Brom, Andy Dobias, Ryan Gilbert, Karley Guidry, Brooke Henderson, Kate Lafrenz, Trent Lyons, Katherine Milke, Simone Mosby, Abbey Olszewski, Sydney Plichta, Keaton Safar, Adam Schaeding, Taylor Thompson, and Alyse Vanacker.

We would also like to thank Joshua Baldwin, who served as the editorial assistant for the book.

Personal Acknowledgements

I owe a great debt to those who have spent time talking with, thinking about, and testing theories of entertainment with me. This includes my current or former colleagues Ron Tamborini, John Sherry, David Ewoldsen, Tilo Hartmann, Benjamin Johnson, Elly Konijn, Morgan Ellithorpe, Rene Weber, as well as the co-authors of this book, Nick Bowman and Matthew Grizzard. I also would like to thank all my students over the years who have given me the privilege of their time and curiosity in developing thoughts on this topic, particularly Lindsay Hahn, Joomi Lee, Britt Hoeksema, and Kevin Kryston. I would also like to acknowledge my husband, Jason Weller, for his constant love and support, and my children, Hazel and Lucas, for their ability to distract me from even the most entertaining media.

—Allison Eden

I was introduced to the study of media entertainment by Ron Tamborini, who showed me how to take seriously and rigorously a topic that most would find trivial and unimportant (those people, of course, have yet to read this book). To Ron, I sincerely enjoyed and appreciated your time and care, and I only hope that this book is evidence that at least some of those lessons stuck. To my family, I am grateful for their unpaid copy-editing and their willingness to be my sounding board: Jaime, Stella, and Izzy are the best support staff that anyone could have. To Mary and David and Nathan, I am thankful for the models of perseverance that you each provide on a daily basis. To my co-authors Allison and Matt, I can think of no more mismatched and perfect of a team for this project, and the next ones.

—Nick Bowman

When I think back to my scholarly journey, I'm reminded of the Talking Heads' song *Once in a Lifetime*: "Well, how did I get here?" The answer to this question for me is my partner in crime, Alison Grizzard. She encouraged me to apply to graduate school, left a good job and moved with me during the Great Recession when I actually got in, stopped me from dropping out during the darkest days of the core, and even worked in the lab helping me to collect data for my dissertation. We've had good times and bad, but through it all she keeps me going.

To my daughter, Violet Jane: Yes, you can be a scientist who studies TV. It's a real job, believe it or not. I love you and your curiosity, and I hope you read this book someday.

To my co-authors: Thank you for being on this journey with me. I'm glad it's over.

—Matt Grizzard

CHAPTER 1

Why Entertainment?

"There are few things less entertaining than trying to define mass entertainment" (Bosshart & Macconi, 1998).

The What, Why, and How of Media Entertainment

What is media entertainment? Are some media, like video games and television, more central to entertainment than others, like books and the Internet? Are specific types of content, like action movies or fantasy novels, more entertaining than others, like documentaries and nonfiction books? What about the responses to content and media? If something made me laugh or cheer, does that mean it is more entertaining than something that made me cry or feel afraid? Is entertainment constantly variable, changing based on who we are with and what we are doing, or how we think about an experience?

These questions have concerned people for centuries. However, with the advent of easily accessible media technology delivering content and entertainment 24 hours a day, they have become even more pressing in today's world. According to recent American Time Use Surveys, media entertainment—including watching TV, playing games, surfing the Internet, or reading—occupies on average 3.5 hours of an average day. More than 90% of the population reports using some form of media for entertainment, relaxation, or leisure during the day. Yet despite the prevalence of entertainment in daily life, defining what entertainment is and understanding how exposure to entertainment influences us continues to pose challenges for scholars and students.

In this book, we will examine the current state of media entertainment research, and couch it in understandings of traditional mass communication and media psychology research. We will attempt to answer the questions posed above, and allow readers the chance to examine their own entertainment use, and the effects of their use. We have worked to frame the text in language and examples that are timely and relevant for today's students, as well as historical examples that have remained and are likely to remain relevant into the near future.

After reading this chapter students will be able to:

- Understand challenges in defining media entertainment
- Clarify how entertainment and enjoyment are related
- Be able to list important definitions of enjoyment used in research

How <u>Not</u> to Define Entertainment

There are several methods that you could take to define entertainment. You might first be tempted to define entertainment based on medium. You might believe, for example, that some media are simply more entertaining than others: Television, video games, and movies are simply more entertaining than books and newspapers. However, this type of definition quickly gets difficult to apply. Is the *Harry Potter* book series less entertaining than educational video games like *Math Blasters* simply because the former is a series of novels and the latter is a series of video games? Can you think of a boring film versus an entertaining film, despite both being the same medium? Can you think of newspapers and other news programming that are, at times, entertaining? Clearly a definition based on medium is not going to work.

Another route that you might be tempted to take is to base the definition on the feelings elicited by the experience. Being sad and scared aren't feelings that we typically think of as positive and rewarding, whereas feeling happy is. Yet, sadness and fear are central emotions to several forms of highly popular and profitable media content. Tearjerkers are routinely nominated for, and often win, the Best Picture category at the Academy Awards, and horror is one of the most profitable genres for movie producers.

Yet, if we can't define entertainment based solely on medium or content, how can we define it? Maybe what is entertainment depends on a host of factors and can't be isolated to any one technology, person, or experience. More on this later, but first let's think about how some major changes in entertainment technology have helped to illustrate the need for a better definition of entertainment.

Entertainment Technology

Consider some of the major technological changes in the past three decades that have altered where we find entertainment: In the 1980s, few would have classified home-computers as entertainment. Early home computers were mainly used for record keeping, accounting, and other calculation-based tasks (**see Sidebar: Fancy Typewriters**). When cellphones gained popularity in the 1990s, their only use was for making phone calls. Unless you were dialing 1–900 numbers, there was little entertainment to be had with a telephone. In the early 2000s, Internet videos were rare; the first viral videos were relatively simplistic, featuring crude animation and graphics, and hosted on an array of sites, usually in a simple flash animation file. YouTube didn't exist until February of 2005, and few predicted it would become an entertainment hub. **Technological convergence**, or the combining of various means of communication into one form, has allowed for various types of entertainment to be delivered through the same device. The Internet and streaming technology, meanwhile, have broken the traditional appointment-viewing model for entertainment, and introduced on-demand entertainment accessible at any moment.

Technological convergence

The combining of various communication and technology media into a single medium or device

---

Sidebar Fancy Typewriters

For most of the students reading this book, it can be difficult to imagine a time in which visual and audio entertainment content wasn't readily available on some sort of computer—a desktop, laptop, tablet, or even a smartphone. Likewise, these different devices have become increasingly more affordable, with functional laptops available for under $200.

However, if you return to the early 1980s, you will see a very different type of computer. Early computers, such as the Sinclair ZX80, looked more like calculators than computers. They plugged into a home television for a monitor (and had about one millionth of the processing power of the smartphone in many people's pockets today). They were also prohibitively expensive. The original Macintosh home

(Continued)

computer was released in 1984 and cost nearly $2,500 (or $6,200 adjusted for inflation by 2018). Those early computers were also very simple. They usually had a basic keyboard interface and some ability to display on-screen text, and were primarily used for data entry. In writing for *BBC Magazine* (reproduced at https://www.historyextra. com/period/20th-century/a-brave-new-world-the-1980s-home-computer-boom/), computer historian Tom Lean explained:

> "Computer enthusiasts used their machines to catalogue record collections, balance household budgets, store recipes, and carry out other domestic chores."

Of course, along with these more domestic tasks, even early computers had entertainment software, including video games (such as Atari's *Adventure*, https://my.ign.com/atari/adventure). As more computers began to enter people's homes—adoption rates were less than 10% of U.S. households in 1984 and increased to more than 50% by 2000 according to the U.S. Census Bureau—developers began to use their increasing technological sophistication to bring new entertainment experiences into people's homes. By many estimates, the global computer games market (which only considers games played on desktop or laptop computers) is expected to reach as much as $33 billion by 2020. Mobile games are an even larger market at more than $70 billion worldwide. Many people use their computers and smartphones to watch television and movies, and to surf the Internet. Those fancy typewriters of the 1980s have grown to provide multimedia experiences that span a range of functional, social, and massively entertaining technologies.

Because the last three decades have seen an uptick of new entertainment technologies and outlets, it may seem that defining or understanding media entertainment is a constantly changing task. But many of these new forms of technology didn't change what we find entertaining, they simply altered what we have access to and how we might experience it. What we hope to illustrate in this textbook is that, by focusing on the *psychological* underpinnings of media entertainment, we can see relatively consistent and stable patterns in how, when, and why people seek out and spend time with media entertainment, as well as systematic patterns in the effects this consumption may have, regardless of which technology is used.

In fact, many of the things that make media entertaining for us are remarkably similar to what humans have found entertaining for millennia. Using a psychological approach to understanding media is broadly known as **media psychology**. This type of approach can be particularly useful for defining entertainment, because even though entertainment technology seems to change at a record pace, our biology and psychology have remained pretty much the same.

media psychology
The study of how media content is related to human thoughts, feelings, and behaviors

Defining Entertainment Using Media Psychology

When you ask yourself, "What do I find entertaining?," the first response probably includes the words "lighthearted," "fun," or "pleasurable." Enjoyment as a concept has been central to media effects research for decades, though an exact definition of the term has, like entertainment, proven difficult. Many researchers have attempted to define entertainment and examining their definitions can help us decide what we mean when we say something is entertainment.

For example, Wurst (2005) simply uses the term "enjoyment:" "[W]hen we look at what entertainment means for those who use the media and expect to be entertained by their content, it is enjoyment that we most often find" (p. 389). Mendelsohn (1966) defines mass entertainment as the experiencing of pleasure from the mass media of communication. There is a general understanding of enjoyment, which encompasses liking, pleasure, attraction to, joy, and delight in media entertainment. We call this positive feeling a **hedonic response**. If you think about media you "enjoy," you probably have a pretty good idea what that looks and feels like.

hedonic response
The basic positive feeling when consuming entertaining media

Bosshart and Macconi (1998) read and studied all research in media entertainment from historical, anthropological, and psychological traditions. They listed the different emotions entertainment may elicit, including psychological relaxation, change and diversion, stimulation, fun, atmosphere, and joy. In psychological terms, they described entertainment as having active, tension-reducing, and positive components. They also tried to address notions of physical presence (think about if you've ever felt like you were in the room with friends during an intense gaming session), personality of the user, and existing social networks. Despite this exhaustive listing of concepts related to entertainment, Bosshart and Macconi ended up defining entertainment primarily in terms of the enjoyment or pleasure: "After all is said and done, entertainment is *pleasure*. It means experiencing pleasure by witnessing or being exposed to something" (Bosshart & Macconi, 1998, p. 5).

However, pleasure doesn't encompass all of entertainment. We can experience great entertainment from watching the trials and tribulations of contestants on public singing or talent contests, or those trudging through dark times in fantasy lands. Watching sports is considered entertaining (although less so if our favorite team or player loses). Therefore, stopping at pleasure doesn't quite get at everything entertainment does or is. Perhaps the most often-used definition that encompasses more than pleasure comes from work by Zillmann and Bryant (1994), who define entertainment as follows:

> "*Any activity designed to delight* and, to a smaller degree, *enlighten* through the exhibition of the *fortunes or misfortunes of others*, but also through the *display of special skills* by other and/or self," a definition that encompasses "any kind of game or play, athletic or not, competitive or not, whether witnessed only, taken part in, or performed alone," including "musical performances by self for self or others, of others for self, or with others" (p. 438, emphasis added).

This definition broadens the notion of entertainment to include tragedy, sport, video games, and public events. Peter Vorderer added to this definition of entertainment by including the notion of **play** as central to understanding media entertainment. He defined entertainment as "a form of playing, that is, a form of coping with reality" (Vorderer, 2001, p. 256). Entertainment, in his view, is ". . . an activity that is most often characterized by different forms of pleasure, but—in certain situations—also by unpleasant aspects. It is an intrinsically motivated action that usually leads to a temporary change in perceived reality and that is repeated quite often by people who are, during this process, less intellectually vivid and attentive than they could be" (p. 257).

In terms of horror and tragedy, specifically, Vorderer, Klimmt, and Ritterfeld (2004) stated that even negative experiences can be termed "enjoyment," as enjoyment is a *multifaceted response to several user and media-based prerequisites that manifest themselves in several distinct emotional and cognitive responses.* Individual reactions may appear to be as diverse as serenity, suspense, sadness, sensory delight, and achievement or self-efficacy and still be considered enjoyable by the user. In order to get

play

A pleasurable activity where individuals change their perceived reality into an imaginative reality enjoyment from media, users must have a willingness to suspend disbelief, a capacity and desire to have affinity or empathy for the characters, an ability to relate to characters, a sense of being present in the media, and an interest in a specific topic, problem, or knowledge domain.

At the same time, other researchers, such as Oliver and Raney (2011), have suggested that negative experiences within entertainment are often more meaningful than experiences that are only positive. Meaningful media experiences are different enough from hedonic understandings of enjoyment that they deserve their own definition as **eudaimonic** media experiences. Eudaimonia is a Greek term meaning someone stretching toward righteousness and well-being. In entertainment research, eudaimonic motivations or gratifications for consuming media are those which do not lead to immediate enjoyment, but may lead to greater well-being over time (**Sidebar: The Paradox of Sad Films**). Hedonic and eudaimonic entertainment can be thought of as complementary to the experience of media entertainment. These experiences are also discussed or defined as enjoyment (hedonic) versus appreciation (eudaimonic) responses to entertainment.

eudaimonic response

A more complex feeling focused on righteousness, well-being, and meaning in life

Sidebar   The Paradox of Sad Films

The American Film Institute maintains a list of movies that are largely regarded as the top 100 greatest American films of all time (https://www.afi.com/100years/movies10.aspx), and on that list you'll quickly recognize several movies it would be difficult to say viewers enjoy from a purely hedonic perspective. Films such as *Citizen Kane* (No. 1), *The Godfather* (No. 2), *Gone with the Wind* (No. 6), and *Schindler's List* (No. 8) are emotionally complicated and complex experiences.

For entertainment scholars, the presence of so many gloomy movies on a top 100 film list presents something of a paradox—why would movies that seem so sad and stressful be so popular, if enjoyment is a positive and fun experience? Although the paradox of tragedy has puzzled philosophers for centuries (see Hume's *On Tragedy* as part of his *Four Dissertations*), media psychologist Mary Beth Oliver studied this question empirically using social science methods in a series of studies in 1993. In those studies, Oliver (1993) developed what she called the Sad Film Scale, which asked people to respond to questions such as "I like watching sad movies because I can relate to the feelings and

(Continued)

emotions of the characters" and "I didn't like the film because I prefer to feel happy than sad while watching a film." The results of this work suggested that many audience saw feeling sad as a facilitator rather than a barrier to enjoying a movie (for example, they might agree with the first statement but not the second one)—especially people with high levels of empathy. For those people (and for others like them), sad films were still very entertaining, even if they weren't enjoyable. From this study, dozens of scholars have begun to explore dimensions of enjoyment such as meaningfulness, elevation, and moral beauty, in addition to pure enjoyment.

You try it! *The YouTube channel "Above Average" prepared a tongue-in-cheek look at the "science" behind Pixar Studio's SadLab (https://www. youtube.com/watch?v=9SXLonaflJw). Give it a view, and see if you can recognize some of the movies in the video. Which ones made you laugh? Which ones made you cry? Did you feel both emotions, or others? Would you say you enjoyed the film?*

Enjoyment: A Functional Perspective

Most recent work has begun to move away from trying to define entertainment and enjoyment. Instead, current perspectives try to focus on what entertainment *does* for people—what we would call a **functional perspective**. Humans are pretty good at situating their environments to suit their basic needs. Typically, our choices for entertainment media are pretty easy for us to control—we can watch a video on demand, or scroll through a social media feed, or play a video game on our mobile phone, or pick up a book. If entertainment was providing little or no benefits to the user, we would not expect it to be so central to so many societies and cultures, nor would we see people using entertainment for such long periods of time. Nor would we expect people to consume entertainment and manage to continue functioning in their day-to-day lives.

Functional perspectives, therefore, recognize that entertainment may be serving a purpose for the user beyond pure escape or pleasure. Enjoyment is thought to be tied to the **intrinsic motivations** that drive individuals to engage in particular activities. In these models, the experience of enjoyment acts a sign to the user that they are doing a good thing—the media either has satisfied or will satisfy basic needs, or will

functional perspective
The idea that outcomes, such as enjoyment, are derived from the fulfillment of individual needs and wants

intrinsic motivations
Any motivation to perform and action that is driven by one's internal desires rather than external forces

be training the viewer for some situation to be encountered later in life. These ideas are based off of understandings of intrinsic motivation as defined by Ryan and Deci's (2000) **Self-Determination Theory**. Self-determination theory suggests that people are motivated to do things which satisfy basic psychological needs for control (autonomy), social interaction (relatedness), and feeling good about their skills (competence). In terms of media, Ryan, Rigby, and Przybylski (2006) surveyed large samples of video gamers and found that video games were particularly good at satisfying these basic psychological needs.

Think of playing a game like *Fortnite*. As noted in the sidebar (**Sidebar: In Praise of Fortnite**), when viewed from a functional, psychological perspective, we can see that this "violent video game" allows players freedom to exercise choices in a new environment, ability to train and get better at specific skills, all while connecting with important friends. When viewed that way, spending time with entertainment is serving a higher psychological purpose, and is potentially functional to the user.

Self-Determination Theory
A theory that argues that psychological well-being is derived from the fulfillment of three intrinsic motivations: autonomy, relatedness, and competence

Sidebar — In Praise of Fortnite

In June 2017, EpicGames released a free-to-play first-person shooter (specifically, a **multiplayer online battle arena, or MOBA**) called *Fortnite*. One of the more popular versions of the game is called *Battle Royale* in which 100 different players are dropped from a flying bus onto a game arena, and must scavenge for weapons so that they can fend off and eventually kill all other players. During gameplay, a fluke storm appears that starts to destroy much of the game's environment, shrinking down the battlefield until the remaining players are in an increasingly smaller combat zone. The final player standing is the winner.

The game was an instant success, being nominated for and winning several awards, including the *2018 Teen Choice Awards* and *2018 Webby Awards* and hosting as many as 125 million players. As the game grew in popularity, many parents expressed concerns that it would harm children, from distracting them from schoolwork to exposing them to strangers with ill intent. However, one blogger Laura Jean Baker wrote for the website "Scary Mommy" that some of these concerns stem from a misunderstanding about *Fortnite* as a source of entertainment. In Baker's blog post (https://www.scarymommy.com/in-praise-of-fortnite/), one

multiplayer online battle arena, or MOBA
A video game genre in which players work in teams to battle each other in a confined environment

(Continued)

of the things that she mentions is that the game is highly collaborative, as players have to work together to help their squads survive. In this way, *Fortnite* can be a very social experience that encourages a sense of relatedness among players in ways not too different than playing sports or engaging in other team activities.

The functional model of entertainment has been expanded upon by Hartmann (2013) in his model of media entertainment as a result of recreation and psychological growth. This model describes entertainment as providing various affective and psychological benefits to the user, for instance by inducing relaxation and a supportive nonthreatening environment, or by providing humor and entertainment in order to promote levels of self-regulation after a hard day of work. Hartmann (2013) specified that media exposure will be enjoyable if it allows users to balance their physiological states and replenish exhausted resources. He suggested that even challenging or negatively valenced media may provide enjoyment to the user as long as the challenge is relevant, engaged in through the user's own volition, and a match for the user's ability and volitional energy.

How to Measure Enjoyment?

There is no standard scale for measuring enjoyment (**Sidebar: Scheming for Enjoyment**). Enjoyment has been most commonly measured either with single-item measures (e.g., "How much did you enjoy/like this?") or with short scales that capture the pleasant and fun dimension of media entertainment. These short scales often contain several items that, when combined, measure a broader sense of enjoyment (e.g., "it was fun for me to watch this movie; this movie was entertaining; I had a good time watching this movie," Oliver & Bartsch, 2010, p. 60; "this game was enjoyable, entertaining, appealing," Tamborini et al., 2011, p. 1030). However, reliance on single-item or short, single-dimension measures of enjoyment has been criticized by leaving out important components of enjoyment, as well as ignoring other dimensions of entertainment broadly. In response to this critique, multidimensional scales for enjoyment and entertainment have been created measuring dimensions such as fun, suspense, moving/thought provoking, and lasting impressions of content.

Sidebar Scheming for Enjoyment

When doing **quantitative research**, one of the challenges that we have is the best way to measure a given concept—such as the notion of enjoyment that you've been reading about in this chapter. There can be lots of ways to try and measure something, but one of the popular ones in **social science** research is to create **scales** in which we ask people to answer a set of similar questions that might seem related to, but aren't exactly, the main concept.

For example, if we were to think of concepts that are related to enjoyment, we can listen to how people talk about things that they enjoy. They might describe those things as being fun, exciting, and arousing . . . and definitely not boring. Those different flavors of enjoyment make up what scientists call the **conceptual scheme** of enjoyment—representing different things that are often associated with the **construct** of enjoyment.

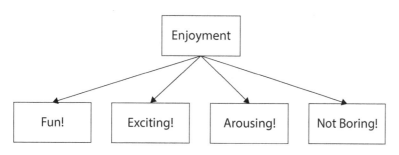

Then, we could convert this conceptual scheme into different items, such as:

- This thing was fun.
- This thing was exciting.
- This thing was arousing.
- This thing was not boring.

And once we have those items? We can ask people how much they agree with each of those items, such as a **Likert scale** or some other way of measuring it. If each item can be answered on a scale from "1: Strongly Disagree" to "7: Strongly Agree" we can then add up or average people's answers and get an estimate of how much they actually enjoyed the thing!

You try it! *If you had to come up with a conceptual scheme for enjoyment, what items would you include that aren't already included above?*

quantitative research

Scientific research that uses numbers to describe and measure phenomena

social science

The study of human behavior using the scientific method

scales

An instrument used to quantify a phenomenon

conceptual scheme

The different components that represent various dimensions of a theoretical construct

construct

A phenomenon that is theoretically understood but may not be directly observable

Likert scale

A measurement that asks individuals to rate how much they agree or disagree with a statement

Psychophysiology
The study of a person's mental processes through observation of physical responses, such as pulse, sweat, and eye movement

functional magnetic resonance imaging
A method for measuring the amount of activity in different brain regions by scanning the amount of oxygen-rich blood in parts of the brain; often used in psychophysiology approaches to research

flow
An intrinsically rewarding experience that occurs when the challenge of an activity is equally matched by a person's skill at performing the activity

These measures are, however, based on the user's ability to accurately report on mental states and emotions after exposure to a media stimulus. Can we measure enjoyment in the brain or body? **Psychophysiology** and brain imaging (via **functional magnetic resonance imaging**) have been proposed as alternatives to self-report measures. In terms of psychophysiology, enjoyment is primarily measured through facial electromyography, which captures involuntary muscle movements at the cheek and brow. Skin conductance can be used to measure arousal levels. These have been correlated with user experiences of enjoyment in video games and film, yet no standard measure of enjoyment via psychophysiological measures yet exists (see Potter & Bolls, 2012, for a comprehensive review).

In terms of measuring enjoyment via brain imaging, simply correlating neural activation with periods of self-expressed enjoyment is perhaps the most obvious way to measure neural enjoyment. Hasson et al. (2004) showed 5 viewers 30 minutes of Sergio Leone's film *The Good, the Bad, and the Ugly* (1966) while subjects lay in an fMRI scanner. While watching the film, all five subjects showed similar patterns of blood flow in the brain—and did not show the same intercorrelation during periods in the scanner when the film was not playing. In follow-up work, Hasson et al. (2008) found the strong intercorrelation while viewers were watching films playing in chronological order—but not for the same images when edited out-of-order. Thus, there seems to be something about cinema that can control viewer's brain responses, and viewers the same story in similar ways.

In terms of video games, Mathiak and Weber (2006) found that, by having players talk aloud as they watched videos of themselves playing a video game in a scanner, positive and negative play experiences in the game could be correlated with brain activation in specific brain areas associated with reward. However, one can also look at links between the activation of different networks. Weber et al. (2009) hypothesized that the experience of **flow** (in general and insofar as it pertains to media enjoyment) could be understood as a synchronization of specialized networks in the brain. To test this idea, Huskey, Wilcox, and Weber (2018) had subjects play a video game (Asteroid Impact) while in an fMRI scanner. Conditions leading to greatest flow experiences were also associated with the greatest network synchrony.

Conclusion

In this chapter, we have introduced the complexity of entertainment, put forth several possible ways to conceptualize and discuss entertainment, linked entertainment with enjoyment, and reviewed definitions of enjoyment. Despite how important entertainment seems to be for the human experience, it has been difficult to define due to sociological or technological forces, and often discounted as a trivial study.

One way to broaden and build entertainment research is by understanding the psychology of entertainment, starting with the emotion of enjoyment. Although early definitions of enjoyment were simple and focused on hedonic responses, alternative definitions later on examined media enjoyment as a complex set of responses to media including behavioral, affective, and cognitive components. Most recently, enjoyment has been conceptualized as a signal that we are satisfying a basic psychological or physiological need via our media behavior.

Media research and theory seem to be moving away from conceptualizations of enjoyment as a simple process, linked only to pleasure, and generated via specific media content. Instead, enjoyment is being conceptualized as a dynamic, individual, and functional signifier of need satisfaction, which may occur over the entire media experience. What remains the same, despite these advancements, is the association of enjoyment with a desirable outcome for the viewer, and the presence of entertainment media as an important driving force of this outcome.

 # Key Terms

Technological convergence The combining of various communication and technology media into a single medium or device

Media psychology The study of how media content is related to human thoughts, feelings, and behaviors

Hedonic Response The basic positive feeling when consuming entertaining media

Play A pleasurable activity where individuals change their perceived reality into an imaginative reality

Eudaimonic Response A more complex feeling focused on righteousness, well-being, and meaning in life

Functional perspective The idea that outcomes, such as enjoyment, are derived from the fulfillment of individual needs and wants

Intrinsic motivation Any motivation to perform and action that is driven by one's internal desires rather than external forces

Self-Determination Theory A theory that argues that psychological well-being is derived from the fulfillment of three intrinsic motivations: autonomy, relatedness, and competence

Multiplayer online battle arena (MOBA) A video game genre in which players work in teams to battle each other in a confined environment

Quantitative research Scientific research that uses numbers to describe and measure phenomena

Social science The study of human behavior using the scientific method

Scale(s) An instrument used to quantify a phenomenon

Conceptual scheme The different components that represent various dimensions of a theoretical construct

Construct A phenomenon that is theoretically understood but may not be directly observable

Likert scale A measurement that asks individuals to rate how much they agree or disagree with a statement

Psychophysiology The study of a person's mental processes through observation of physical responses, such as pulse, sweat, and eye movement

Functional magnetic resonance imaging (fMRI) A method for measuring the amount of activity in different brain regions by scanning the amount of oxygen-rich blood in parts of the brain; often used in psychophysiology approaches to research

Flow An intrinsically rewarding experience that occurs when the challenge of an activity is equally matched by a person's skill at performing the activity

References

Bosshart, L., & Macconi, I. (1998). Defining "entertainment." *Communication Research Trends, 18*(3), 3–6.

Hartmann, T. (2013). Media entertainment as a result of recreation and psychological growth. In E. Scharrer (Ed.), *Media effects/media psychology, Vol. 5. The international encyclopedia of media studies*, A. Valdivia (Gen. Ed.) (pp. 170–188). Boston, MA: Wiley-Blackwell.

Hasson, U., Nir, Y., Levy, I., Fuhrmann, G., & Malach, R. (2004). Intersubject synchronization of cortical activity during natural vision. *Science, 303*(5664), 1634–1640. https://doi.org/10.1126/science.1089506

Hasson, U., Yang, E., Vallines, I., Heeger, D. J., & Rubin, N. (2008). A hierarchy of temporal receptive windows in human cortex. *The Journal of Neuroscience, 28*(10), 2539–2550. doi: 10.1523/JNEUROSCI.5487-07.2008

Huskey, R., Wilcox, S., & Weber, R. (2018). Network neuroscience reveals distinct neuromarkers of flow during media use. *Journal of Communication, 68*(5), 872–895. doi: 10.1093/joc/jqy043

Mathiak, K., & Weber, R. (2006). Toward brain correlates of natural behavior: fMRI during violent video games. *Human Brain Mapping, 27*(12), 948–956. https://doi-org.proxy2.cl.msu.edu/10.1002/hbm.20234

Mendelsohn, H. (1966). Mass entertainment. New Haven, CT: College & University Press.

Oliver, M. B. (1993). Exploring the paradox of the enjoyment of sad films. *Human Communication Research, 19*(3), 315–342. doi: 10.1111/j.1468-2958.1993.tb00304.x

Oliver, M. B., & Bartsch, A. (2010). Appreciation as audience response: Exploring entertainment gratifications beyond hedonism. *Human Communication Research, 36*(1), 53–81. doi:10.1111/j.1468-2958.2009.01368.x

Oliver, M. B., & Raney, A. A. (2011). Entertainment as pleasurable and meaningful: Identifying hedonic and eudaimonic motivations for entertainment consumption. *Journal of Communication, 61*(5), 984–1004. doi:10.1111/j.1460-2466.2011.01585.x

Potter, R. F., & Bolls, P. (2012). *Psychophysiological measurement and meaning: Cognitive and emotional processing of media.* New York: Routledge.

Ryan, R. M., & Deci, E. L. (2000). Self-determination theory and the facilitation of intrinsic motivation, social development, and well-being. *American Psychologist, 55*(1), 68–78. doi: 10.1037//0003-066x.55.1.68

Ryan, R. M., Rigby, C. S., & Przybylski, A. (2006). The motivational pull of video games: A self-determination theory approach. *Motivation and Emotion, 30*(4), 344–360. doi: 10.1007/s11031-006-9051-8

Tamborini, R., Grizzard, M., David Bowman, N., Reinecke, L., Lewis, R. J., & Eden, A. (2011). Media enjoyment as need satisfaction: The contribution of hedonic and nonhedonic needs. *Journal of Communication, 61*(6), 1025–1042. doi:10.1111/j.1460-2466.2011.01593.x

Vorderer, P. (2001). It's all entertainment—sure. But what exactly is entertainment? Communication research, media psychology, and the explanation of entertainment experiences. *Poetics, 29*(4-5), 247–261. doi: 10.1016/s0304-422x(01)00037-7

Vorderer, P., Klimmt, C., & Ritterfeld, U. (2004). Enjoyment: At the heart of media entertainment. *Communication Theory, 14*(4), 388–408. doi: 10.1111/j.1468-2885.2004.tb00321.x

Weber, R., Tamborini, R., Westcott-Baker, A., & Kantor, B. (2009). Theorizing flow and media enjoyment as cognitive synchronization of attentional and reward networks. *Communication Theory, 19*(4), 397–422. doi: 10.1111/j.1468-2885.2009.01352.x

Wurst, K. A. (2005). *Fabricating Pleasure: Fashion, Entertainment, and Cultural Consumption in Germany, 1780–1830.* Detroit: Wayne State University Press.

Zillmann, D., Bryant, J., 1994. Entertainment as media effect. In J. Bryant, D. Zillmann. (Eds.), *Media effects: Advances in theory and research.* Lawrence Erlbaum Associates, Hillsdale, NJ, pp. 437–461.

Suggested Readings

Hasson, U., Landesman, O., Knappmeyer, B., Vallines, I., Rubin, N., & Heeger, D. J. (2008). Neurocinematics: The neuroscience of film. *Projections: The Journal of Movies and Mind, 2*(1), 1–26. doi: 10.3167/proj.2008.020102

Hume, D. (1757). *Four dissertations.* London: A. Millar.

United States. (2017). *American time use survey.* Washington, DC: U.S. Bureau of Labor Statistics.

CHAPTER 2

Early Understandings of Entertainment Selection

"The expansion of choice has become an explosion of choice"

—Sheena Iyengar

As of this writing, Netflix has over 4,000 movies and over 1,600 TV series in its streaming catalog, with an estimated 34,000 hours of programming (Pressman, 2015). If you binge-watched Netflix for 8 hours a day, 7 days a week, it would take you 11 years, 235 days to watch everything available for streaming. The media landscape has become saturated with content. There are still all the major players producing content, from film studios, to cable and network television, to book publishers. But, added to that are new media outlets which feature self-published books on Amazon, web series on YouTube, and the streaming services' original programming. But even in this saturated entertainment mediascape, we still manage to find and select programs to watch, games to play, and books to read. How does this happen? What drives selection of certain programs over others, and why do people develop systematic preferences for one type versus another? This chapter will examine media selection and choice models, with a focus on how people develop their preferences and select shows to watch, as well as the underlying mechanisms of selection behavior.

Objectives

After reading this chapter students will be able to:

➤ List and describe dominant theories of media selection
➤ Understand under which contexts and circumstances particular theories will apply
➤ Describe their own media use based on these theories

Describing media selection has been a goal of mass communication research since the earliest days of the discipline. For example, in their landmark study on transmission of political attitudes via radio and newspaper exposure, Lazarsfeld, Berelson, and Gaudet (1948) note that "actual exposure does *not* parallel availability. Availability *plus* predispositions determines exposure" (p. 89, emphasis in original.) In other words, media consumers are selective in what they choose to view, listen to, or read from available media. Moreover, our selectivity relates to our predispositions, which might include values, interests, and experiences. Notably, selective exposure to media content can occur even if one only received one channel: He or she could choose to watch only certain programs or nothing at all.

Media choice therefore is not a theory in and of itself—instead, media choice is a behavior, and understanding this behavior means drawing from *other* theories of human behavior to understand why and how people make choices.

The most important models for explaining media selection can be categorized based on their underlying assumptions. Uses and Gratifications approaches assume that viewers select content and channels to satisfy different motivational and psychological needs. Mood management theory (MMT) and the selective exposure paradigm formulated by Zillmann argues that mood regulation and reducing cognitive dissonance are major forces which determine our media choice behavior. The habit model argues that media selection is more of a habit—an unthinking decision that is influenced by past behaviors and current psychological state. Finally, there are cognitive decision models that argue media choice is a rational decision, and like other decisions it is influenced by heuristic decision-making, or decision-making based on cognitive shortcuts, as well as more deliberative decision-making. Although there are other theories, these broad categories cover those most frequently discussed in terms of entertainment selection and preference, and we describe each in more detail in the following sections.

Uses and Gratifications of Entertainment

One of the most prolific mass communication theories to deal with media selection is Uses and Gratifications (Katz, Blumler, & Gurevitch, 1973). Uses and gratifications comes from a **functional approach** to understanding media. Functional approaches of media selection seek to understand the intents and purposes that media can serve in a consumer's life. Katz et al. (1973) explained the Uses and Gratifications approach as understanding "the social and psychological origins of needs, which generate expectations of the mass media or other sources, which lead to differential patterns of media exposure (or engagement in other activities), resulting in need gratifications and other consequences, perhaps mostly unintended ones." They also described six assumptions of the Uses and Gratifications approach which is displayed graphically below and described in detail on the following pages.

functional approach

A school of thought that argues that media use serves as a gratification of one's needs or wants

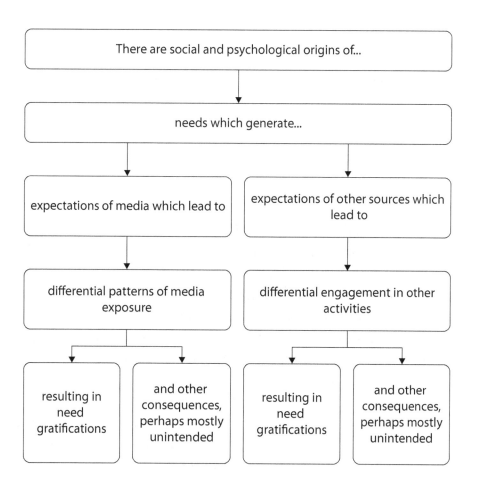

Assumptions of the Uses and Gratifications Approach

The Uses and Gratifications approach makes six assumptions about media and people. The first is that media use is *goal oriented and motivated*. That means that unintentional exposure to entertainment, such as catching a show while you pop in to talk to friends, would neither be selected for a use nor expected to satisfy your gratifications the way a show you selected yourself would have. The second assumption is that media users are *relatively active participants who select media that best Fulfill their needs*.

The third, fourth, and fifth assumptions deal with media effects. The third assumption is that media and content are *sources of influence among other potential sources*. In other words, although we may believe the media messages we consume have a strong effect, they are only one message among all the other possible messages you get during the day, such as face-to-face conversations with friends. Coupled rather than couple with assumption three, assumption four maintains that *media compete with other channels (i.e., alternatives) for need satisfaction*. If we have a psychological need for food, we are more likely to seek out food than turn to the Food Network. Assumption five is that *people are more influential than the media in the media effects process*. So while a movie might portray cigarette smoking as cool, if your family, friends, and work are all sending strong should be anti-smoking messages, you will be receiving a multitude of messages about one topic, from a variety of sources, and may not show a strong direct effect of watching media on your attitudes about smoking.

The sixth and final assumption is that *audience members can describe their needs in terms of motivations*. In other words, consumers of media can explain why and for what reason they made their media choice. This is critical for understanding Uses and Gratifications research methods. Remember Chapter 1? We discussed how hard it is to measure enjoyment. Yet Uses and Gratifications researchers assume that audiences can voice their motivations and gratifications from media, so self-report measures are accepted as a valid way to measure audience responses.

Lasswell (1948) suggested that all media serve one of three purposes for individuals: surveillance, or informing the viewer about the world; correlation, or helping the viewer to understand the relationship between events; and transmission, or educating the viewer about specific topics and helping to pass on cultural heritage. In the same book,

Lazarsfeld and Merton (1948) added the notion of entertainment to the three functions of mass media, but rather than categorize it as another function, they described it as a "narcotizing dysfunction." Media entertainment, in Lazarsfeld and Merton's view—distracted us from the more important things in the world and rather than help us and society function better, it led to distraction and impairments. Today, some types of media entertainment content are still often considered "bad" or "damaging" among certain groups (see Chapter 5). Although it would be unwise to completely ignore potential negatives related to media entertainment content, researchers now generally consider that there are positives associated with exposure to media entertainment as well. Indeed only two decades later, Wright (1960) discussed the role of entertainment as a critical and useful function of the mass media.

If media serve certain functions, Uses and Gratifications research is partially devoted to identifying what the functions are. Researchers have come up with multiple varied lists of uses and gratifications for all different kinds of media. The standard methodology for identifying uses and gratifications from media is to bring a bunch of users together, ask them what they use a medium for and what they get out of it, and then create a list of possible uses and gratifications out of that discussion. Then, researchers make that list into a survey, and give it to another set of folks who use that medium, to test out how best to categorize or group those uses and gratifications. Despite the invention of new media platforms since Lazarsfeld and Merton (1948), the four initial functions of media entertainment are ever present (**Sidebar: Smartphones and Gratifications**).

Sidebar   Smartphones and Gratifications

In Chapter 1, we discussed the notion of technological convergence, or combining several different means of communication into a single form or device. Perhaps no device represents convergence better than the smartphone. Market research firm eMarketer estimates that over 95% of Americans aged 18 to 34 own these devices, and use them for a variety of different functions: communicating with family and friends, checking emails and online documents, listening to music, watching streaming television and movie content, or even playing video games.

(Continued)

Perhaps one of the most telling signs that smartphones have long evolved from being mobile phones and now serve a wide variety of functions can be found in industry data into voice and data traffic patterns. For example, from 2013 through the third quarter of 2019, while voice traffic has remained rather flat (increasing by less than one-quarter of 1% each year), data traffic has grown dramatically during the same time period (Ericcson, 2018). This rapid increase in data traffic is a clear indicator that smartphones are serving a variety of uses beyond making phone calls—and probably, serving a variety of different gratifications beyond interpersonal communication. Consider that streaming 1 hour of Netflix takes about 1 gigabyte of data (3 GB if streamed in high definition), and browsing Instagram for 1 hour can use as much as 100 megabytes of data. Indeed, each of the more than two million apps available in Apple's App Market (or one million apps available in Google's Play Store) all require some amount of data to download, install, and operate efficiently. Far more than phones today, smartphones are used by billions daily to learn about the day's events (surveillance), make sense of their environment (correlation), feel connected to society at large (transmission), or simply take a break from a stressful day (entertainment).

You try it!   *Pick any app from your smartphone. How do you use that app? For what types of information or entertainment do you access that app? Now, think about the emotional gratifications you get from the app? Can you separate the two? Which model of uses and gratifications is closest to how you use that particular application?*

We can also think of uses and gratifications as broader categories of how we interact with and understand media. For example, Atkin (1985), characterizes uses of media as anticipated pragmatic goals—we may log onto an educational website with the hopes of learning something, or check the weather app to know what to wear that day. Gratifications, in Atkin's model, are the fleeting emotional responses that result from media so pleasure, arousal, relaxation, or satisfying a habit would all fall under this type of gratification. Rubin (1984) looked at uses as instrumental or active use of media for entertainment or information. He suggested uses can be characterized by a focus on specific content, information motivations, and higher perceived realism and attention. The gratifications aspect Rubin characterizes as being associated with habitual and time-consuming exposure with a focus on the medium, diffuse motives, less intentional or conscious selection, and heavier viewing patterns.

The Uses and Gratifications model was a reaction to a commonly held notion during the 1950s and 1960s that the audience was a passive receptacle for media messages. The primary question guiding these passive audience perspectives was, "What are media doing to us?" Uses and Gratifications perspectives flipped this question on its head. Assuming an active audience engaged in conscious selection, Uses and Gratifications researchers asked, "What are we doing with media?" Clearly viewers are selective about what they expose themselves too. But are viewers always aware of why they choose what they choose? Or, might there be forces that influence us that occur below conscious awareness? Let's turn now to media selection models which do not necessarily assume conscious selection—MMT and the Theory of Media Habits.

Mood Management Theory and The Selective Exposure Paradigm

To this point, we have been talking about media choices as being active and purposeful. This makes sense, because at some point a person has to do something in order to use media: Fire up a video game console, turn on a television set, scroll through a streaming music service, or surf the web (although increasingly, we can play games, watch TV, or listen to music all on the same device). Of course, once we've gained access to the media channel we want, we're usually faced with numerous different choices. We might have a dozen or so games to pick from, thousands of television or music channels, and half a billion or so different websites. After we've made the choice for media, how do we determine what we want to watch, play, or listen to?

Say you just came home from a long day of work. You are tired and frustrated with the office environment. While flipping through the channels, you come across a show about refurbishing old houses. This seems like the ticket! After a few minutes with the show, you are feeling more relaxed, less frustrated with your life, and you may even feel more energy returning. Yet, the next day, after a good night's sleep and while reading the morning news, you decide that show is just too boring, and instead select a show about sharks attacking pirates. What just happened? Why are your media choices so different from one state to the next?

Mood Management Theory

An entertainment selection theory which predicts that people will select media content to maximize positive feelings and minimize negative feelings

Selective Exposure Theory

A process of choosing what media content you will watch or listen to

mood(s)

(A) persistent emotional state

pleasure principle

The notion that people are motivated to maximize pleasure and to minimize pain; central to MMT

excitatory homeostasis

The process of maintaining an optimal (i.e., not too high or too low) level of arousal

In the 1980s, media psychologists Dolf Zillmann and Jennings Bryant (we've mentioned them quite a few times, in this book) proposed the affect-dependent theory of stimulus arrangement—now more commonly referred to as **Mood Management Theory** and discussed in conjunction with **Selective Exposure Theory** (SET; Zillmann & Bryant, 1985). They explained that often, even when we are not aware of it, our **moods** and emotions (see Chapter 6) can influence some of the impulsive decisions that we make. Consider how we tend to act when we are particularly stressed or bored. Stressed people will often seek a target to "let it all out" (a stress ball, punching bag, or maybe just screaming really loud for a moment) and bored people will often seek out any distraction to avoid falling asleep (doodling in a notebook or textbook, or daydreaming). None of these behaviors are particularly purposive, and we don't often plan them in advance. They just sort of happen. These behaviors represent people making subconscious choices and some involve rearranging their environment to try and disrupt noxious mood states. Since we have a great deal of control over which media programs we want to use, media is one way people can easily disrupt their mood states.

MMT was an initial attempt to explain how a person's mood might subconsciously influence their media selections. The theory is based on a concept called the **pleasure principle**, which suggests that people are motivated to maximize pleasure and minimize pain. For a person who is particularly bored (boredom often being marked by very low levels of arousal), a show with sharks might be just what the doctor (or at least, the media psychologist) ordered to shake off boredom and increase arousal to a pleasurable level. Similarly, for a person who is particularly stressed, a show about fixing up an old house might help reduce arousal from an unpleasantly high level to a moderately low pleasurably relaxed level. This process is simple, but there is bit more nuance to it than is easily explained by just shaking off bad moods.

In fact, there are four core components of MMT and SET that are critical to understanding the perspective. The first is called **excitatory homeostasis**, which suggests that people are driven toward an optimal, or balanced level of arousal. Being bored (i.e., an extremely low level of arousal) and being stressed (i.e., an extremely high level of arousal) are not particularly pleasant. A moderate, Goldilocks (not too stressed, not too bored) level of arousal is preferred. This idea is among one of the older discoveries on psychology, first proposed by Yerkes and Dodson (1908). Broadly, it suggests that a balanced mood state is one that is not too arousing but arousing enough to avoid very low levels of energy. From this perspective, the **excitatory potential** of a message—that is, the level of arousal that we would expect a message to cause—plays an important role in whether or not we would engage it, with bored individuals probably more likely to want content with a high excitatory potential, and stressed individuals more likely to want content with a low excitatory potential. If you come home from work stressed, you are more likely to choose a show that is soothing and predictable, versus one that has a high level of excitement.

excitatory potential
The ability of a media message to increase or decrease arousal

The second component is the **intervention potential** of the message, or the message's ability to attract our attention and hold it. Some forms of **interactive** media can be very demanding of our attention—Bowman (2018) argues that video games can be particularly demanding of our attention on cognitive, emotional, physical, and even social dimensions. Indeed, it can be very hard to imagine trying to play a video game and do chores around the house at the same time, or sometimes even be aware of what's happening in the room next to you! When we are in noxious mood states (i.e., states that we want to change rather than prolong) we are likely to seek out messages that require us to pay attention, because as we devote more attention to the messages themselves, we don't have as many attentional resources left over to ruminate on our moods. In this way, we can use entertainment media to distract us from our bad mood, and thus forget whatever it was that was causing our bad mood to begin with.

intervention potential
The ability of a media message to distract one's attention and intervene in an existing mood state

A third component of MMT/SET is the **behavioral** or **semantic affinity** of the message, in relation to the root causes of our mood. This component is very much focused on the extent to which the on-screen content is similar (i.e., high semantic affinity) or dissimilar (i.e., low semantic affinity) to events in the viewer's own life—in particular, the events that might have caused the noxious mood in the first place. For example, we suggested that a home-renovation show may be able to soothe noxious moods caused by work—but probably not for someone who works in real estate! They may be more likely to pick a relaxing show that does not center around homes. Because of this dissimilarity, the message has the potential to grab our attention because it won't simply remind us of our boredom and thus, could help us shift our mood.

The fourth component of MMT is the **hedonic affinity** of the message, or the tone of the message in terms of it being more positive or negative. Generally speaking, messages with a more positive tone, such

hedonic affinity
The extent to which a message matches the user's current mood state

as comedies, are higher in hedonic affinity and are better at perpetuating mood states—essentially, they make us feel good and thus, help us sustain positive moods. Messages with more negative tones, such as tragedies or horror films, are lower in hedonic affinity and thus, are more likely to grab our attention as they tend to activate more basic (and often, more arousing) human emotions, such as fear or anger (Izard, 1977).

Some researchers have suggested that we do not just select media in response to our moods, but that we can also select media in terms of how we wish to feel. Known as Mood-adjustment Theory (MAT; Knobloch-Westerwick, 2003), this theory suggests we don't always want a hedonically optimized (positive) mood, but instead we strive for the mood that best fits our particular situation. For example, if you were about to go out for a night on the town, you may prepare by listening to high-energy, dance-like, or positively valenced music. In contrast, if you are preparing to attend church or a funeral, you may pick slower, more serious-feeling music to "get you in the mood."

Media Choice as Habit

media habits

Automaticity in media selection that persists over time given stable circumstances

Another way to think about media choice is by looking at **media habits** (LaRose, 2010). A media habit is "a form of automaticity in media consumption that develops as people repeat media consumption behavior in stable circumstances." (p. 194). Media habits are different from other types of media selection discussed previously because they do not assume an active audience. Instead, media habits determine choice when audiences are under conditions of depleted self-regulation, such as being tired, distracted, or having little control over their consumption. Under these conditions, we are likely to rely on our media habits to determine what kind of entertainment we consume. In fact, media habits are something that is rather well-understood by producers. For example with broadcast television, many television stations take advantage of **audience flow** effects (first identified by Williams, 1974) by programming less popular shows to broadcast either right before or right after a popular show. The idea here is that audiences are so routine in how they watch their favorite programs that they might also tune into the same channel a bit early or watch the channel for a bit longer, which could expose them to other programs essentially by accident. Of course, this type of media habit might be less relevant in an age of television streaming, where audiences no longer watch the same channel for hours but instead, might watch only very specific programs.

audience flow

When audiences for one show continue to watch another, different show because the shows are broadcast in a sequential manner

How are media habits formed? We build a media habit based on how *frequently* we engage in a media behavior, how *stable our circumstances* are, how *stable the context* is, and the *stability of the goal* we are meeting. For example, someone who reads the comics in the newspaper every morning while drinking coffee has a specific media selection (comics) that they engage in in a stable context (morning, coffee) and for similar reasons each morning (mood management). If suddenly the person gives up coffee, changes schedule because of catching an earlier train, or the paper stops printing comics in the daily paper, the reader may find their media habit quite disrupted.

Two things to note: First, because habits actually diminish choices, habitual media use may take its toll. That is, habitual users are less thoughtful about their "decisions" than those who are operating from a nonhabitual place. If the comics are no longer funny, but the reader keeps reading the comics searching for that amusement, then the habit has become dysfunctional rather than functional. Second, bad habits can also be regulated, if they are reflected (made conscious) and revised by investing willpower, or by altering the context. Although we may not worry about our breakfast paper-reader, consider an unemployed man who lives at his parent's home, and habitually plays video games until the wee hours of the morning while drinking soda and eating chips. If this person must suddenly change his habit, due to perhaps acquiring an early-morning job, it may require also moving away from his parent's home and leaving the game console behind in order to break the contexts under which this dysfunctional media habit occurs.

Sidebar   What are Your Media Habits?

You try it!   *Keep a media diary of your entertainment screen time over 5 days. This can be a complex diary system, or a simple excel chart. In one class, students used a chart like the one below to track entertainment consumption:*

Day	Time Started	Time End	Content	Media	Second screening?	Comments

(Continued)

At the end of the day, sum up the time spent by type of content (group by social media, series/television, movies, games, or music). Break out the time you spend second screening (that is, with multiple entertainment screens open, such as book + phone, movie + music, etc.) By the end of 5 days, you will have a pretty good snapshot of what your entertainment diet looks like.

Things to consider: Would you characterize your media use as more habitual or intentional? Do you "fall back" into media or consume entertainment as part of other activities? Are you selecting entertainment when you are supposed to be doing other things—like driving, working, or spending time with family? What does your media diary tell you about how we select and consume entertainment?

Media Selection as a Rational Process

Moving away from models of media choice which are based in emotional response and regulation, we can consider models of media choice based on cognitive models of decision-making. Perhaps the most commonly applied model of cognitive decision-making used in media selection studies is based on heuristic models of media choice. These models are based on the idea that humans make rational decisions in two ways. The first way is if we consider human decision-making as a product of perfect knowledge, unlimited time, and tons of available energy to consider alternatives. This is known as **unbounded rationality**, because in this situation we are able to make completely rational decisions about what media would best meet our emotional, cognitive, and social needs—in other words, there isn't anything "bounding" or restricting our ability to make decisions. However, think of the last time you had unlimited time, perfect knowledge of all possible products, and tons of energy to consider alternatives. It is probably tough to think about a time like this, given the number of entertainment options and the limited leisure time most of us have to spare. Therefore, humans tend to make decisions under conditions of **bounded rationality**—where we aren't sure of all the options, we have limited time, and therefore we rely on shortcuts to make decisions. We call these shortcuts **heuristics**, and understanding which heuristics come into play when choosing entertainment can give us a lot of insight into how and why people make entertainment choices in the way they do.

unbounded rationality

The idea that humans will choose the most logical and rational option when provided with infinite resources, time, and/or information

bounded rationality

The idea that humans will use mental shortcuts in decision making when resources, time, and/or information are limited

heuristics

Mental shortcuts used to process information quickly

For example, consider the question "Which movie is better: *Snow White and the Huntsman* (2012) or *Mirror Mirror* (2012)?" Both movies are retelling the fairy tale of Snow White and the Seven Dwarves, and both feature pairs of well-known actresses (Kristen Stewart/Charlize Theron and Lily Collins/Julia Roberts, respectively). However, *Snow White* made about twice the money that *Mirror Mirror* made, despite comparable release dates and ratings. Why did people flock to one and not the other film? Marewski, Galesic, and Gigerenzer (2009) suggested that we use similar heuristics to decide which movie to see as we do in other decision tasks.

One such heuristic (which we also discuss in Chapter 4) is called the **recognition heuristic**. This means we search among possible options until one is recognized, stop once we have recognized one, and then pick the one we have recognized. In this case, Julia Roberts was coming from a long time being away from movies, while Kristen Stewart was coming off a successful run as the lead actress in the *Twilight* movies. So when comparing "Snow White" movies, audiences may have simply picked the more recognized actress and gone from there. We can also consider the **fluency heuristic**: Which alternative is retrieved more quickly when I ask you to name Snow White movie adaptations? If *Snow White and the Huntsman* is more easily retrieved than *Mirror Mirror*, you pick the one that comes to mind first.

Finally, say you also know of yet another Snow White adaptation from the same year (2012 was apparently a good year for fairy tales): *Grimm's Snow White*. This movie featured Eliza Bennet as the titular Snow White, and Jane March as the Evil Queen. When deciding between three relatively similar potential movies, you may use the **take-the-best approach**. This approach relies on viewers splitting entertainment into its corresponding features (central actress, genre, ratings, release date) and comparing content along each feature until a decision is made. In this case, if we look at ratings from IMDb, *Snow White and the Huntsman* is at 6.1/10, and *Mirror Mirror* is 5.6/10, whereas *Grimm's Snow White* is at a measly 3.5/10. So you may eliminate the third film, and then compare the first two on another feature, such as box office take, director, or fan reviews. In this sense you are taking the best option from the cues which can best discriminate between your entertainment choices. These heuristics can be useful in many other places as well, such as when using your mobile phone (**Sidebar: There are thousands of apps for that**).

recognition heuristic
When people judge an object or event simply based on whether or not they recognize it or not

fluency heuristic
When people judge an object simply based on how quickly it is remembered

take-the-best approach
A selection strategy in which a person compares two choices based on corresponding features until a decision is made

Sidebar   There Are Thousands of Apps for That

For most smartphone users, it might seem as if there is an app for almost everything one can imagine. For sure, smartphones can serve numerous users far beyond making phone calls and helping us communicate with our friends. However convenient apps might be, there are also numerous apps available to today's consumers. Statistica estimates that by 2013, there were one million different apps available on the Google Play Store (apps for any Android-based phones), and by the end of 2017 this number had climbed to over 3.5 million. Such a market can be incredibly difficult to navigate, because it suggests that there could well be dozens of different apps, for even the most basic functions.

Consider something as simple as a flashlight app, which you might use to activate the camera flash on your phone to operate as a flashlight. Searching the app market for the term "flashlight" will return several dozen different options, from any number of different creators and companies, with all manner of functions and options. For something as simple as a flashlight, how do we choose between so many options? German media economist Leyla Dogruel and her colleagues looked at the issue by trying to understand the different heuristics that smartphone users might engage during the app search process. They invited a few dozen U.S. and German smartphone users to search for three different apps (flashlight, running, and dictionary apps) and asked them to use a special smartphone that would track all of the on-screen search behaviors—including their finger swipes and touches. What they found was evidence of a "take-the-first" heuristic by which users largely ignored any of the other apps on-screen. Rather, they would usually choose one of the first apps that showed up on the list and spent little time considering any other alternatives (the average number of apps that we viewed by participants was 1.28, suggesting that very few people ever looked at more than one). Most users would select the first app they saw and immediately install it, assuming that highly rated apps by others suggested a quality app, and this entire installation process, on average, took less than a minute.

You try it!   *If you have a smartphone, take a moment and open up the app market on your phone—Google Play Store or Apple's App Store—and try to find a flashlight, running, or dictionary app (or perhaps, your class* *can come up with any other app to search for). When you search, take note of how you navigated the market. How many options were available to you? How many of them did you look at, before choosing an app? How much time did this entire process take? How much time should it have taken?*

Conclusion

In conclusion, this chapter has looked at the most common models of media selection and given you an overview of each one. We pick media entertainment in a variety of different ways. Sometimes we think carefully about what we want from media, sometimes our bodies tell us what we want, and sometimes we pick things purely out of habit. Depending on these situations we find ourselves in, one or more of the models may help to explain our selections. Importantly, understanding why we choose what we choose can be an important way to make better choices and feel better about them.

 # Key Terms

Functional approach   A school of thought that argues that media use serves as a gratification of one's needs or wants

Mood management theory (MMT)   An entertainment selection theory which predicts that people will select media content to maximize positive feelings and minimize negative feelings

Selective exposure (SE)   A process of choosing what media content you will watch or listen to

Mood(s)   (A) persistent emotional state

Pleasure principle   The notion that people are motivated to maximize pleasure and to minimize pain; central to MMT

Excitatory homeostasis   The process of maintaining an optimal (i.e., not too high or too low) level of arousal

Excitatory potential   The ability of a media message to increase or decrease arousal

Intervention potential   The ability of a media message to distract one's attention and intervene in an existing mood state

Hedonic affinity   The extent to which a message matches the user's current mood state

Media habits   Automaticity in media selection that persists over time given stable circumstances

Audience flow   When audiences for one show continue to watch another, different show because the shows are broadcast in a sequential manner

Unbounded rationality   The idea that humans will choose the most logical and rational option when provided with infinite resources, time, and/or information

Bounded rationality   The idea that humans will use mental shortcuts in decision making when resources, time, and/or information are limited

Heuristics   Mental shortcuts used to process information quickly

Recognition heuristic   When people judge an object or event simply based on whether or not they recognize it or not

Fluency heuristic   When people judge an object simply based on how quickly it is remembered

Take-the-best approach   A selection strategy in which a person compares two choices based on corresponding features until a decision is made

References

Atkin C (1985). Informational utility and selective exposure to entertainment media. In D. Zillmann & J. Bryant (Eds.), *Selective exposure to communication.* (pp. 63–92). Hillsdale, NJ: LEA.

Bowman, N. D. (2018). *Video games: A medium that demands our attention* (Ed.). New York: Routledge. ISBN: 978-0-81537-687-9

Ericcson. (2018, November). Mobile data and voice traffic (quarterly), Q12015 to Q32018. Retrieved from https://www.ericsson.com/en/mobility-report/mobility-visualizer?f=9&ft=1&r=1&t=8&s=4&u=3&y=2013,2018&c=5

Izard, C. E. (1977). *Human emotions.* New York: Penguin.

Katz, E., Blumler, J. G., & Gurevitch, M. (1973). Uses and gratifications research. *Public Opinion Quarterly, 37*(4), pp. 509–523. doi: 10.1086/268109

Knobloch-Westerwick, S. (2003). Mood adjustment via mass communication. *Journal of Communication, 53*(2), 233–250. doi: 10.1111/j.1460-2466.2003.tb02588.x

LaRose, R. (2010). The problem of media habits. *Communication Theory, 20*(2), 194–222. doi:10.1111/j.1468-2885.2010.01360.x

Lasswell, H. (1948). The structure and function of communication in society. In L. Bryson (Ed.), *The communication of ideas* (pp. 37–51). New York: Institute for Religious and Social Sciences.

Lazarsfeld, P. F., Berelson, B.,& Gaudet, H. (1948). *The people's choice.* New York: Columbia University Press.

Lazarsfeld, P. F., & Merton, R, K. (1948). Mass communication, popular taste, and organized social action. In L. Bryson (Ed.), *The communication of ideas* (pp. 95–118). New York: Institute for Religious and Social Sciences.

Marewski, J. N., Galesic, M., & Gigerenzer, G. (2009). Fast and frugal media choices. Media choice: A theoretical and empirical overview. In *Media Choice* (T. Hartmann, Ed.) pp 107–128.

Pressman, L. (2015, Aug. 26). Netflix Statistics: How Many Hours Does the Catalog Hold? [blog post]. Retrieved from <u>https://automatedinsights.com/blog/netflix-statistics-how-many-hours-does-catalog-hold/</u>

Rubin, A. M. (1984). Ritualized and instrumental television viewing. *Journal of Communication*, 34(3), 67–77.

Williams, R. (1974). *Television: Technology and cultural form*. London: Fontana.

Wright, C. R. (1960). Functional analysis and mass communication. *Public Opinion Quarterly*, 24(4), 605–620.

Yerkes, R., & Dodson, J. (1908). The relation of strength of stimulus to rapidity of habit formation. *Journal of Comparative and Neurological Psychology*, 18, 429–482.

Zillmann, D., & Bryant, J. (1985). Affect, mood, and emotion as determinants of selective exposure. In D. Zillmann & J. Bryant (Eds.), *Selective exposure to communication*. (pp. 157–190). Hillsdale, NJ: LEA

 # Suggested Readings

Bowman, N. D. (2017). Selectivity: Selective exposure effects. In P. Roessler (Ed.), *International encyclopedia of media effects*. Hoboken, NJ: Wiley-Blackwell.

Dogruel, L., Joeckel, S., & Bowman, N. D. (2015). Choosing the right app: An exploratory perspective on heuristic decision processes for smartphone app selection. *Mobile Media & Communication*, 3(1), 125–144. doi:10.1177/2050157914557509

Knobloch-Westerwick, S. (2015). *Choice in preference in media us: Advances in selective exposure theory and research*. New York: Routledge.

CHAPTER 3

From Escapism to Entertainment

Streaming, online, on-demand, on-the-go—technological convergence has created an entirely new media landscape where entertainment is instantly accessible. The smartphones that many of us now carry in our pockets are powerful enough for gaming and accessing the Internet and fast enough to instantly stream music, movies, and television. How has this always-on access changed how people use and respond to media entertainment? How have the uses and functions of media entertainment changed or stayed the same as our lives have transitioned to being always online? At what point does "use" become "overuse?" Likewise, when does "overuse" become a harmful compulsion or addiction? If media can be used to entertain us, is there a point at which this entertainment becomes an escape from reality . . . and is this necessarily a bad thing? These are the questions we will ask and attempt to answer in the following chapter.

Objectives

After reading this chapter students will be able to:

➤ Understand the push and pull of media entertainment in everyday life

➤ Differentiate between displacement, escapism, multitasking, and addiction

➤ Summarize key arguments related to media use and media overuse

➤ Analyze the costs and benefits of entertainment media on well-being

American Time Use Survey

A US government-sponsored survey that measures the different patterns by which Americans use their time for work, leisure, and self-preservation

autotelic or **intrinsic motivation**

When a person is self-motivated to perform a task

extrinsic motivation

When a person is motivated by external reward or benefit to perform a task

normative debate

An value-based argument about how something should or ought to be

displacement hypothesis

The idea that the time a person uses media takes up time for other activities

Recent data from the **American Time Use Survey** suggest that the amount of leisure time available to the average American increased over the years 2007 to 2017. More than two-thirds of that leisure time is spent watching television in some form or another. Our consumption of entertainment media is generally **autotelic** or **intrinsically motivated**—in other words, done for its own purpose. Other activities, like going to school or work, are activities that we engage in for **extrinsic motivations**; we go to school to potentially get a job, and we go to work to earn money. Why might we spend so much time with an activity that has no purpose beyond itself? Media entertainment provides us access to different spaces and place through compelling stories, characters, and worlds—and it does so using all forms of technology. This type of intrinsic reward can be highly appealing. At the same time, the appeal of entertainment media is concerning to many. Since the Industrial Revolution, when modern laborers first found themselves with time not devoted to work or sleep, there have been debates about how to best spend one's leisure time. However, even in these **normative debates**, the concept of overusing entertainment is a critical one that can be thought of in four broad lines of reasoning that have dominated research: displacement, escapism, multitasking, and addiction.

Displacement Hypothesis

Concern about the amount of time people spend with entertainment is not new. As you remember from Chapter 2, early researchers were concerned that the escapism provided by media entertainment distracted us from more important things. The idea that media entertainment would somehow displace the things we *should* be doing is at the heart of the **displacement hypothesis**. The displacement hypothesis states, "media consumption will displace some other activity or activities, such as exercise of social interaction, or even shift time from one medium to another." Time is, unfortunately, a limited resource, and if we are spending our time with media entertainment, we are not spending it doing other more worthwhile things (**Sidebar: Why Some Men Don't Work**).

However, the idea that media displaces more important activities has not yet been well-supported in research and literature. For example, media use typically displaces other mediated activities rather than nonmediated ones (for example, surfing the Internet replaces television viewing, rather than playing outside). At the same time, understanding features of media and how we as users interact with them can help us predict what will and what will not get displaced. Four common features considered in research are: functional similarity, transformation, marginal fringe activities, and physical proximity.

Sidebar Why Some Men Don't Work

A group of researchers from the National Bureau of Economic Research (NBER) made startling claims in 2017 about the distracting nature of video games. By their observations, the average number of weekly hours of leisure time available to US workers aged 21 to 55 increased by between 1 and 2 hours per week, in part due to an economic recession. While most groups (younger and older women, and older men) seemed to use that extra leisure time on sleeping, eating, and personal care activities, younger men (those aged between 21 and 30) spend over 60% of this time playing video games; younger men also had the greatest increase in weekly leisure time (nearly 2.3 hours per week) and thus, did not seem to be returning to work at the same rate as other groups. Those researchers claimed that video games are essentially responsible for keeping young men home from work between 15 to 30 hours over the course of a year.

Are video games more attractive than working? One argument that the NBER economists put forward is that the quality of video games has improved dramatically in the last few decades, from crude graphics and sounds in the 1980s to the immersive and social online worlds of today. Modern games have vivid graphics and provide highly interactive environments (some with photorealistic graphics), and many also provide for social interactions that are critical to many leisure activities. However, others have been critical of the NBER claims for assuming video games to be a less worthwhile leisure activity than other forms of entertainment.

You try it!   *For Hoche and the NBER economists, entertainment media might distract us from our daily work. What do you think about these conclusions? Read the full article of the NBER research from the New York Times, online at https://www.nytimes.com/2017/07/03/upshot/why-some-men-dont-work-video-games-have-gotten-really-good.html. Do you see other trends in their data that might be interesting to talk about, in terms of changes in leisure time for other groups? How do these data reflect your current leisure time?*

Functional similarity: If two media perform the same function, the media that best (or most easily) satisfies the given need will typically be selected. Think of how many people used to have a membership at movie rental stores, such as Blockbuster (at one time, nearly 50 million U.S. households were Blockbuster members). Now consider how many users switched to Netflix or numerous other online platforms when streaming video rental became available. Blockbuster went bankrupt in 2010, and Netflix is a multimillion-dollar company (estimated to earn more than $1B in 2018), serving over 125 million customers worldwide. The two services were functionally similar, but Netflix eliminated the need to drive to a store, pick out a movie, and return the movie after watching.

Transformation: If a displaced medium is to survive, its function must change. We can think about the transformation radio underwent following the introduction of TV. Radio used to be a "one stop shop" for news, music, and even narrative entertainment, like plays and soap operas. After television became popular, radio focused on its strengths—music and news delivery—while marginalizing other entertainment content—narratives and stories—which television could deliver in a more appealing format. We can also consider the counter-example of public pay phones. In areas where most people are on mobile phones, we see the once-ubiquitous pay phone disappearing, as it cannot shift its function to differentiate itself sufficiently.

Physical and psychological proximity. If two competing activities occupy the same physical or psychological space, the one that provides greater satisfaction will most often be selected. We can consider here the use of laptop computers for streaming media. Many students now rely on their laptop for work and entertainment media use, sometimes giving up the separate television screen entirely. With limited time, budget, and dorm space, we gravitate to the technology that best meets our needs in a given space.

Marginal fringe activities. When we discuss displacement, we have to consider that entertainment media do not necessarily replace specific activities. Instead, they might simply displace what the U.S. Bureau of Labor Statistics refers to as "relaxing and thinking" time. This is an intentionally broad category of leisure time, but the core idea is that this is time essentially not spent doing anything in particular. Walking around a park, sitting in a coffee shop, or even simply relaxing on a patio or a couch, just contemplating the day (or perhaps, not contemplating anything at all) would all be considered relaxing and thinking time. With newer technologies that encourage users to be "permanently online" and "permanently connected" (Vorderer, Hefner, Reinecke, & Klimmt, 2017), we might see that "relaxing and thinking" time has gone the way of the pay phone. This would be the claim of technology critics such as Sherry Turkle, who argue that access to networked technologies such as smartphones takes away from our ability to be alone.

Displacement and the family

Most research examining the effects of displacement has focused on negative effects for children such as decreased physical activity, family interaction, and time spent on homework. Although there is some support for a negative relationship between television viewing and physical activity, the effects are quite small. In terms of family interaction and schoolwork, children tend to do best (or at least, avoid negative effects) when their parents or guardians play an "active mediation" role with their television and gaming time. That is, research has found that watching television and playing games as a family can be a meaningful activity when families watch and play together (**Sidebar: Mario and My Family**).

We can also consider that the activities being displaced by entertainment may not be positive and prosocial activities such as exercise or family time, but instead may be violent or antisocial activities such as crime and vandalism. In this way, media displacement might actually be keeping children away from harm. Some have pointed to crime data in the United States as potential support of this claim, showing that while video game sales have steadily increased over the last decades, violent crimes have steadily decreased.

Sidebar — Mario and My Family

"My dad died when I was 10 so [playing *Mario Kart* with him] is one of my best memories of him"

—research participant, from Wulf et al. (2018)

For many of our students, memories such as the one above are quite common. Video games have grown into one of the most prominent forms of entertainment media and likewise, gamers span nearly every age bracket—industry estimates suggest that the average age of a video game player in 2017 was 35 years! old

(Continued)

Because of these age patterns, it might not be surprising that children and parents are both playing video games . . . and playing them together. In fact, the video game company Nintendo is rather well-known for making video games that are more family friendly, with much of the marketing behind the Nintendo Switch console aimed at making Nintendo "part of the family" (https://www.nintendo.com/switch/family-fun/). Even the original design of the Nintendo Entertainment System from 1984 was meant to make it look more like a living room appliance (similar to a VCR) so that families would be more likely to put the console in living rooms.

One aspect of parents and children playing video games together is that it adds to an interesting psychological aspect of gaming: **nostalgia**. When we think of nostalgia, we normally think of those bittersweet recollections of our past. With media, this usually means remembering retro or classic media properties, such as our favorite cartoon characters, comic books, or video games. However, in their research on video game nostalgia in particular, Wulf et al. (2018) found that many of the players discussing nostalgic experience also discussed sharing those experiences with family and friends. One of the strongest correlates of nostalgia for a gaming memory was the extent to which that memory helped encourage a feeling of relatedness with others. Put these two findings together, and their research suggests that much of the nostalgia that people report feeling toward video games might be less about the games themselves, and more about the social context of those bygone gaming experiences.

You try it! *When you were growing up, did you ever play video games with family members? What do you remember from those experiences? How do they make you feel today? Do those experiences differ from times that you might have used other media, such as watched television or read books together?*

nostalgia
An emotional and cognitive process where one feels bittersweet about specific past events

multitasking
The execution of two or more processing activities at the same time

simultaneous cognitive processing
The act of engaging with and perceiving two different stimuli at the same time

Multitasking

If we are not displacing other activities while using media, yet we keep increasing our screen time, then how are we managing to function at all? Most of us perform what we call **multitasking**, or the execution of two or more processing activities at the same time. Most of us multitask without even considering we are doing something exceptional.

However, engaging in two things at once—what we call **simultaneous cognitive processing**—is incredibly difficult. Instead, multitasking involves switching quickly between one task and another over and over again—a process commonly referred to as **task switching**. Task switching can occur across any sorts of activities, leading to media multitasking being studied in terms of *multiple media* (having your radio on while you watch TV), *multiple screens* (having multiple tabs open on one screen), or *using media while doing another task* (such as watching TV while studying).

When we switch from one task to another, we incur a **switch cost**—the delay it takes for our attention and processing to catch up to the new stimulus. This leads to greater inefficiency, more time to complete a task, and more mistakes in both tasks than when we simply focus on one thing at a time. Anyone who has ever tried to read a book chapter while playing a video game or watching television can attest to how difficult this all can be . . . and if you don't believe us, try it with this chapter!

So if multitasking is hard and it slows us down, then why do we do it? Several studies have suggested we multitask to help with our mood management (Wang & Tchernev, 2012). When we are engaged in a boring or frustrating task, such as work or homework, we are likely to look for a pleasant second task to add—think of flipping on the television or radio while writing an essay for class. Media entertainment is often employed as the secondary, pleasant task. Given our discussion above, it might not seem like a very productive idea to watch television while doing homework, but the flip-side of this process is that we might feel better during the experience, which could encourage us to complete the essay.

However, relying on entertainment as a hedonic mood boost during homework or school can have negative effects. Multitasking seems to "scatter" attention, leading to reduced attention for both tasks. This means easy tasks can become difficult and difficult tasks nearly impossible when we multitask. But, are there long-term effects? Some researchers talk about GenM (those born after 1995) as the "multitasking generation"—digital natives who are able to juggle multiple tasks with ease. Yet, multitasking practice seems to be unrelated to long-term, fundamental cognitive abilities such as working memory and ability to task switch (van der Schuur, Baumgartner, Sumter, & Valkenburg, 2015). In other words, there is no boost from multitasking on memory or ability to multitask. GenM is a fiction of the imagination, and likely today's youth are no more skilled with their technological devices than previous youth were skilled at the devices of their times.

task switching

The act of switching, usually quickly, between two tasks

switch cost

The delay it takes for our attention and processing to catch up to the new task when we engage in task switching

Escapism

The displacement of nonmediated activities was not the only concern of early media scholars. They were also worried about **escapism**, or the urge to simply ignore the immediate problems of the "real world" and disappear into a fantasy world provided by entertainment. The **Frankfurt School** of media criticism was particularly concerned that escapism was a natural effect of living in a capitalist society. The main function of media, according to key researchers Horkheimer and Adorno (1947) was to provide an entertaining, dream-like world, which narcotizes the anxious capitalist citizen. Thus, media can act as a stabilizing force. These concerns are echoed in popular fiction such as the Soma drug in Aldous Huxley's *Brave New World* (1932) which encourages happy thoughts that distract from the reality of dictatorship, and Neil Postman's *Amusing Ourselves to Death* (1985), an academic writing that claims entertainment media to be a root cause of social isolation among people who would rather spend time at home with television than in public with each other.

We can see concerns involving escapism in early uses and gratifications work (discussed in Chapter 2), as well (**Sidebar: Oxydol's Own Ma Perkins**). McQuail, Blumler, and Brown (1972) suggested three uses of media to escape: To *escape from daily routines, to escape from problems in your life*, and *to escape from noxious emotions*. Katz and Foulkes (1962) similarly suggested that people turn to the media when they have serious problems for three reasons—to escape the problem itself (*escapism as avoidance*), to avoid emotional pain (*escapism as mood management*), and to maintain the illusion that the problem has been solved (*escapism as wishful fantasizing*). When we attempt to escape our problems, often the content we choose will be fictional, feature a biased or extreme reality (think of *Keeping up with the Kardashians*), or offer the viewer an opportunity for wishful identification and vicarious experiences with superordinary characters (e.g., wizards in Harry Potter, or the complicated love lives of soap opera characters).

Sidebar　Oxydol's Own Ma Perkins

On Monday, December 4, 1933, the first episode of *Oxydol's Own Ma Perkins* was aired. It was the first daytime serial narrative on a network radio sponsored by Procter & Gamble soap. Oxydol was a popular soap product for washday, which in the 1930s could often take hours as people typically

(Continued)

washed clothes using washboard, water, and elbow grease. Ma Perkins was the central character in a serial narrative, which covered the trials and tribulations of Ma Perkins and her family. Ma Perkins was a young widow with a big heart and down-home philosophy, and her stories took place across over 7,000 different episodes—more than enough content to get through the wash day. And thus, the first **soap opera** was born!

In addition to being the first soap opera, *Ma Perkins* was also the subject of the first uses and gratifications study, which examined the role of soap operas in the lives of daily listeners. Escapism was a key draw for listeners (remember, they would often be engaged in the wash as they listened, and this task could take hours). There appeared to be no vacuum or great dystopian angst in the lives of listeners—instead listeners tuned into Ma Perkins and her family to escape via wishful thinking " . . . these serials provide the more naive individual with a much-desired, though vicarious, contact with human affairs which the more sophisticated person obtains at first hand through her wider range of experience."

soap opera
A televised drama that is traditionally aired midday; its name comes from the first programs being sponsored by soap companies

You try it! If you'd like to hear Ma Perkins, the entire archive is available online at this website: *https://archive.org/details/MaPerkins01Misc12Eps.* Be sure to listen for the Oxydol advertisements, and imagine yourself scrubbing along with the laundry almost 90 years ago.

Escapism may also function as a **thought-blocker**. Although people differ in their tendency to ruminate about themselves, rumination—such as thinking constantly about one's problems and struggles, focusing on discrepancies to the ideal self, and dealing with other stressors—can be harmful to well-being. Thus, escapism via media can be a tool used by viewers to block harmful rumination about the self. In one study, Moskalenko and Heine (2003) found that people who received false negative feedback on a task, spent a longer time watching television than those who received positive or no feedback. In this case, television seemed to act as a buffer from the negative feedback.

thought-blocker
The act of using media to remove a person's unpleasant thoughts

Finally, what might look like the use of media as a form of escapism to some might not actually be escapism at all. Johnson and Knobloch (as well as others) have suggested that while people do turn to the media during times of stress and strain, people also turn to the media to address the source of their problems, an activity known as **coping** (Johnson & Knobloch, 2017). Knobloch suggests that people may cope with problems by using media to find information, seek guidance, find reassurance, all of which are **approach-oriented coping**

coping
Any psychological or behavioral process used to deal with a stressor

approach-oriented coping
A way to cope with stressors by confronting them either directly or indirectly

strategies, or those that are based in user activity. So, for example, if you are struggling to lose or gain weight, you may start watching shows illustrating healthy habits and choices, or documenting others' weight loss journeys. However, some forms of coping are **avoidance-based**, and may look like behavioral and mental disengagement, or classic escapism. For example, you may turn off *The Biggest Loser* and watch shows unrelated to health or lifestyle. These avoidance-based strategies, although resembling classic escapism, may also help the viewer emotionally process or deal with unavoidable or uncomfortable information for which no solution exists.

avoidance-based coping

A way to cope with stressors by staying away from them

Addiction, Problematic Behavior, and Binge-Watching

Displacement and escapism are perhaps more relevant today as we grapple with new, always-on entertainment technology that most of us carry in our pockets. As discussed earlier with the displacement of marginal and friend activities, being permanently online and permanently connected has raised questions again about technological addiction, dependence, and recovery. People struggle to manage their time with entertainment and leisure activities, in a way that can feel much like other addictive substances, such as drugs or alcohol. But what does it mean to be addicted to entertainment media?

Addiction versus Problematic Behavior. The American Society of Addiction Medicine defines addiction as a "chronic disease of brain reward, motivation, memory, and related circuitry . . . characterized by the inability to consistently abstain, impairment in behavioral control, [and] craving" that continues despite the resulting destruction of relationships, economic conditions, and health. Media addiction is not a chemical dependence, such as those that can develop with addictive drugs or alcohol. However, media may fall into a category known as "behavioral disorders," such as gambling. These behavioral disorders involve a compulsion to engage in rewarding behavior, despite negative consequences to person's health or well-being. The term **psychological dependence** replaced addiction in the 1960s to refer to the craving for a drug without physical dependence; the term is now used to describe habitual behavior in the absence of proof for physical addiction. Although popular opinion now favors the traditional conceptualization of addiction, the term dependence remains in its place.

psychological dependence

A craving for a behavior or substance

Some researchers caution against using any sort of medical terms to describe media behavior. They suggest that treating media as an addiction or medical condition **over-pathologizes** a range of otherwise-normal human behavior (LaRose, Lin, & Eastin, 2003); after all, entertainment media usage is among the most popular forms of leisure. These researchers suggest that symptoms of media addiction may be indicators of a deficiency in **self-regulation**, or the ability to control one's behavior. While patterns of "media addiction" lie at one extreme of a continuum of unregulated media behavior, unregulated media behaviors are experienced in all media consumers to some extent under some circumstances.

Researchers have yet to determine if excessive time spent with media qualifies as a pathology, but many have agreed it can indeed be **problematic** for some users. The American Psychiatric Society lists both "social media addiction" and "Internet addiction disorder" as "conditions for further study," suggesting that while neither should be recognized as an addiction, both require additional investigations regarding their potential clinical relevance and, if necessary, treatment. We turn now to look at specific qualities of different entertainment media and how they have been linked to problematic behavior.

Internet addiction. Media and technology companies work hard to keep us tuned in and focused on the apps and entertainment available to us through their platforms. As we discussed last chapter, humans are inherently social creatures, and technology companies center their offerings around staying connected (Facebook, Snapchat), getting back in touch with lost friends or family (Ancestry.com), or meeting new people (Tinder). We are also driven by a need to feel like we are good at things, and getting likes and comments on social platforms can often feel like a reason to keep using the apps. Some research has even linked the neurological response to the "likes" we receive through these apps to reward centers in the brain, indicating that validation via a mediated social platform acts like a reward in real life. These combined forces can lead to those who quit social platforms to feel "**FOMO**" or **Fear of Missing Out**—that nagging feeling that something better is happening online, or that there's a party somewhere people are Instagramming, and you aren't there!

Vicarious virtual rewards have made self-regulating Internet usage very difficult for some users. In fact, the American Society of Addiction Medicine lists "Internet addiction" as a behavioral disorder based on criteria similar to those used with pathological gambling, the only

over-pathologize
The trend to diagnose otherwise normal or common behaviors as medical conditions

self-regulation
The ability to control one's behavior

problematic
When a given behavior interferes with normal human functioning

Fear of Missing Out (FOMO)
The anxiety that comes when a person feels excluded from their social group; often discussed in relation to social media usage

recognized behavioral addiction. These criteria have been isolated into six core elements which characterize a problematic behavior: 1) *salience*, or thinking excessively about the behavior, 2) *tolerance*, or needing more and more of the behavior to have the same effect, 3) *mood regulation*, or using the behavior to regulate mood states, 4) *relapse*, where you struggle to maintain abstinence from the behavior, 5) *withdrawal*, or experiencing negative effects from stopping the behavior, and 6) *conflicts*, or experiencing compromises in social activities and relationships (Griffiths, 2005). Cognitive behavioral therapy is a recognized treatment for Internet addiction, and involves changing underlying thoughts and habits surrounding the behavior.

Video game addiction. Different terms like "video game addiction," "compulsive video game use," "problematic game use," "pathological gaming," and "excessive game behavior" have been used since the arcade days of the 1970s. Again, "pathological gambling" serves as a model for the concept of video game addiction, in which the player experiences a "persistent and excessive involvement with video games which cannot be controlled, despite associated social and/or emotional problems" (Lemmens, Valkenburg, & Peter, 2009). However, there are problems with this approach to behavioral addiction. For example, there is great variation between criteria and cut-off points. When does a behavior become "problematic"? Behavior which creates problems for some users may be entirely tolerable for others. Because of these issues, some researchers suggest thinking about gaming as engagement (focusing more on how often one engages an activity, voluntarily) versus addiction (focusing more on how often one engages an activity, involuntarily).

There are recognized risk factors for developing problematic gaming behaviors. For example, adolescent boys spend more time gaming than girls, and are thus at higher risk. Players who are introverted, show high impulsivity and neuroticism, and feel lonely are also at higher risk. Moreover, players who do exhibit problematic behaviors often develop other severe consequences including sleep disruption, stress, and social isolation. Treatment so far is relegated to cognitive therapy and desensitizing players to the withdrawal process. As recently as September 2018, the **World Health Organization (WHO)** has formally recognized gaming disorder in the **International Classification of Diseases.**

Television addiction. Concerns about the ability to quit media behavior is not solely a function of newer media technology, but also pertains to "older" entertainment such as television. We can see this

World Health Organization (WHO)
A United Nations agency that monitors and addresses public health concerns

International Classification of Diseases
A reference text to diagnose human diseases; maintained and published by the WHO

reflected in early cultivation work examining the difference between "heavy" and "light" television viewers (discussed in more detail, in Chapter 4). However, systematic study of the issue was relatively rare until the early 2000s, perhaps due to the low prevalence of self-determined television addiction (~.04%, Horvath, 2004). In 2004, Horvath created a problematic viewing scale by identifying four factors linked to problematic television use: **heavy viewing**, or watching a lot of television; **problem viewing**, or when television viewing caused conflicts with goals or family members; **craving for viewing**, which includes attempts to quit; and **withdrawal**, or the extent to which people can imagine a life without television. People scoring high on the scale were more often male, older, and less educated than those scoring lower on the scale.

This research was conducted just as television was moving away from **appointment viewing**, or watching a program at a set time, toward **time-shifted viewing**, or viewing television when convenient for the viewer. Much like problematic Internet and gaming behavior, the always-on, always available mentality has shifted how viewers manage their entertainment and leisure time. The phenomenon known as **binge-watching**, in which viewers watch three or more episodes of a favorite show in a row (and **hyper-binging**, where viewers watch more than nine episodes in a row) has taken hold of public imagination and personal leisure time (**Sidebar: How much do you stream?**).

Sidebar — How Much do You Stream?

You may have already done the media diary study in Chapter 2, but did you know that most streaming services will allow you to download your own viewing habits in order to see what, when, and how much you've watched?

You try it! *To download your Netflix viewing activity, follow the steps below:*

1) Sign in to Netflix.com and choose the profile you'd like to download the viewing history for. 2) Visit netflix.com/viewingactivity. 3) Scroll to the bottom of the My activity page and select Download all. The file can opened using any spreadsheet software that supports CSV (or comma-separated value) file format.

(Continued)

Not covering everything you've watched? Try looking up some of the shows that you watch on the Binge Clock (www.bingeclock.com) to find out how long it will take to watch your favorite series and movies. Popular shows such as the *Office* (4 days, 3 hours, 30 minutes) to *Game of Thrones* (2 days, 22 hours, 15 minutes) are featured. You can use these time estimates to answer provide an estimated answer for the question: How much time have you spent in front of the tube?

Recovery and Challenge

Despite the relatively negative picture we have painted in terms of entertainment use in this chapter so far, in truth most people use media entertainment with few problems. One area which has come under recent investigation is how people use media entertainment to recover from challenging or fatiguing work days. Sonnentag and Fritz (2007) discuss that people must recover from stress by a **recovery experience**, which contains four core components: (1) *psychological detachment* (2) *relaxation, including mood regulation*, (3) *mastery experience*, and (4) *control*.

recovery experience
The experience of restoring psychological and physiological resources

Leisure activities which facilitate recovery, or meet all of these needs, can be termed **resource-providing activities**, while those which get in the way of recovery or prolonged stress responses are **resource-consuming**. Not surprisingly, house- and child-care activities fall into resource-consuming leisure category, whereas social activities, exercise, and even media fall into resource-providing category.

resource-providing activity
Any activity which facilitates recovery from fatigue and stress

resource-consuming activity
Any activity which prevents recovery from, or prolongs, fatigue and stress

A number of studies have started to explore entertainment as resource-consuming or resource-providing. Early survey studies explored the use of video games for recovery purposes, suggesting that video games can elicit all four facets of recovery dimension and are used to recover from stress and strain (Reinecke, 2009). These correlational results have been significantly extended by recent experimental study designs addressing media-induced recovery (see Reinecke & Eden, 2016, for a review of this literature). The recovery results elicited by media include indicators of subjective well-being, such as vitality and perceived energy, but also reduced fatigue and increased cognitive performance. Findings on the use of video games as a recovery-providing activity are particularly interesting, given that video games are often thought of as being rather taxing, given their requirements on attention and performance (**Sidebar: Games: The cause of, and solution to, all of the stress**).

Sidebar	Games: The Cause of, and Solution to, All of the Stress

Games require the user to be fully engaged in the on-screen action, which has a lot of implications for how they might help us escape from the stressors of everyday life. On the one hand, games require so much of our focus and attention that they are probably very good at distracting us from our stress and other root causes of bad moods. On the other hand, may video game players have suffered from "gamer rage" after losing at the same challenge or level, several times.

A study by Bowman and colleagues (2013) looked at the mood recovery potential of games, to see if playing video games would be more effective than watching television for mood repair. In the study, they recorded footage of a flight simulator video game, and compared the experience of watching that footage to playing the same game with varying levels of control: Some players only had to use a simple joystick to fly their airplane, and other players had to use a more complex control system that mimicked what you might find in a real plane. Before playing the game, the researchers had people in the study spend nearly 20 minutes on a very boring task (putting metal rings on a piece of string) or a very stressful task (taking a paper-and-pencil college competency exam) leading to participants feeling either bored or stressed before they played.

Did the video games help with alleviating the negative moods brought about by the pregame tasks? They did, and they didn't. For all participants, playing the video games with the simplified controls resulted in improved mood levels than people who only watched the game footage. But for the people who were stressed, playing the video game with the more complex controls made their moods a little bit worse after play. Why is that? Essentially, the more complex game required a great deal more out of participants, and the researchers concluded that the game became its own source of stress. Another way of thinking about this is that the complex controls were resource-consuming, which might have wiped out the potential recovery experience that others in the study benefited from.

Do you ever play video games when you're stressed out? *If so, what sort of video games do you play, and how do you feel after playing them? Do you feel that your mood changes depending on how well you do at the game? Do you feel differently about the same games when you're bored or feeling a different sort of mood? Share your thoughts with your classmates.*

Further work has suggested that the type of media content may also play a role in recovery. Both survey and experimental work has demonstrated that when fatigued, users will select media that is less intellectually and less emotionally challenging than when they are full of energy (Eden, Johnson, & Hartmann, 2018). That is, when exhausted we are more likely to binge *House Hunters*, with formulaic stories and predictable endings, than shows full of suspense and intrigue like *Game of Thrones*. This type of "low effort" viewing may lead to short-term mood management but may not lead to recovery of vitality or energy. Also, when viewing these low-challenge offerings, users may feel guilt for not doing something more meaningful, which can block the hedonic and recovery benefits of entertainment. Therefore, more research is needed to better understand the relationship between fatigue, content, and subsequent recovery of psychological and physiological resources.

Conclusion

While fears of media overuse have been centered in time- and value-based arguments, we can see that most people use entertainment media in functional ways that enhance their everyday lives. Although some people will overuse media to the extent that it becomes a source of interpersonal or goal conflict, the majority of healthy individuals are able to pull back from causing themselves serious life and relational problems. That said, media companies are capitalizing on our attention and eyeballs, so media presence and availability will not lessen in the future.

Key Terms

American Time Use Survey A US government-sponsored survey that measures the different patterns by which Americans use their time for work, leisure, and self-preservation

Autotelic or **intrinsic motivation** When a person is self-motivated to perform a task

Extrinsic motivation When a person is motivated by external reward or benefit to perform a task

Normative debate An value-based argument about how something should or ought to be

Displacement hypothesis The idea that the time a person uses media takes up time for other activities

Nostalgia An emotional and cognitive process where one feels bittersweet about specific past events

Multitasking The execution of two or more processing activities at the same time

Simultaneous cognitive processing The act of engaging with and perceiving two different stimuli at the same time

Task switching   The act of switching, usually quickly, between two tasks

Switch cost   The delay it takes for our attention and processing to catch up to the new task when we engage in task switching

Escapism   The desire to leave "real world" problems and disappear into another world, such as those provided in an entertainment media product

Frankfurt School   A scholarly tradition and perspective that originated from the Institute for Social Research at the University of Frankfurt in the early 20th Century.

Soap opera   A televised drama that is traditionally aired midday; its name comes from the first programs being sponsored by soap companies

Thought-blocker   The act of using media to remove a person's unpleasant thoughts

Coping   Any psychological or behavioral process used to deal with a stressor

Approach-oriented coping   A way to cope with stressors by confronting them either directly or indirectly

Avoidance-based coping   A way to cope with stressors by staying away from them

Psychological dependence   A craving for a behavior or substance

Over-pathologize   The trend to diagnose otherwise normal or common behaviors as medical conditions

Self-regulation   The ability to control one's behavior

Problematic   When a given behavior interferes with normal human functioning

Fear of Missing Out (FOMO)   The anxiety that comes when a person feels excluded from their social group; often discussed in relation to social media usage

World Health Organization (WHO)   A United Nations agency that monitors and addresses public health concerns

International Classification of Diseases   A reference text to diagnose human diseases; maintained and published by the WHO

Recovery experience   The experience of restoring psychological and physiological resources

Resource-providing activity   Any activity which facilitates recovery from fatigue and stress

Resource-consuming activity   Any activity which prevents recovery from, or prolongs, fatigue and stress

 # References

Bowman, N. D., Weber, R., Tamborini, R., & Sherry, J. L. (2013). Facilitating game play: How others affect performance at and enjoyment of video games. *Media Psychology, 16*(1), 39–64. doi: 10.1080/15213269.2012.742360

Eden, A., Johnson, B. K., & Hartmann, T. (2018). Entertainment as a creature comfort: Self-control and selection of challenging media. *Media Psychology, 21*(3), 352–376. doi: 10.1080/15213269.2017.1345640

Griffiths, M. (2005). A 'components' model of addiction within a biopsychosocial framework. *Journal of Substance Use, 10*(4), 191–197. doi: 10.1080/14659890500114359

Grodal, T. (2000). Video games and the pleasures of control. In D. Zillmann & P. Vorderer (Eds.), *Media entertainment: The psychology of its appeal* (pp. 197–213). Mahwah, NJ: LEA.

Horkheimer, M., & Adorno, T. W. (1947/2002). Dialectic of enlightenment: Philosophical fragments (E. Jephcott, Trans.). *Cultural memory in the present.* Palo Alto, California: Stanford University Press.

Horvath, C. W. (2004). Measuring television addiction. *Journal of Broadcasting & Electronic Media, 48*(3), 378–398. doi: 10.1207/s15506878jobem4803_3

Johnson, B. K., & Knobloch-Westerwick, S. (2017). Steer clear or get ready: How coping styles moderate the effect of informational utility. *Journal of Broadcasting & Electronic Media, 61*(2), 332–350. doi: 10.1080/08838151.2017.1309408

Katz, E., & Foulkes, D. (1962). On the use of the mass media as "escape": Clarification of a concept. *Public Opinion Quarterly, 26*(3), 377–388

LaRose, R., Lin, C. A., & Eastin, M. S. (2003). Unregulated Internet usage: Addiction, habit, or deficient self-regulation? *Media Psychology, 5*(3), 225–253. doi: 10.1207/S1532785XMEP0503_01

Lemmens, J. S., Valkenburg, P. M., & Peter, J. (2009). Development and validation of a game addiction scale for adolescents. *Media Psychology, 12*(1), 77–95. doi: 10.1080/15213260802669458

McQuail, D., Blumler, J. G., & Brown, J. R. (1972). The television audience: A revised perspective. In P. Marris & S. Thornham (Eds.), *Media studies: A reader* (pp. 438–454). New York: NYU Press.

Moskalenko, S., & Heine, S. J. (2003). Watching your troubles away: Television viewing as a stimulus for subjective self-awareness. *Personality and Social Psychology Bulletin, 29*(1), 76–85. doi: 10.1177/0146167202238373

Reinecke, L. (2009). Games and recovery: The use of video and computer games to recuperate from stress and strain. *Journal of Media Psychology, 21*(3), 126–142. doi: 10.1027/1864-1105.21.3.126

Reinecke, L., & Eden, A. (2016). Media-induced recovery as a link between media exposure and well-being. In L. Reinecke & M. B. Oliver (Eds.), *The Routledge handbook of media use and well-being: International perspectives on theory and research on positive media effects* (pp. 106–117). New York: Routledge.

Sonnentag, S. & Fritz, C. (2007). The recovery experience questionnaire: Development and validation of a measure for assessing recuperation and unwinding from work. *Journal of Occupational Health Psychology, 12*(3), 204–221. doi: 10.1037/1076-8998.12.3.204

Van Der Schuur, W. A., Baumgartner, S. E., Sumter, S. R., & Valkenburg, P. M. (2015). The consequences of media multitasking for youth: A review. *Computers in Human Behavior, 53*, 204–215. doi: 10.1016/j.chb.2015.06.035

Vorderer, P., Hefner, D., Reinecke, L., & Klimmt, C. (Eds.). (2017). *Permanently online, permanently connected: Living and communicating in a popc world.* New York: Routledge.

Wang, Z., & Tchernev, J. M. (2012). The "myth" of media multitasking: Reciprocal dynamics of media multitasking, personal needs, and gratifications. *Journal of Communication, 62*(3), 493–513. doi: 10.1111/j.1460-2466.2012.01641.x

Wulf, T., Bowman, N. D., Velez, J., & Breuer, J. (2018). Once upon a game: Exploring video game nostalgia and its impact on well-being. *Psychology of Popular Media Culture.* doi: 10.1037/ppm00000208

 # Suggested Readings

Juul, J. (2001). Games telling stories? A brief not on games and narratives. *Game Studies, 1*(1). Retrieved from http://www.gamestudies.org/0101/juul-gts/

Reinecke, L., & Oliver, M. B. (Eds.). (2016). *The Routledge handbook of media use and well-being: International perspectives on theory and research on positive media effects.* New York: Routledge.

Turkle, S. (2012). *Alone together: Why we expect more from technology and less from each other.* New York: Basic Books.

CHAPTER 4

Entertainment and Perceptions of Social Reality

"Human beings are unique to other species in that we live in a world that is created by the stories we tell. Most of what we know, or think we know, we have never personally experienced; we learned about it through stories." Gerbner, 1997, p. 4)

—Gerbner, G. (1997). TV as Storyteller.
Media Education Foundation.

Introduction

Most of the perceptions we have about the world are derived from our actual experiences. Most of us have had a soft drink, ridden a bike, or been out to eat at a restaurant. Our own experiences help us to figure out how the world works and what things are like. But there are other things that we "know" about the world, even though we have no direct experience with them whatsoever. For example, we might think that Russia is a very cold place, even if we've never been there before. This perception might have been developed through watching the news, reading a book, or seeing Russian settings in movies, like *From Russia with Love*. Perhaps this is why Sochi seemed like an obvious choice to host the 2014 Winter Olympics. It might surprise you, however, to learn that Sochi can be quite warm, as it has a humid subtropical climate similar to the southern United States. The average temperature in February, its coldest month, is 42.8° F, and its average temperature in August, its warmest month, is 74.5° F—hardly cold at all. In fact, much of the snow for the 2014 Winter Olympics was artificially created. Why is there such a discrepancy between our perception of reality and actual reality?

As we will read in Chapter 4, we learn a great deal from the stories we're told, even if we're not aware that we're learning. Stories shape how we view the world around us, for better or for worse, and some of the most important storytellers of the modern age are the mass media. This chapter will examine the role that media entertainment plays in shaping our understanding of reality.

Objectives

After reading and studying the concepts in this chapter, students should be able to:

➤ Understand the role that entertainment media play in shaping our view of our social environment.

➤ Identify key theoretical perspectives that describe, explain, and predict the impacts of entertainment media on social reality.

➤ Critique the intended and unintended effects of entertainment-based social portrayals on audiences.

➤ Discuss the role of emerging communication technologies in influencing the social realities portrayed in entertainment media.

pseudo-environment
The constructed environment in one's mind that is derived from nonphysical observations, such as mediated observations

mediated experience
Any experience derived from media content; usually contrasted with a lived or real world experience

Mediated Reality

Walter Lippmann, a journalist and media commentator of the early 20th century, wrote in his book *Public Opinion* (1922) that in a society with mass communication there are two environments: The real physical environment in which we live and work, and the **pseudo-environment**, which is a constructed reality that exists in our minds. The pseudo-environment is a combination of both our direct experiences—those things that we actually have first-hand experience with—and our indirect experiences—those things that we have experience with through second-hand sources. Since this indirect experience has to go through someone (such as other people) or something (such as a television screen) we call this indirect knowledge of the world **mediated experience**.

For the most part, our mediated experience is far more diverse than anything we could ever hope to experience in our daily lives. Media entertainment provides us with contact with people, places, and things that we can't experience directly, and so it is likely to have an important role in shaping our perceptions of how the world is. The stories we hear or see help us to understand what something is like. We have knowledge (or at least, a perception) of what the mafia is like through movies and TV shows, such as *The Sopranos* and *The Godfather*. We have an idea of what making and selling methamphetamine is like thanks to *Breaking Bad*. We know what prison is like because of *Orange is the New Black*. We know what criminal cases look like thanks to *CSI* (**Sidebar, the CSI Effect**). Whether these shows are fictional or not is somewhat inconsequential. They depict relationships and settings, and those depictions can influence our perceptions of social reality even when we know they aren't "real."

Sidebar   The CSI Effect

Crime dramas is one of the most classic and popular genres of entertainment television. In these shows, clever police detectives and other investigators, who are usually the protagonists, are presented with murders and other serious crimes and tasked with solving the on-screen crime, with very few clues. One of the more popular franchises from this genre is *CSI: Crime Scene Investigation*, which aired in some version for nearly 16 years, from 2000 to 2016. *CSI* was a particularly interesting crime drama, because it placed a heavy focus on advanced technologies and forensic evidence, such as advanced fingerprinting and deoxyribonucleic acid (DNA) evidence.

As early as 2004, major news media outlets such as *USA Today* (Willing, 2004) began reporting on the **CSI Effect**. Trial juries seemed to expect the same sort of technologies and evidence that were used in television crime dramas to be presented on the cases they were hearing. When there was no "forensic evidence" presented, juries were more likely to find criminal defendants not guilty. In reality, it is very unlikely that DNA evidence or even fingerprint evidence is gathered during the course of a normal investigation due to high costs and lack of common expertise. However, the mediated reality of television crime dramas indicated that forensic

(Continued)

evidence had become commonplace, leading state prosecutors to become concerned that the CSI Effect might explain acquittals for capital crimes. In his *USA Today* article from 2004 (https://usatoday30.usatoday.com/news/nation/2004-08-05-csi-effect_x.htm), Willing discussed a trial in Arizona in which jurors demanded DNA testing of a bloody coat found at the scene of a murder, while the judge had to remind jurors that DNA evidence is not necessary when the identity of the murderer (who was wearing the coat) had already been established.

However, scientific research into the CSI Effect is not as strong as anecdotal reports. For example, Kim, Barak, and Shelton (2016) found that watching CSI did not really have any direct impact on jurors' verdicts, although they did find that frequent viewers of such shows placed less value on circumstantial evidence despite the fact that such evidence is used extensively in criminal convictions.

stalagmite theories

A family of media theories that predict that perception effects such as attitude change are small or undetectable in the immediate term yet cumulative and large over time

When talking about the influence of entertainment on social reality, we often refer to them as **stalagmite theories**, a metaphor for media effects based on a geological process. Stalagmites are the calcite mounds that form in underground caves. These mounds grow slowly over millennia from minerals contained in water dripping from a cave's ceiling. If you sat and watched the drops of water, you wouldn't be able to perceive any effect whatsoever. Over time though, there would be a large stalagmite thanks to the many, many drops of water which fell. Geology and media entertainment might not seem to have much in common, but we can think of some effects of entertainment media as being slow and gradual, but powerful over long amounts of time and repeated exposure. After all, the average American watches 5 hours of television per day, or 76 days of television per year. The individual vicarious experiences that we have with mediated worlds, when added together, can influence how we see the "real" world around us. In the following paragraphs, we'll discuss several such stalagmite perspectives including cultivation, social learning theory/social cognitive theory, and exemplification theory.

Cultivation and the Cultural Indicators Project

In the mid-1960s, George Gerbner and his colleagues at the Annenberg School of Communication at the University of Pennsylvania were fascinated by the increasingly prominent role that the television set was playing in American households, referring to television as the great storyteller of a generation. Shows such as the western drama *Gunsmoke* and images of the Vietnam War were nightly beamed into the homes of a sizeable portion of the U.S. population. What effect were those messages having on the viewers? It is important to note that at that same time, societal unrest was growing in the form of protests and demonstrations across the country. President Lyndon B. Johnson commissioned the **Cultural Indicators Project** with Gerbner at the helm to determine whether television violence could be a contributing factor.

The Cultural Indicators Project took a three-pronged approach to studying media. The first step (institutional process analysis) examined the institutions that create media. The second step (message system analysis) required a careful study of the messages that those institutions actually produced. The third step (cultivation analysis) involved examining perceptions of violence in the population and determining what effect media had on those perceptions.

The **institutional process analysis** arm of research tried to answer three questions: Who is producing content, for whom, and for what reasons? In the United States and around the world, entertainment media is often produced with a profit motive; content is produced by investors interested in making money off of the content. But, this is not the case for all content, such as public-access and government or education-funded networks. Things get even more different when we look at content produced world-wide. For example, the European Union have adopted quota systems to ensure content is being produced by culturally relevant sources. The EU's Audiovisual Media Services Directive protects a certain share of any given country's media market from American or other foreign content. In France, for example, the government reserves 60% of broadcast time for European programming and 40% for French-produced and French-language programming. In implementing this system, the French government has made a bold statement about which kinds of stories may be told on-air, in which language, and from which type of creators.

The second arm of the project was **message system analysis.** This message system analysis was essentially a **content analysis** of the content on major broadcast networks of the time (ABC, CBS, and NBC). The shows were cataloged and watched, with acts of violence being counted. Among their findings, Gerbner and colleagues discovered that more than half of television programs were classified as "action" programs—crime, westerns, and adventure shows—that usually featured violent conflicts between people. Of course, simply

Cultural Indicators Project

A research project focused on quantifying the content and effects of television on the general population

content analysis

A social scientific method in which researchers systematically quantify and describe properties of media content counting the violent content in popular programming is not enough to establish if the content is having any effect. However, the method can help us understand who and what is on screen. Content analysis have, for example, shown that ethnic minorities are often underrepresented on screen compared to their proportions of the population. Or, that women and men are shown doing very different types of jobs on screen (**See Sidebar: Who stays home and drinks coffee?**).

Sidebar Who Stays Home and Drinks Coffee?

As noted by Morgan, Shanahan, and Signorielli (2015), masculinity and femininity are portrayed consistently across many different types of entertainment media, which might cultivate specific attitudes about traditional gender roles. In two special issues of the journal *Sex Roles*, the portrayal of women in television was examined and quantified. As reported by Collins (2011), women on television are often underrepresented, portrayed in sexualized clothing, shown as subordinate, or shown in traditionally feminine roles, such as homemakers, wives, and parents.

What effect is this having on viewers? Scharrer and Blackburn (2018) found that U.S. adults who watch more sitcoms, police and detective programs, sports, and reality shows are more likely to endorse masculine social norms, such as "a man should never admit when others hurt his feelings," "Men should watch football games instead of soap operas," and "A man should always be the boss." These findings suggest that to the extent that entertainment programming reinforces specific attitudes on-screen, heavy viewers become more likely to share those views.

---

cultivation differential
The difference in beliefs and attitudes between heavy and light television viewers; thought to result from the prevalence of beliefs and attitudes presented on television

To examine potential effects of violent content may be "cultivating" in the audience, Gerbner and Gross (1976) followed up their content analysis with a survey of television viewers, their viewing habits (i.e., how much and how often they watched television), and their perceptions of violence in the world. The researchers compared light (watching less than 4 hours of TV per day) and heavy (watching more than 4 hours of TV per day) television viewers' perceptions of reality in what is known as the **cultivation differential**. Gerbner and Gross (1976) found that heavy viewers overestimated their chances of being personally involved in violence, and were more likely to agree with statements such as "Most people are just looking out for themselves,"

"You can't be too careful in dealing with people," and "Most people would take advantage of you if they got the chance." These findings led to Gerbner's development of the **Mean World Index**, in which his research team argued that the sheer amount of violence on television was causing heavy viewers of television to overestimate how dangerous the world around them really was. Gerbner argued that the similarity between the stories on television and the exposure of the limited set of stories found on television to a large population would lead to audiences sharing a similar perception of the world. Cultivation describes this process as **mainstreaming**.

Cultivation theory, especially in the new media environment, has had to expand and change to fit the times. Some recent tests of the theory have specified differences between **first-order cultivation effects** (effects on viewer's statistical descriptions of the world) and **second-order cultivation effects** (effects on how they see the world, generally). For example, Jamieson and Romer (2014) found that increased rates of violence on television from the 70s to the early 2000s had a strong impact on audience's views of a mean world (second-order effects), but had no impact on their perceptions of actual crime rates (first-order effects). Grabe and Drew (2007) found that while news and entertainment television both had second-order cultivation effects (related to perceptions of crime), only news content had first-order effects.

Cultivation has rather fallen out of favor in media psychology due to the difficulty of translating what began as a sociological (or societal-level) theory to the individual level of analysis. Current cultivation research has moved from societal-level analysis to understanding how concepts are retained in memory and expressed in behavior by means of other processes and theories (e.g., priming, see Chapter 5, and exemplification covered in this chapter). However, alternate theories for how entertainment could affect our understanding of social reality advanced in relatively short order to examine how media can affect an individual's perceptions of the world in which they live.

Social Learning Theory and Social Cognitive Theory

The next theory we discuss in terms of media shaping social reality is one that was not really designed to be a theory of media effects. Instead it stemmed from research on **vicarious learning**, that is, the notion that we can learn from observing others. As noted psychologist

Mean World Index

A self-report measurement that asks people how dangerous they believe the world to be

mainstreaming

A phenomenon by which individual differences in beliefs and attitudes more closely resemble the world on television than would otherwise be expected

first-order cultivation effects

Cultivation effects on general beliefs about the world; usually related to factual or statistical information

second-order cultivation effects

Cultivation effects on specific beliefs about the world; usually about an individual's own environment or situation

vicarious learning

Learning a behavior by watching another person engage in it, rather through experiencing directly-direct experience

Albert Bandura (1977) quipped, "Learning would be exceedingly laborious, not to mention hazardous, if people had to rely solely on the effects of their own actions to inform them what to do."

In terms of learning from media, Bandura noticed that children seem to model—or copy—many of the things that they see in their environment, and he wanted to develop a more systematic explanation for how this vicarious learning works. The need for such a model was critical, because it is not the case that children model everything that they see. Yet, children absolutely have a capacity to observe and learn behaviors they see even when these behaviors are mediated.

Bandura hypothesized that what encourages children to model some behaviors and not others is how they feel about the person modeling the behavior—Bandura called this **model attractiveness.** For example, if a particular child sees a character such as Hugh Jackman's Wolverine or Scarlett Johansson's Black Widow as attractive or interesting, then they are more likely to model the behaviors that those characters engage in. Of course, this modeling could be more prosocial, such as both characters' deep devotion and loyalty to their friends and colleagues in times of need. But, it can also be very antisocial, such as both characters' use of brutal violence. Likewise, children can find both "bad" characters and "good" characters attractive (**Sidebar: Goofus, or Gallant?**)

model attractiveness

The extent to which a person performing a behavior is perceived positively or negatively by observers

didactic

Of or pertaining to teaching

Sidebar   Goofus, or Gallant?

For many children in the United States, the characters Goofus and Gallant have been a **didactic** behavioral model since the 1940s. Featured in *Highlights for Children* magazine (although they first appeared in *Children's Activities*), the two characters have been used as behavioral models for good (Gallant) and poor (Goofus) behaviors. The comics are always drawn as two separate panels, like so:

- Goofus never helps wash the dishes at home but Gallant always helps with house chores.
- Goofus changes the channels on the television without asking but Gallant always asks before changing program.
- Goofus repeats bad jokes that he hears online but Gallant always asks his parents to explain the jokes, before he repeats them.

(Continued)

Curiously, the characters Goofus and Gallant have also been drawn at various ages, although they have always been drawn as Caucasian males, which could be an opportunity for future research and production of the characters—especially given that model attractiveness can be influence by how similar or dissimilar the model is to the individual viewer. An engaging history of Goofus and Gallant was gathered by the website *Mental Floss*, along with several facts about the long-running series: http://mental floss.com/article/503615/7-engaging-facts-about-goofus-and-gallant.

You try it!   *Assume that you've been asked to put together a Goofus and Gallant cartoon for your campus, to try to demonstrate good and bad community behaviors. What sort of behaviors would you display? What sort of characteristics would Goofus and Gallant have? Consider pitching the idea to your campus and share your cartoons with each other. If you need help, several Pinterest boards and other online archives have classic and contemporary Goofus and Gallant cartoons. You can even submit your own Goofus and Gallant examples to Highlights for Children, at https://www. highlightskids.com/asks/ask-us/goofus-and-gallant.*

The social learning process (Bandura later renamed it as a social cognitive process) has four critical stages. The first is the **attention** stage: The viewer must pay attention to what is happening on-screen and in particular, the model that they are likely to learn from. Next is the **retention** stage: The viewer must remember the behavior that was just enacted on-screen. If the viewer has both paid attention to and stored into memory the modeled behavior, they then must learn how to **reproduce** the actual behavior in question. Some behaviors such as shouting at another person, punching a person, or hugging a close friend are probably very easy to reproduce; other behaviors such as racing through traffic on a crowded highway or using a set of nunchakus, are quite complex. Finally, if the viewer has paid attention, remembered the behavior, and has the skills to reproduce the behavior, there is still no guarantee that they will actually model it. The final stage of Bandura's model is the **motivation** stage, where the individual considers the consequences of their actions. This is perhaps the most critical aspect of Bandura's model, because it suggests that people have a **self-reflective capacity** in which they can carefully consider whether or not there is a reason for engaging the learned behavior.

These four stages are critical because they provide a systematic explanation for the conditions under which audiences do and do not learn from media. For example, a certain media narrative might consistently punish all characters that use violence to solve their problems and from this, viewers would not be likely to want to reproduce violent behavior. Another narrative might consistently reward all characters that use violence in the same manner and thus, viewers are more likely to want to reproduce the behavior. Bandura found that a lack of explicit punishment for a behavior tends to be interpreted as a reward. Notably, modeling is more likely to occur when the behaviors are conducted by attractive models as compared to unattractive models. Here, attractive doesn't necessarily have to refer to being physically attractive but rather, can also refer to an individually being socially attractive (or popular) as well as task attractive (well-suited for a particular action or scenario).

Social cognitive theory has been criticized for being too vague, or unspecified. This means that it can explain every instance of behavior by the above stages, and yet cannot predict when and why particular characters will be seen as particularly attractive by particular viewers, or how viewers make sense of particular characters. Therefore, we turn now to discussing **exemplification theory** (Zillmann, 2009), which does just that.

Exemplification Theory

Which is more likely to bite you, a shark or a dog? If you are like most readers, who have grown up with the legacy of *Jaws* and annual summer blockbuster movies featuring killer marine fish, you are likely to say a shark, despite dogs being the animal most often implicated in human attacks. Yet, even knowing the facts, we are still less likely to be scared of entering a dog park than swimming in an unknown ocean. What is it about *Jaws* that has shifted so many people's perception of the relative risk of sharks versus dogs?

Throughout history, humans have had to make sense of a very complex and changing world around them in a very short amount of time. For this reason, we tend to use vital "chunks" of information to form quick judgments about potential threats and rewards. These chunks, over time, form patterns of thinking known as **heuristics**, and two in particular are very important to understanding how we learn from media.

The first heuristic is the **recognition heuristic**, which says "the thing I have heard of is the most important" (**Sidebar: The Fast and the Frugal**). Yet recognition isn't everything. If I asked you whether more words in English start with 'r' or have 'r' as the third letter, you'd probably start thinking of words that start with 'r' and words that have 'r' as the third letter, and from there compare lists to find words that appear on both (matches which are, indeed, quite "rare"). How easily each came to mind would probably influence your judgment about which has more. This is known as the **availability heuristic**, and it's a function of how information is stored in memory and how it is retrieved.

Sidebar   The Fast and the Frugal

Which city has a larger population: San Diego or San Antonio? Psychologist Gerd Gigerenzer and his colleagues posted this question to a group of college students in the United States and in Germany. Sixty two percent of U.S. students correctly answered San Diego, while 100% of the German students gave the same answer. How could this be? Gigerenzer reasoned that the German students were more efficient in their thinking because they used a very basic **recognition heuristic**—they had heard of San Diego, but not of San Antonio. Conversely, U.S. students had likely heard of both cities and in a sense, had *too much* information with which to decide. Both cities are rather well known to most Americans: both have major airports, popular professional sports teams, and similar population sizes.

The above finding—which has been replicated in numerous different forms and varieties—is an example of a human capacity to engage in what Gigerenzer called **ecological rationality**. The argument is that there are scenarios in which having only some information about a topic can be useful. For judging the sizes (in population) of different cities, we might correctly assume that if we've heard of a city, then that city is probably larger than another that we haven't heard of.

In fact, many maps will use this very heuristic. Very small towns aren't listed at all, and larger cities are written in larger fonts and in bold. So long as larger cities are more likely to be features on maps, in media programming, and in daily conversations (often times, people who grow up near major cities will just say that they're from the name of the city, then their specific town name), it's likely that the recognition heuristic will be an effective way for you to win trivia games and other arguments about major cities and their population.

ecological rationality
An argument that states that rationality comes from weighing the amount of information one knows and does not know in a given situation

(Continued)

You try it!   *Can you think of other types of facts and information for which the recognition heuristic would apply very well? If you were to think of cities from your home state or country, do you think you could replicate Gigerenzer's findings?*

exemplar

An instance of an event population that shares essential features with all other instances from the group of events

model of intuitive morality and exemplars (MIME)

A theory that proposes media exemplars can prime short-term morality accessibility and shape individual chronic morality accessibility over multiple media exposures

base-rate information

The probability of an event actually occurring

Why is this important? Our brains don't really distinguish mediated content from nonmediated content. Moreover, we often remember information but forget where or how we learned about it. So mere exposure to information, through the media or elsewhere, can lead to deeper and broader memory stores which in turn influence our judgments. Media representations can alter our social reality by increasing the recognition and availability of specific examples provided in the media. These stores are known as **exemplars**, and over time we begin to rely on these exemplars to make decisions and attributions about real-life events (Zillmann, 2009).

Zillmann (2009) lays out three assumptions of how exemplars form. First, *events of some consequence attract more attention and are remembered better than inconsequential events.* When a dog bites someone, it is not likely to be in the newspapers, and there are very few blockbusters about killer dogs (save perhaps *Cujo*). However, there is often at least one blockbuster shark attack movie a year, and when a shark bites someone it attracts considerable media attention. Second, *it is much easier for audiences to comprehend and remember concrete events than abstract events.* Seeing Jaws attack helpless swimmers on screen, with incredibly graphic and realistic images and the sounds is more likely to stay in our memories than simply reading statistics about dog bites. These effects are especially strong when an event being portrayed is emotionally engaging. Finally, when we do remember exemplars, we often incorrectly remember the frequency of those exemplars happening. We base our own quantitative assessments on our memories, rather than **base-rate information**—or the extent to which these events happen in reality.

To summarize, exemplification theory would suggest that concrete, iconic, emotionally salient exemplars foster overestimation of specific events, as well as undue attention paid to specific events. In most cases, these exemplars do not represent social reality, yet they can come to alter audience's perceptions of social reality by shaping and shifting the examples upon which people draw. One way this can occur is by shifting our examples of what is morally right or wrong: The focus of the **model of intuitive morality and exemplars** (MIME; Tamborini, 2011).

The MIME provides a systematic explanation of how audience's views on morality might be shaped by media entertainment. The MIME borrows from **moral foundations theory** (Haidt & Joseph, 2007), which suggests that people implicitly engage one (or more) of five different concepts of morality when they encounter a given scenario: care/harm, fairness/cheating, loyalty/betrayal, authority/subversion, and sanctity/degradation (all described in more detail, at https://www. moralfoundations.org/). These foundations are found in cultures all over the world, but various cultural groups (such as different countries, or people with different political philosophies) pay more attention to some of these foundations and less attention to others.

We can use these moral foundations to understand the different types of entertainment media people might enjoy, as well as their responses to the content. For example, we know from Haidt's work that political liberals in the US tend to place more importance on issues of care/harm and fairness/cheating than US political conservatives—in a sense, they see the world very differently on these dimensions. These different worldviews might explain why political liberals seem more likely to enjoy shows with diverse cast members (such as *Will and Grace*) while political conservatives may be more likely to watch shows that feature themes of justice (such as *Blue Bloods*; Santiago, 2017). However, exposure to entertainment can also alter perceptions of moral content. For example, in a series of studies (Eden et al., 2014; Tamborini et al., 2010) students watched several weeks of soap opera in their class. Over time, the moral intuitions of the viewers nudged closer to the moral views expressed on screen by the characters. The MIME illustrates how exemplars can influence media selection while also shaping our social reality in specific ways.

moral foundations theory (MFT)
A theory that suggests individuals have variable accessibility to different types of preconscious moral intuitions; this accessibility to some over other intuitions influences how individuals process media content.

Conclusion

We live in a mediated reality, in which entertainment consumption can have a subtle yet lasting effect on our attitudes and cognitions about the world around us. In this chapter we discussed the notion of entertainment as a pseudo-experience, which can replace real experience in some instances. We covered the Cultural Indicators Project and the three-pronged attempt to understand media effects from production, message content, and effects perspective, as well as the mainstreaming and Mean World hypothesis. We then turned to social cognitive theory and how we learn from social actors in media content. Finally, we focused on individual psychology, looking at how exemplification—or the process of chunking information into relevant and salient bits—can be formed by entertainment experiences. Taken together, these different theories and perspectives suggest that while entertainment media might simply be something that we do to pass the time, there is a great deal of influence that those mediated experience can have on us, both good and bad. In the rest of the book, we will continue to revisit the many ways that entertainment media can influence our thoughts, feelings, and behaviors.

Key Terms

Pseudo-environment   The constructed environment in one's mind that is derived from nonphysical observations, such as mediated observations

Mediated experience   Any experience derived from media content; usually contrasted with a lived or real world experience

Stalagmite theories   A family of media theories that predict that perception effects such as attitude change are small or undetectable in the immediate term yet cumulative and large over time

Cultural Indicators Project   A research project focused on quantifying the content and effects of television on the general population

Content analysis   A social scientific method in which researchers systematically quantify and describe properties of media content

Cultivation differential   The difference in beliefs and attitudes between heavy and light television viewers; thought to result from the prevalence of beliefs and attitudes presented on television

Mean World Index   A self-report measurement that asks people how dangerous they believe the world to be

Mainstreaming   A phenomenon by which individual differences in beliefs and attitudes more closely resemble the world on television than would otherwise be expected

First-order cultivation effects   Cultivation effects on general beliefs about the world; usually related to factual or statistical information

Second-order cultivation effects   Cultivation effects on specific beliefs about the world; usually about an individual's own environment or situation

Vicarious learning   Learning a behavior by watching another person engage in it, rather through experiencing directly-direct experience

Model attractiveness   The extent to which a person performing a behavior is perceived positively or negatively by observers

Didactic   Of or pertaining to teaching

Ecological rationality   An argument that states that rationality comes from weighing the amount of information one knows and does not know in a given situation

Exemplar   An instance of an event population that shares essential features with all other instances from the group of events

Base-rate information   The probability of an event actually occurring

Model of intuitive morality and exemplars (MIME)   A theory that proposes media exemplars can prime short-term morality accessibility and shape individual chronic morality accessibility over multiple media exposures

Moral foundations theory (MFT)   A theory that suggests individuals have variable accessibility to different types of preconscious moral intuitions; this accessibility to some over other intuitions influences how individuals process media content

References

Anderson, C. A., & Bushman, B. J. (2002). Human aggression. *Annual Review of Psychology, 53,* 27–51. doi: 10.1146.annurev.psych.53.100901.135231

Bandura, A. (1977). *Social Learning Theory.* New York: General Learning Press.

Bowman, N. D., Knight, J. Schlue, L., & Cohen, E. L. (2018). What if it happened to me? Socially conscious music videos can address campus assault: Narrative comprehension and rape myth acceptance. *Psychology of Popular Media Culture.*

Bryant, J. (1986). The road most traveled: Yet another cultivation critique. *Journal of Broadcasting & Electronic Media, 30*(2), 231–235. doi: 10.1080/08838158609386621

Collins, R. L. (2011). Content analysis of gender roles in media: Where are we now and where should we go? *Sex Roles, 64,* 290–298. doi:10.1007/s11199-010-9929-5

Eden, A., Tamborini, R., Grizzard, M., Lewis, R., Weber, R., & Prabhu, S. (2014). Repeated exposure to narrative entertainment and the salience of moral intuitions. *Journal of Communication, 64*(3), 501–520. doi: 10.1111/jcom.12098

Gerbner, G., & Gross, L. (1976). Living with television: The violence profile. *Journal of Communication, 26*(2), 173–199. doi: 10.1111/j.1460-2466.1976.tb01397.x

Grabe, M. E., & Drew, D. G. (2007). Crime cultivation: Comparisons across media genres and channels. *Journal of Broadcasting & Electronic Media, 51*(1), 147–171. doi: 10.1080/0883815 0701308143

Haidt, J. & Joseph, C. (2007). The moral mind: How five sets of innate intuitions guide the development of many culture-specific virtues, and perhaps even modules. In P. Carruthers, S. Laurence, & S. Stich (Eds.), *The innate mind* (Vol 3., pp. 367–391). New York: Oxford University Press.

Holbrook, R. A., & Hill, T. G. (2006). Agenda-setting and priming in prime time television: Crime dramas as political cues. *Political Communication, 22*(3), 277–295. doi: 10.1080/10584600591006519

Jamieson, P. E., & Romer, D. (2014). Violence in popular U.S. prime time tv dramas and the cultivation of fear: A time series analysis. *Media and Communication, 2*(2), 31–41.

Kim, Y. S., Barak, G., & Shelton, D. E. (2016). Examining the "CSI-effect" in the cases of circumstantial evidence and eyewitness testimony: Multivariate and path analyses. *Journal of Criminal Justice, 37*(5), 452–460. doi: 10.1016/j.crimjus.2009.07.005

Lasswell, H. D. (1948) The structure and function of communication in society. In W. Schramm (Ed.), *Mass communications, 2nd Ed.* (pp. 117–129). Urbana, IL: University of Illinois Press.

Mastro, D., Enriquez, M., Bowman, N. D., Prabhu, S., & Tamborini, R. (2012). Morality subcultures and media production: How Hollywood minds the morals of its audience. In R. Tamborini (Ed.), *Media and the moral mind* (pp. 75–92). London: Routledge.

McCombs, M. E., & Shaw, D. L. (1972). The agenda-setting function of mass media. *Public Opinion Quarterly, 36*(2), 176–187. doi: 10.1086/267990

Morgan, M., Shanahan, J., & Signorielli, N. (2015). Yesterday's new cultivation, tomorrow. *Mass Communication & Society, 18*(5), 674–699. doi: 10.1080/15205436.2015.1072725

Santiago, A. L. H. (2017). Conservatives and liberals love wildly different TV shows—here are the top series across the political spectrum. *Business Insider.* Retrieved from https://www.businessinsider.com/conservative-v-liberal-shows-2017-9

Scharrer, E., & Blackburn, G. (2018). Cultivating conceptions of masculinity: Television and perceptions of masculine gender role norms. *Mass Communication & Society, 21*(2), 149–177. doi: 10.1080/1520543.2017.1406118

Schiappa, E., Gregg, P. B., & Hewes, D. E. (2005). The parasocial contact hypothesis. *Communication Monographs, 72*(1), 92–115. doi: 10.1080/036775052000342544

Tamborini, R. (2011). Moral intuition and media entertainment. *Journal of Media Psychology, 23,* 39–45. doi: 10.1027/1864-1105/a000031

Tamborini, R., Weber, R., Eden, A., Bowman, N. D., & Grizzard, M. (2010). Repeated exposure to daytime soap opera and shifts in moral judgment toward social convention. *Journal of Broadcasting & Electronic Media, 54*(4), 621–640. doi:10.1080/08838151.2010.519806

Vezzali, L., Stathi, S., Giovannini, D., Capozza, D., & Trifiletti, E. (2015). The greatest magic of Harry Potter: Reducing prejudice. *Journal of Applied Social Psychology, 45*(2), 105–121. doi: 10.1111/jasp.12279

Willing, R. (2004). 'CSI effect' has juries wanting more evidence. *USA Today.* Retrieved from http://usatoday30.usatoday.com/news/nation/2004-08-05-csi-effect_x.htm

Wright, C. R. (1960). Functional analysis and mass communication. *Public Opinion Quarterly, 24*(4), 605–620. doi: 10.1086/266976

Zillmann, D. (2009). Exemplification theory: Judging the whole by some of its parts. *Media Psychology, 1*(1), 69–94. doi: 10.1207/s1532785xmep0101_5

Further Reading

Allport, G. W. 1954. *The Nature of Prejudice.* New York: Doubleday.

Bandura A. (2001). Social cognitive theory of mass communication. *Media Psychology, 3,* 265–299. doi: 10.1207/S1532785XMEP0303_03

Goldstein, D. G., & Gigerenzer, G. (1999). The recognition heuristic: How ignorance makes us smart. In G. Gigerenzer, & P. Todd (Eds.), *Simple heuristics that make us smart* (pp. 37–58). New York: Oxford University Press.

Lippmann. W. (1922). *Public opinion.* New York: Macmillan.

Tamborini, R. C. (Ed.). (2013). *Media and the moral mind.* London: Routledge.

Zillmann, D., & Bryant, J. (1985). *Selective exposure to communication:* Hillsdale, NJ: LEA.

CHAPTER 5
The Dark Side of Entertainment

"I shall not today attempt further to define the kinds of material I understand to be embraced within that shorthand description ["hard-core pornography"], and perhaps I could never succeed in intelligibly doing so. But I know it when I see it, and the motion picture involved in this case is not that."

—Justice Potter Stewart on his threshold test for obscenity, Jacobellis v. Ohio, 1964.

In 1966, John Lennon stated in an interview with a British journalist that "The Beatles were more popular than Jesus." In the United States, Christian groups, primarily in the south, began to protest the "Fab Four" leading to the burning and destruction of many Beatles' records and memorabilia. Ministers, DJs, and various other cultural critics were concerned that The Beatles might undermine the youth's faith in Christianity and the only response to such an imminent threat was a boycott of The Beatles!

The ministers and DJs involved in the boycott of The Beatles—along with many other infamous book bannings and burnings throughout history—were likely engaging in a **moral panic**, a scenario defined by Elson and Ferguson (2013) as when one part of society considers another part of society to be a threat or risk to society as a whole. Similar moral panics have been observed with other entertainment media. The 1950s saw comic books lambasted by psychiatrist Fredric Wertham for seducing innocent readers into juvenile delinquency (with examples of comics with erotic and violent content). Video game violence first appeared in the culture wars in the

moral panic
When one part of society considers another part of society or a specific behavior to be a threat or risk to society as a whole, based on little or contradictory evidence

1970s with the release of the video game *Death Race,* where players were allowed to drive their car over humanoid "gremlins" for point. Could such a game make murderers out of normal high school students? The 1980s linked satanism with Role Playing Games and heavy metal music. Today, many in society are worried about cell phones and social media destroying our ability to interact with in-the-flesh social contacts.

The view that entertainment harms society is *not* new. But how much truth underlies the hype? The goal of this chapter is to outline and describe some potential negative effects associated with entertainment media.

Objectives

After reading and studying the concepts in this chapter, students should be able to:

➤ Identify what types of content may be considered concerning.

➤ Understand how concerning content is portrayed in entertainment media.

➤ Describe key theoretical perspectives regarding potential effects of concerning content.

➤ Be able to critique the moral panic perspective on concerning content.

"Concerning" Content

Most research on the negative effects of media entertainment has focused on specific types of content thought to be most likely to lead to harmful outcomes. The three types of content that have received the most intense scrutiny are sexual content, violent content, and content that features psychotropic (i.e., mind altering) substances, such as drugs, alcohol, and tobacco. Of particular concern are the effects of exposure to these types of content on children. At the same time, adult audiences are not presumed to be immune to the potential negative effects of this content either. In the following section, we illustrate what we know about particular kinds of concerning or controversial content in entertainment media—the presence of sexual content, pornography, violence, and substance use across television, film, and music entertainment.

Sexual content. In the United States, sex is still a fairly taboo conversation (**Sidebar: Fifty Shades of Grey**). You might talk to a classmate about the details of their workout regime, but you're probably unlikely to strike up a conversation about their techniques in the bedroom. Most of what we know about the quantity of sexual content in television comes from a series of studies commissioned by the Kaiser Family Foundation in four reports from 1997 to 2005 (Sex on TV). **Sexual content** was defined broadly and included talk about sex (two friends talking about their sex lives, or a couple talking about whether to have sex), as well as sexual behaviors, ranging from passionate kissing to intercourse (either depicted or strongly implied). A team of researchers, led by Dale Kunkel of the University of California, Santa Barbara, worked to quantify what kinds of sexual content was portrayed on television, how much of it was there, and how frequent it occurred in different genres.

Sexual content
Media content that
includes any type of
sexual intimacy

Results from their latest study (2005), which examined over 1,000 hours of programming content across 1,100 shows, demonstrated that most entertainment (70%) contains some form of sexual content, and during prime time that percentage increases to 77%. This number has been increasing over time, in the 1996 study only 56% of the programs contained sexual content. The number of sex scenes in shows has also increased (to as many as five sex scenes per hour of programming). Movies included the most, with 92% of movies showing some sexual content, whereas reality television (including shows like extreme home makeover) had the least (26%). The Kaiser Family report was also concerned with what kinds of sexual messages were targeted to teenagers and adults. References to safe sex or sexual risks and responsibilities were rare, with only 14% of all sexual content referring to or mentioning negative consequences from sexual behavior. Only 1% of shows focus on sexual risks during the entire episode. Sexual content is likely to be depicted between young characters (under 25) who have just met (think of the movie *Knocked Up*).

Sidebar   Fifty Shades of Grey

"We weren't criticizing [the book] from any literary standpoint because that's not why anyone's reading it."

—Cleveland radio DJ Alan Cox, on organizing a
burning of the book Fifty Shades of Grey.

(Continued)

In 2011, British novelist E. L. James released an erotic romance novel called Fifty Shades of Grey. The book (part of a trilogy) focuses on a secretive love affair between a young woman, Anastasia Steele, and a wealthy man, Christian Grey. A significant part of Anastasia's and Christian's romance is a nondisclosure agreement (signed by Anastasia, at Christian's request) to keep the specific details of their sexual encounters private. In particular, the two engage in explicitly described sadomasochistic sex.

As an erotic romance novel, discussions of sexual behavior are expected. For many, however, the book's keen focus on bondage and sadomasochism was too much. Groups in Michigan and Ohio organized public book burnings to protest the offensive sexual lifestyles depicted in the book. Both events were organized by male radio DJs in the two areas.

In the United Kingdom, a domestic abuse charity Wearside Women in Need organized their own book burning to protest what they saw as a piece of literature that encouraged sexual abuse and in particular, abuse of women.

Notably, the American Library Association and the American Civil Liberties Union both spoke out against censoring or destroying the book. As of 2015, the book has sold nearly 125 million copies worldwide, and has been translated into more than 50 different world languages. In 2015, the book was given a film adaptation, which has earned nearly $600 million worldwide. Similar to the book, the film has also faced resistance. It was banned in several nations, including Cambodia, India, Indonesia, Kenya, Malaysia, and the United Arab Emirates.

pornography
Media content that includes graphic and explicit depictions of sexual activity

Pornography. A subset of sexual content is **pornography**, which is defined as the graphic and explicit depiction of sexual activity. Anthropologists and historians are able to find evidence of pornographic media in almost every culture and sexually explicit imagery predates written history (Lenz, 2016). Of course, pornography is also a prominent feature of today's media landscape as well. In their annual report on viewing trends, Pornhub.com (the 28th most visited web page in the world as of 2018) reports over 28.5 billion annual visits to its webpage, with more than 25 billion searches performed and enough video content (3,700 petabytes) to completely fill the memory of every iPhone currently in use around the world. The digital revolution has revolutionized pornography production and consumption, however most of the research to date has been focused on negative effects of pornography viewing rather than quantifying the type of content that exists.

Violence. Another area that researchers and philosophers alike have examined in detail is why humans are attracted to, yet also disgusted by, violence. One reason that individuals might be attracted to violence is related to morbid curiosity and evolutionary fitness. Violence is a potential cause of death, and so being aware of it and how it unfolds is likely to provide some evolutionary advantage. When we see or hear something potentially life-threatening, it causes high arousal and we quickly orient to it—that is, we focus our senses to quickly assessing if we are in danger. Violence, including explosions, threats, and force, is a way for writers and producers to quickly grab our attention. Another explanation is that we may simply like the sounds that things make or the way things look like when they break, blow up, or are destroyed, which is known as "**the aesthetic theory of destruction**" (Allen & Greenberger, 1978).

Violence is quite prevalent in media content, even content targeted toward children. Comic violence is more common in movies rated PG, such as *Home Alone*. But PG-13 movies contain grittier violence and a large number of guns (Romer, Jamieson, & Jamieson, 2017). Ironically, parents tend to be more accepting of violence when it is justified when research suggests justified violence is actually more harmful in terms of increasing aggression. Across the age ranges though, media tends to portray violence as a means to achieving one's goals. The biggest blockbusters (**see Sidebar: Count the Cuts**) feature dramatic conflict that is often solved only through violent means.

the aesthetic theory of destruction

The idea that people may be attracted to and enjoy watching the destruction of objects

---

Sidebar   Count the Cuts

It seems simple enough to define media violence, doesn't it? One could watch a television show with a notebook in hand, and write down every time that one character punches or shoots another. Or, maybe for something to be counted as "violent" the action has to result in a death (the webpage www.moviebodycounts.com can track this for you, with *Lord of the Rings: Return of the King* currently marked as having the highest "body count" at 836). Perhaps only *graphic* violence should be included, such as when violence is accompanied by blood and gore; after all, this type of graphicness can trigger an arousal reaction which can intensify subsequent behavior (Potter & Smith, 2010). Or is justification for violence more important than graphicness (Tamborini et al., 2013)?

(Continued)

The point of the discussion above is that media violence is something that is remarkably complicated and multifaceted. While we all might invoke our inner Justice Stewart (from the introduction of this chapter) and say that "we know it when we see it," we often don't even agree on what we see—as consumers, researchers, and policy-makers.

> **You try it!** *Imagine for a moment that you were going to do a study designed to quantify the number of violent acts in a well-known movie or television show. How would you decide what counts and what does not count as violence? Would you include violence against nonhumans? Violence that happens as the result of accidents? Would verbal aggression and bullying count as violence? What about acts of nature? Discuss your approach with classmates or your instructor, and compare how differences in your definitions might result in a very different numbers regarding how violent that movie or TV show is considered to be.*

The prevalence of violence likely relates to the ease with which it translates to various languages and cultures. Comedy is often culturally dependent, and so a comedic film produced in one language would likely have a difficult time finding an audience in another. However, explosions sound the same in every language. So just how prevalent is violence? Some studies suggest that 60% of all TV shows contain violence. With premium channels like HBO and Showtime, more than 85% of the shows contain violence. Only about 4% of shows have antiviolence messages. According to the American Psychiatric Association (as cited by Muscari, 2002), by the late 1990s the average child watching TV in the United States is likely to see 200,000 acts of violence and 18,000 murders by the time they reach 18!

virtual violence

Violence that occurs in a virtual environment, such as virtual reality or a video game

Equally prevalent is **virtual violence**, defined as any user behavior with the intention of doing harm to other social characters in a video game, given that the other game characters are motivated to avoid having the harm done to them. Smith et al. (2003) content analyzed over 1,300 violent interactions in 60 violent video games finding that 23% featured violence against women, and that 77% of games included "justified" violence, that is, violence that is somehow excused as being on the part of the moral justice system of the game or serving the interests of the player. Heintz-Knowles (2001) found that violence in games, particularly killing other characters, is almost always rewarded in the game (**Sidebar: Grand Theft Auto: Satire or Murder Simulator?**).

Sidebar Grand Theft Auto: Mature Audiences Only?

To even the casual gamers, the video game series *Grand Theft Auto* is one of the most well-known, and maligned, video game series in the history of the medium. The *GTA* video games are well-known for their over-the-top portrayals of gun violence and vehicular manslaughter, with narratives heavily steeped in criminal activities from assassinations and drug deals to racially motivated crimes and prostitution. In most cases, the player is asked to break the law for any number of motivations, with earlier versions of the game more focused on accumulating points and personal achievements (like more traditional video games), and later versions of the game taking on more serious and emotional narratives (more similar to Hollywood films). Due to this type of hyper-violent content, all iterations of the games have been rated "M" for mature audiences only.

The game's references to popular media franchises such as *The Godfather, Scarface*, and *Miami Vice* are often sarcastic or nostalgic, and older audiences are likely to see these parallels and understand them in context. The tongue-in-cheek themes within the game are often highly critical of real-world processes and biases (e.g., the in-game Weazel News serves as a right-wing media outlet, as a satire of Fox News). However, the game is remarkably popular with younger audiences that might not have the developmental skills and the media experiences necessary to place the content in a more appropriate context. This can be particularly problematic if the content portrays racial or gender stereotypes. Scholars Anna Everett and S. Craig Watkins refer to such games as **racialized pedagogical zones** and argue that the inherent learning nature of video games also serves as experience-driven laboratories in which children in particular might learn and enact racial and ethnic stereotypes that could transfer to their real world.

You try it! *Consider playing one of the many video games in GTA series, or watch videos of in-game footage on websites such as Twitch.tv or YouTube Gaming. What sorts of content are you seeing in these games? Do you think that the content is meant to be taken at face value or simply included for shock value? Is the content earnest or is it more satirical and critical in nature? If you were in charge of rating video games, how old do you think that somebody should be, in order to play this game? Why?*

racialized pedagogical zones The idea that interactive media (such as video games)s allow players to practice enacting racial and ethnic stereotypes that could transfer to the real world

Alcohol. By far the most frequent drug portrayed in media entertainment is alcohol. Think of the recent hit *A Star is Born* (2018) about a musician dealing with alcoholism, or the award-winning similar story told in *Leaving Las Vegas* (1995). Despite these films that focus on the negative effects of alcohol, drinking is often portrayed as normative with G and PG-rated movies containing scenes of characters drinking alcohol. Gerbner (2001) found that alcohol is portrayed in a scene on television once every 22 minutes, and up to once every 14 minutes in music videos. In the movies, a content analysis of top U.S. box office hits from 1998 to 2003 found that most movies (83%, including 57% of G/PG-rated movies) depicted alcohol use (Dal Cin, Worth, Dalton, and Sargent, 2008). Similar to portrayals of sexual content, rarely are any negative consequences shown for alcohol consumption on television, and it is often portrayed as humorous or sociable.

Tobacco. In the early days of TV, cigarette companies often advertised in family programming and in the cinema. Up to 88% of films in the 1930s contained tobacco use. For example, an advertisement on the *Flintstones* featured Fred and Barney enjoying a Winston cigarette. Since 1998's Master Settlement Agreement, tobacco companies have been unable to market their products by name in media entertainment. However, popular programs, such as *Mad Men, Stranger Things,* and video games such as *Grand Theft Auto* feature a great deal of cigarette consumption. In a recent study, 79% of shows popular with youth aged 15 to 24 (key ages for adoption of smoking habits) depict smoking. In the movies, a concerted effort between the U.S. government, researchers at Harvard, and researchers at University of California San Francisco have worked to monitor the number of tobacco incidents in movies. From 2002—the beginning of the program—to 2016, the percentage of G, PG, and PG-13 rated films depicting tobacco use fell from 65% to 38%. However, half of all PG-13-rated films contain tobacco use, in part due to a "biographical exception" granted for films portraying people who, in real life, smoked cigarettes. In response to mounting criticism from anti-tobacco groups such, popular media streaming service Netflix announced in mid-2019 that they will substantially cut back on how often characters are shown smoking on-screen.

Although the use of e-cigarettes (vaping) is growing in popularity, and has been featured prominently in some mainstream films (*The Tourist*, 2010), and series (notably Kevin Spacey's character in *House of Cards*) it has not received the same scholarly attention to date.

Other drugs. Illicit drug use is somewhat less common than tobacco and alcohol. Research in the 1990s indicated that only 3% of TV shows included illicit drug use, and almost every instance was associated with negative consequences (Christenson, Henriksen, & Roberts, 2000). Music and movies, however, were more likely to feature illicit drugs, with some 20% of movies and songs containing a reference to illicit drugs (Roberts, Henriksen, & Christenson, 1999). These patterns have likely increased given the increasing prevalence of more mature content on television (a la *Breaking Bad* and *Weeds*), and the more relaxed social attitudes toward some illicit drugs like marijuana. Rating organizations such as the MPAA restrict drug usage other than alcohol to content rated R. Other forms of entertainment media, such as comic books, have also incorporated illicit drug use into their storylines— usually with the intent to tell antidrug messages, albeit not without controversy (**Sidebar: Spidey and a Web of Drugs**).

Sidebar   Spidey and a Web of Drugs

For most people, comic books are thought of as a light-hearted medium for children, usually featuring colorful heroes and villains in fantasy environments. For these folks and many others, three issues of *Amazing Spider-Man* published in the 1970s were quite a shock, as they placed a spotlight on an issue of considerable social concern at the time: drug use. According to Marvel Comics publisher Stan Lee, the U.S. Department of Health, Education, and Welfare approached him about the possibility of incorporating a **public service announcement** into an upcoming issue of *Amazing Spider-Man*, which was one of the most popular comics among children at the time. Lee seized the opportunity, and his office wrote a three-issue narrative arc in which one of Spider-Man's longtime friends, Harry Osborn, turns to illicit drugs (unnamed pills) to cope with being dumped by long-time love interest Mary Jane Watson.

Lee's storyline was considered too salacious for the time, and the Comics Code Authority (CCA) refused to offer the comic it's seal of approval. Marvel Comics decided to sell the comics anyways, and the issues received numerous accolades, including recognition in the *New York Times* as well as parents' groups and other civic organizations.

A lasting legacy of those issues of *Amazing Spider-Man* is that they opened the doors for other publishers to work illicit drug use into their own storylines. DC Comics released a similar story in the 1970s, with a controversial front cover showing the Green Arrow's side-kick Speedy

public service announcement (PSA) A message that is design to promote a social good; central to the concept of social marketing

(Continued)

network models of memory
A theory that argues that memories are organized and connected to each other in the brain.

spreading activation
The notion that when one concept is accessed in memory, related concepts will also be activated. The closer the concepts are to each other in either conceptual or semantic terms, the more quickly concepts will be activated.

priming
A short-term effect that activates associations and relations in the brain

intensity
The frequency and duration of a prime

recency
The amount of time since a person was exposed to a prime

using heroin on the cover of Green Lantern Number 85, with the tagline "DC Attacks Youth's Greatest Problem . . . DRUGS!" This time around, the comic was able to receive a CCA stamp of approval, and likewise was widely praised for its antidrug message in an unexpected medium: comic books.

You can read more about the history of drug depictions in comic books from the Comic Book Legal Defense Fund, at http://cbldf. org/2012/07/tales-from-the-code-spidey-fights-drugs-and-the-comics-code-authority/

Effects of Exposure to Concerning Content

Social critics often make claims against popular media entertainment and how its content can lead to negative effects. Although you have likely heard your parents or elders talk about some of these effects, you might wonder whether there are psychological mechanisms that would indeed lead to such outcomes. The answer is yes. However, these mechanisms are more complex than they are often portrayed in the news or by social critics. We have already touched on cultivation, exemplification, and social learning in Chapter 4.

However, much research on the role of specific types of content is based on specific models of memory we have not covered yet, particularly **network models of memory**. Network models assume that memory is formed of specific nodes, each representing a concept. Nodes are connected via associative pathways to each other, so that when a node is activated, it can influence how quickly other nodes around it are activated, in a process known as **spreading activation**. When we activate a memory node, this is known as **priming** (much like priming a pump so it will work). The extent of a prime's effect depends on both the **intensity** and the **recency** of a prime. Intensity depends on frequency or duration of a prime, with more frequent and longer-exposure primes having more intensity. Recency depends on how long ago the viewer saw the prime. It is important to note that priming is a short-term effect, only lasting for up to about an hour (maximum).

In psychological research, priming is how our exposure to a given stimulus, such as entertainment media content, can subconsciously influence how we think and behave (Roskos-Ewoldsen et al. 2006).

Berkowitz's (1984) **neoassociationistic model** specifically applied this model to violence in the media, demonstrating that shortly after exposure to violent films or video games, people are more likely to have aggressive thoughts or perform aggressive actions. The **general aggression model** (Anderson & Bushman, 2002) extends the neo-associationistic model to explain why individuals might respond to social encounters with aggression, especially when they are provoked or otherwise agitated. For example, while short-term exposure to violent media might cause a person to have aggressive thoughts toward others, repeated exposure to media characters that use violence to solve their problems might train a person to think that violence is the right and proper solution to provocation.

Given these models of spreading activation, it makes sense why some researchers are concerned about exposure to particular types of content. In general, the proposed effects underlying the claims break down into ABC effects, which stand for Affect, Behavior, and Cognition. **Affect**, or **emotion**, is feeling, **behavior** is doing, and **cognition** is thinking. In the following section we break down the effects of different types of content based on ABC.

Attitudinal/Affective Effects

The aforementioned associative learning mechanisms can also be responsible for creating or changing attitudes. Creating an attitude is easier than changing an already existing one. So media entertainment can be particularly powerful in creating attitudes toward objects with which the viewer doesn't have past experience. When some new thing is experienced in media entertainment, how it is depicted (e.g., as a good thing or as a bad thing) can sway an attitude more positively or negatively.

Changing an attitude is more difficult. But still media can alter previously held attitudes. One method of altering such attitudes is through a process called **disinhibition**. Consider the following example. A child learns from his parents and school that smoking is bad and not something that should be done. If the child learns this lesson well, then an inhibition has been created against smoking. However, if the child watches lots of TV and sees attractive characters smoking, then the previously learned restraints against the behavior can be weakened. This weakened effect can be quite small, but through repeated exposure, the small effects might accumulate.

neo-associationistic model of aggression

A model that predicts that people will have more aggressive thoughts and behaviors after consuming violent media

general aggression model

A model that predicts how violent media in conjunction with personality, cultural, and social variables may lead to aggressive thoughts and behaviors

Affect or **emotion**

A concept used in psychology to describe the experience of feeling

behavior

The way in which a person or animal acts in response to a situation or stimulus

cognition

A concept used to describe the process of thinking, perception, or learning

disinhibition

The weakening of a person's inhibitions

desensitization

The process of feeling a weaker emotional reaction toward media content the more a person consumes or is exposed to the same type of content

Habituation

The lessened response to the same stimulus (in this case, media content) after multiple viewings

Generalization

The ability of habituation to transfer between similar media content

excitation transfer

When arousal created by one event can be transferred to and added upon another event even if the two events differ in cause or result in different feelings (e.g., positive vs. negative)

An affective effect that might occur through entertainment media is **desensitization**. Desensitization is a combination of two psychological processes: **habituation** and **generalization**. When we first encounter an emotion-inducing stimulus (e.g., a gory scene in a horror film or an arousing scene in a pornographic film), we experience an emotional response. However, every time we are exposed to that stimulus after the initial exposure, the "emotion-inducing" potential of the stimulus is reduced. The film *Halloween* is probably less scary the 10th time you watch it as compared to the first. This is the process of habituation and it applies to repeated exposure to the *same* stimulus.

Generalization is a related process that sometimes coincides with habituation, but extends the response to other *similar* stimuli. So if you watch *Halloween* 10 times and then watch some other scary movie, like *Nightmare on Elm Street*, *Nightmare on Elm Street* may be less scary to you than if you had never watched *Halloween*. These effects aren't limited to horror. Repeated exposure to pornography can lead to desensitization not only to pornography but also to other forms of sexual activity, including interaction with a real significant other. Repeated exposure to violent video games can lead to desensitization not only to virtual violence, but to violence in general. When our emotional responsiveness is reduced to one stimulus, our emotional responsiveness to other similar stimuli may also be reduced.

A third affective response that can occur is called **excitation transfer**. When we encounter some emotion-inducing or arousing stimulus, we might have our heart rate increase and a surge of hormones like adrenaline course through our veins. This type of response is completely normal, and you've likely experienced it. Sometimes the spike in arousal is so strong and sudden that it is noticeable. Arousal is a physiological response that comes on fast, but decreases slowly. If you've ever gone for a run you know that increases in your heart and respiration rate happen fast, but if you suddenly stop running, they don't decrease as fast. The comedown is slower. Because of this lag, we can transfer our arousal from one event to another. Imagine someone stepped on your ankle as you were leaving a theater. If you had just seen the newest action film, *Blow 'Em Up Real Good Part 2*, the arousal from the film might lead to a stronger and more aggressive response than if you had just left the romantic drama, *Lovers Who Are Also Sad*. Residual arousal can intensify whatever response your feeling. Coupled with the cognitive effect of **priming**, your response might be stronger and more aggressive after watching *Blow 'Em Up Real Good Part 2*.

Behavioral Effects

In addition to cognitive and affective effects, there is also widespread concern that media entertainment can alter behavior. In order to change behavior we must first change beliefs and then change attitudes. Thus, the effects we have already described are thought to underlie and support behavioral effects.

For sex and substance abuse, behavioral effects that draw the most concern are **imitation** of behavior. For example, with regard to sex, the concern is that exposure to sexual activity depicted in mainstream entertainment content such as TV shows and song lyrics will result in sexual experimentation at an earlier age. For violence, the concern is that depictions that glorify and endorse violent behavior will lead to more violent behavior in viewers.

Another behavioral effect that has garnered a lot of interest and debate is **catharsis**. Catharsis is a term derived from ancient Greek philosophy and a term meaning "purification" or "cleansing." Some philosophers argue that exposure to violence or sex in media can lead to a purging of negative emotions. For example, if you want to hit your boss, you might come home and play *Grand Theft Auto* for several hours and feel better afterward. Empirical studies of catharsis, however, do not provide good evidence that it works as believed and may even exacerbate problems. For example, individuals who are trying to quit smoking cigarettes are more likely to fail when they encounter images of smokers. Seeing others smoke can increase urges for smoking. Catharsis of course would argue the opposite; that we could purge our desires for smoking by witnessing others smoke. With regard to media violence, catharsis also has poor empirical evidence. In laboratory studies, individuals who are provoked are more likely to retaliate aggressively if they watch violent media programming than if they watch nonviolent programming.

imitation
When a person copies a behavior seen on screen

catharsis
The argument that one can purge negative feelings and behaviors by watching entertainment content directly related to those behaviors

Sidebar   Murder Simulators

"From a military and law enforcement perspective, violent videogames are "murder simulators" that train kids to kill."

—Lieutenant Colonel (Retired) Dave Grossman, US Army

(Continued)

Many modern video games feature violence as a core aspect of gameplay. In 2017, of the top 10 video games in the United States by sales, three of them featured gun violence as core to gameplay: *Destiny 2*, *Grand Theft Auto V,* and *Tom Clancy's Ghost Recon: Wildlands.* Because of the popularity of these games, parents and policy-makers and others express concern that players—especially younger children—might learn antisocial behaviors from them (we'll explore some of the theories and debates in detail, in Chapters 4 and 8).

Of course, not all video games are violent. In fact, the original video games were largely nonviolent. The earliest games were two-player and more akin to other bar games like pool or foosball. They also focused on cognitive challenges, such as testing players **eye-hand coordination** by asking them to avoid (but sometimes, eat) ghosts in the mazes of *Pac-Man.* Games scholar Carly Kocurek argues that it wasn't until the 1970s that concerns about video game violence came about, following the release of a driving simulator called *Death Race* in which players used a **naturally mapped** steering wheel, gas and brake pedal, and gear-shift to chase down and run over "gremlins" on-screen. For Kocurek (2012), this game marked the beginning of the video game violence debates, as psychologists began a fierce debate about the antisocial influences of video games on children of all ages. As of 2018, a quick Google News search of "video game violence" will return several hundred articles, opinions, and podcasts debating the dangers (or lack thereof) of video games. Given the size of the video game industry in the United States—video games are the most prominent and profitable form of entertainment media, even more popular (and profitable) than Hollywood movies—it is unlikely that these debates will be silenced soon. That society is so engaged in this question suggests that there is great social value in studying how entertainment media products can affect people's thoughts, feelings, and behaviors—for better, or for worse.

eye-hand coordination

The ability to react to visual inputs with bodily responses

naturally mapped

Any interface that is designed for the five human senses: touch, taste, sight, smell, and sound

Cognitive Effects

Cognitive effects relate to how our brains work and the judgments that we make. For example, how prevalent is adultery? How violent and dangerous is the world? Do other people think like me? These questions all relate to cognition. With regard to sex, if you watch a lot of pornography, you might think that certain sex acts, such as group sex or sadomasochism, are more common than they are (this was one of the complaints that some had about *Fifty Shades of Grey*, discussed earlier in this chapter). Zillmann's (1982) early research on pornography suggests that this is the case. Repeated nonviolent pornography exposure led a sample of students to have unrealistic expectations about the frequency and type of sexual intercourse they were likely to encounter in everyday life.

The other cognitive effect that people are concerned about relates to learning. One learning effect is explained through **observational or vicarious learning**. Witnessing a character in a narrative engage in a behavior and then observing some kind of reward afterward can lead to a more positive appraisal of the behavior (e.g., thinking that the behavior is good). If punishment comes after a behavior, then more negative appraisals of the behavior are likely. Another learning effect relates to **associative learning**. Repeatedly observing two things together creates an association between them. The more often two things occur together, the stronger the association. If members of a certain race are repeatedly depicted as criminals within media entertainment, then prejudiced beliefs can emerge related to the association of that race with criminal.

observational or **vicarious learning**

Learning a behavior by watching another person instead of trial and error

associative learning

Learning about a connection between two things by repeatedly observing them together

Limitations to Understanding Effects of "Controversial" Content

The effects of entertainment media, and especially controversial media content such as the sex, drugs, and other salacious behaviors described in this chapter, are not as strong as many might perceive them to be. For example, there have been over 300 experimental studies published in the literature that examine how violent media can influence viewers. **Meta-analyses**—a method of examining the overall effect across various individual studies—typically indicate that media violence has a small but positive effect on aggressive outcomes, such as aggressive thoughts, attitudes, and behaviors.

This would put the exposure to controversial content squarely in the **limited effects paradigm**. What this means is that the direct influence of any media content, both prosocial or antisocial in nature, tends to be rather small. In fact, some of the earliest communication

Meta-analysis

A type of study that gathers multiple previous studies together about the same topic and compare the effect sizes of each

limited effects paradigm

A paradigm in media studies in which it is assumed that media has little effect on thoughts and behaviors scholarship was already writing about this expectation of limited effects, with Berelson (1948) penning a rather famous line, "some kinds of communication on some kinds of issues, brought to the attention of some kinds of people under some kinds of conditions, have some kinds of effects (148)."

Beyond the notion that media effects simply might not be very strong, there could also be some methodological issues with the research itself. For example, many scholars have claimed that with respect to entertainment media, there is evidence of **publication bias** in which (a) studies that detect statistically significant effects are more likely to be published than studies that do not demonstrate media effects, and in turn, (b) studies that do not demonstrate media effects are usually never submitted to academic journals and publications in the first place. This latter effect is also called the **file-drawer effect** and is based on an assumption that nonsignificant effects are not informative. An analysis of video game violence research by Ferguson (2007) found evidence of publication bias in the literature, which he interpreted as "concern that researchers in the area of video game studies have become more concerned with 'proving' the presence of effects, rather than testing theory" (p. 481), such as those discussed to this point, in the chapter. In many ways, Ferguson's concerns here related to the notion of moral panics introduced at the start of the chapter, in that researchers might be assuming video games (and other types of media) to have corrosive effects on users, prior to generating evidence to that effect.

Yet another confusion that we face in understanding the behavioral effects of media entertainment is that many of the studies that have been published have conflicting results. One way that researchers try to get around this is by conducting meta-analyses where they try to summarize the results of several studies—the Ferguson (2007) study described earlier is an example of such a meta-analysis. However, even these meta-analyses can lead to conflicting results, depending on which studies the researchers choose to include or exclude in their analysis. In an article for *Science* magazine, de Vries (2018) discussed many of the debates around meta-analyses and their role in science. One general conclusion is that while they are good for summarizing large bodies of literature, they are only useful when they systematically include all published (and even unpublished) research results on a topic

publication bias

In media psychology research, studies that detect media effects are more likely to be published that studies that do not

file-drawer effect

The problem in which studies that do not detect media effects are usually never submitted for publications; related to publication bias

Conclusion

Between methodological limitations and the increased likelihood that entertainment media effects (at least on their own) are likely not that strong, it can therefore be easy to reject any concerns about "dark" entertainment media as being moral panics. However, this too would be a mistake, because it is not the case that small effects are trivial ones. Children and adults alike learn from the media, and under certain conditions these effects can be quite strong—ideas can definitely start on-screen. As media researchers shift their attention to the "nexus of mediating and moderating variables" that explain the effects, we should not forget that the process often starts with a single, well-timed, and popular entertainment media message.

 # Key Terms

Moral panic   When one part of society considers another part of society or a specific behavior to be a threat or risk to society as a whole, based on little or contradictory evidence

Sexual content   Media content that includes any type of sexual intimacy

Pornography   Media content that includes graphic and explicit depictions of sexual activity

The aesthetic theory of destruction   The idea that people may be attracted to and enjoy watching the destruction of objects

Virtual violence   Violence that occurs in a virtual environment, such as virtual reality or a video game

Racialized pedagogical zones   The idea that interactive media (such as video games)s allow players to practice enacting racial and ethnic stereotypes that could transfer to the real world

Public service announcement (PSA)   A message that is design to promote a social good; central to the concept of social marketing

Network models of memory   A theory that argues that memories are organized and connected to each other in the brain.

Spreading activation   The notion that when one concept is accessed in memory, related concepts will also be activated. The closer the concepts are to each other in either conceptual or semantic terms, the more quickly concepts will be activated.

Priming   A short-term effect that activates associations and relations in the brain

Intensity   The frequency and duration of a prime

Recency   The amount of time since a person was exposed to a prime

Neo-associationistic model of aggression   A model that predicts that people will have more aggressive thoughts and behaviors after consuming violent media

General aggression model   A model that predicts how violent media in conjunction with personality, cultural, and social variables may lead to aggressive thoughts and behaviors

Affect or **emotion**   A concept used in psychology to describe the experience of feeling

Behavior   The way in which a person or animal acts in response to a situation or stimulus

Cognition   A concept used to describe the process of thinking, perception, or learning

Disinhibition   The weakening of a person's inhibitions

Desensitization   The process of feeling a weaker emotional reaction toward media content the more a person consumes or is exposed to the same type of content

Habituation   The lessened response to the same stimulus (in this case, media content) after multiple viewings

Generalization   The ability of habituation to transfer between similar media content

Excitation transfer   When arousal created by one event can be transferred to and added upon another event even if the two events differ in cause or result in different feelings (e.g., positive vs. negative)

Imitation   When a person copies a behavior seen on screen

Catharsis   The argument that one can purge negative feelings and behaviors by watching entertainment content directly related to those behaviors

Eye-hand coordination   The ability to react to visual inputs with bodily responses

Naturally mapped   Any interface that is designed for the five human senses: touch, taste, sight, smell, and sound

Observational or **vicarious learning** Learning a behavior by watching another person instead of trial and error

Associative learning   Learning about a connection between two things by repeatedly observing them together

Meta-analysis   A type of study that gathers multiple previous studies together about the same topic and compare the effect sizes of each

Limited effects paradigm   A paradigm in media studies in which it is assumed that media has little effect on thoughts and behaviors

Publication bias   In media psychology research, studies that detect media effects are more likely to be published that studies that do not

File-Drawer Effect   The problem in which studies that do not detect media effects are usually never submitted for publications; related to publication bias

 # References

Allen, M., D'Alessio, D., & Brezgel, K. (1995). A meta-analysis summarizing the effects of pornography II: Aggression after exposure. *Human Communication Research, 22*(2), 258–283. doi: 10.1111/j.1468-2958.1995.tb00368.x

Allen, V. L., & Greenberger, D. B. (1978). An aesthetic theory of vandalism. *Crime & Delinquency, 24*(3), 309–321. doi: 10.1177/001112877802400305

Anderson, C. A., & Bushman, B. J. (2002). The effects of media violence on society. *Science, 295*(5564), 2377–2379. doi: 10.1126/science.1070765

Berelson, B. (1948) Communication and public opinion, In W. Schramm (Ed.), *Communication in modern society* (pp. 167–185). Urbana, IL: University of Illinois Press.

Berkowitz, L. (1984). Some effects of thoughts on anti-and prosocial influences of media events: A cognitive-neoassociation analysis. *Psychological Bulletin, 95*(3), 410–427. doi: 10.1037//0033-2909.95.3.410

Christenson, P. G., Henriksen, L., & Roberts, D. F. (2000). *Substance use in popular prime-time television.* Washington, D.C: Office of national Drug Control Policy.

Dal Cin, S., Worth, K. A., Dalton, M. A., & Sargent, J. D. (2008). Youth exposure to alcohol use and brand appearances in popular contemporary movies. *Addiction, 103*(12), 1925–1932. doi: 10.1111/j.1360-0443.2008.02304.x

de Vries, J. (2018). Meta-analyses were supposed to end scientific debates. Often, they only cause more controversy. *Science.* doi: 10.1126/science.aav4617

Elson, M., & Ferguson, C. (2013). Gun violence and media effects: Challenges for science and public policy. *The British Journal of Psychiatry, 203,* 322–324. doi: 10.1192/bjp.bp.113.128652

Ferguson, C. (2007). Evidence for publication bias in video game violence effects literature: A meta-analytic review. *Aggression and Violent Behavior, 12*(4), 470–482. doi: 10.1016/j.avb.2007.01.001

Gerbner, G. (2001). Drugs in television, movies, and music videos. In Y. R. Kamalipour & K. R. Rampal (Eds.), *Media, sex, violence, and drugs in the global village* (pp. 69–75). Lanham, MD: Rowman & Littlefield.

Heintz-Knowles, K., Henderson, J., Glaubke, C., Miller, P., Parker, M. A., & Espejo, E. (2001). Fair play? Violence, gender and race in video games. *Children Now.*

Kocurek, C. A. (2012). The agony and the exidy: A history of video game violence and the legacy of death race. *The International Journal of Computer Game Research, 12*(1).

Kunkel, D., Eyal, K., Finnerty, K., Biely, E., & Donnerstein, E. (2005). *Sex on TV 4 2005: A Kaiser Family Foundation report.* San Francisco: Kaiser Family Fund

Lenz, L. (2016). A brief and incredible history of porn. *The Daily Dot.* Retrieved from https://www.dailydot.com/irl/history-of-porn/

Muscari, M. (2002). Media violence: Advice for parents. *Pediatric Nursing, 28*(6), 585–591.

Potter, W. J. & Smith, S. (2000). The context of graphic portrayals of television violence. *Journal of Broadcasting & Electronic Media, 44*(2), 301–323. doi: 10.1207/s15506878jobem4402_9

Roberts, D. F., Henriksen, L., & Christenson, P. G. (1999). *Substance use in popular movies and music.* Washington, D.C.: Office of National Drug Control Policy.

Romer, D., Jamieson, P. E., & Jamieson, K. H. (2017). The continuing rise of gun violence in PG-13 movies, 1985 to 2015. *Pediatrics,* e20162891. doi: 10.1542/peds.2016-2891

Roskos-Ewoldsen, D. R., Roskos-Ewoldsen, B., Carpentier, F. D. (2009). Media priming: An updated synthesis. In J. Bryant & M. B. Oliver (Eds.) *Media effects: Advances in theory and research* (pp. 90–109). Routledge.

Smith, S. L., Lachlan, K., & Tamborini, R. (2003). Popular video games: Quantifying the presentation of violence and its context. *Journal of Broadcasting & Electronic Media, 47*(1), 58–76. doi: 10.1207/s15506878jobem4701_4

Tamborini, R., Weber, R., Bowman, N. D., Eden, A., & Skalski, P. (2013). "Violence is a many-splintered thing:" The importance of realism, justification, and graphicness in understanding perceptions of and preferences for violent films and video games. *Projections: The Journal for Movies and Mind, 7*(1), 100–118. doi: 10.3167/proj.2013.070108

Zillmann, D., & Bryant, J. (1988). Effects of prolonged consumption of pornography on family values. *Journal of Family Issues, 9*(4), 518–544. doi: 10.1177/019251388009004006

Zillmann, D., & Bryant, J. (1982). Pornography and sexual callousness, and the trivialization of rape. *Journal of Communication, 32*(4), 10–21. doi: 10.1111/j.1460-2466.1982.tb02514.x

Suggested Readings

Scott, D. T. (2018). *Pathology and technology: Killer apps and sick users.* New York: Peter Lang Publishing.

Tilley, C. L. (2012). Seducing the innocent: Fredric Wertham and the falsifications that helped condemn comics. *Information & Culture, 47*(4), 383–413.

CHAPTER 6

Entertainment and Emotions

"How can we be moved by the fate of Anna Karenina?"

—(Radford & Weston, 1975).

At the end of *Star Wars: The Force Awakens*, Kylo Ren and his father Han Solo have an emotional confrontation. Han is trying to convince his son that it's not too late for him to return to the light side of the force, while Kylo believes that he is beyond saving. Just as it appears that Han will be successful, Kylo turns on his lightsaber killing his father. This gripping scene represented the death of Han Solo and left many fans sad. But why? Harrison Ford, the actor who plays Han, didn't die, and Han Solo is a purely fictional character who isn't based on any real person. In 1975, Radford and Weston asked this very question in a paper titled, "How can we be moved by the fate of Anna Karenina?" based on the titular character from Leo Tolstoy's famous novel. This question, in essence, is what we now call the **paradox of fiction**, and it has been explored by philosophers as early as Plato and Aristotle. The basic premise of the paradox can be described as follows: In order to feel emotions when reading or watching narratives, we have to first believe that the characters are real. The characters are obviously fictional, yet we feel emotions anyway (**Sidebar: Suspension of disbelief?**).

paradox of fiction
The idea that feeling emotions in response to fictional narratives is irrational because the events and characters are not real

91

Sidebar   Suspension of disbelief?

Several explanations have been offered to explain why we feel emotions when watching obviously fictional content. Samuel Coleridge explained the solution to the paradox of fiction in terms of the willing suspension of disbelief. The basics of the Coleridge's solution was that the writer of fiction can craft an environment so real that the reader will not question the reality of the fictional world. They will accept the reality that is given to them if it is skillfully crafted by the author. Dolf Zillmann argued that this latter definition does not make good sense. If viewers of fiction had to suspend their disbelief in order to enjoy a story, they would be engaging in a lot of cognitive effort.

Moreover, we seem to respond to mediated environments as if they were real. Reeves and Nass described this tendency to not distinguish between media and the real world in their book *The Media Equation*. Their book was more focused on treating comptuers as if they were people, but they (and others) suggest that because we evolved long before media entertainment existed, we don't distinguish mediated images from real images. Even though we know that a mediated image is just an image, it still activates the same psychological processes as nonmediated images do. We simply don't have a "media lobe" in the brain to process mediated images differently than real images.

Just about everyone has had a strong emotional reaction to some particular movie, song, TV show, book, or video game. If you didn't jump at a horror film, if the ending of *Marley & Me* or the beginning of *Up* never made you tear up, or if you didn't feel "warm fuzzies" while watching *The Incredibles*, then you are probably in the minority of viewers. Media entertainment has incredibly close ties to emotional responses. According to Zillmann, the functions of entertainment are to "delight and enlighten." Thus, media entertainment is often valued and judged by how strongly it made us feel a specific emotion. Scary horror films are enjoyed more than tame ones, and funny comedies are enjoyed more than boring ones.

In the following chapter, we'll describe emotions and what elicits them. We'll also talk about various types of entertainment media and how they exploit our perceptions and other psychological processes leading to strong emotional responses.

Objectives

After reading this chapter students will be able to:

➤ Define what emotions are.

➤ Explain how media can cause us to feel emotions even when we know it is false.

➤ Understand the potential effects, both short-term and long-term, related to emotions elicited by media entertainment.

What are Emotions?

The central and important role of emotions in media entertainment has its basis in the earliest studies of media psychology. From early film research investigating how we respond to characters (Munsterberg, 1916), through seminal radio studies exploring attractions to radio narratives (Cantril & Allport, 1935), to understanding the role of fear in attention to war persuasion videos (Hovland, Janis, & Kelley, 1953), understanding emotion has been central to understanding the effects of all types of media. But what are emotions? Emotions are something that we all feel, but are surprisingly hard to define.

Although most researchers view emotions as unique as compared to behaviors and cognition, there are many models and theories of emotions that rely on different definitions. Two basic models, the **dimensional model** and the **discrete model**, are the foundation for much research in media entertainment. Dimensional models consider emotions to be a motivational state characterized by valence (positive to negative) and degree of arousal (high to low). For example, the **circumplex model of affect** posited by Russell (1980) holds that emotions are a combination of positive/negative affect and low/high arousal. Low arousal and negative affect might be categorized as feeling bored, whereas low arousal and positive affect might be categorized as feeling relaxed. High arousal and negative affect might be categorized as feeling stressed, whereas high arousal and positive affect might be categorized as feeling excited. For the dimensional models, there would not necessarily be a unique name for each emotion. Instead, all emotional states would be just a combination of affect and arousal. In addition, cultures might have vastly different labels and experiences for the unique states in the dimensional model.

Discrete emotion models consider individual emotional states as being delineated by the cognitive appraisals, or thought patterns,

---

discrete model (of emotion)

An argument proposing that discrete emotional states can be identified by independent appraisals and neural architecture underlying these basic emotions

dimensional model (of emotion)

An argument proposing that emotions can be defined through a combinations of psychological factors, namely arousal and valence

circumplex model of affect

A dimensional model of emotion that understand emotions as a combination of positive or negative affect and high or low arousal

Discrete emotion(s)

A small group of unique, distinct, and universally felt emotions (based on a discrete model of emotions) that include including anger, disgust, fear, happiness, sadness, and surprise underlying them. Discrete emotion perspectives suggest that there are a small number of unique and distinct emotions. Much of this work has links to Charles Darwin's research on emotions as signalling devices; emotions help others understand whether we are happy or sad. In this perspective, all humans will demonstrate and experience similar emotions due to the way we evolved to communicate, as a social animal. In support of this perspective, Paul Ekman, a psychologist who studied facial expressions, has argued that six basic emotions exist across all cultures: Anger, disgust, fear, happiness, sadness, and surprise. In Ekman's model, all emotional states can be boiled down to one of these six basic emotions or a combination of these basic emotions.

Both views are relevant when we think about how emotion can play a role in entertainment selection, reception, and subsequent effects. However, we may also consider models of how emotions affect us more broadly. In 2008, Robin Nabi and Werner Wirth coedited a special issue of the scholarly journal *Media Psychology* that focused on the role of emotion in media effects. They began with an overview of emotion, describing emotions as complex concepts encompassing affective, cognitive, **conative**, **physiological**, and **motivational** components. The affective component includes the subjective experience of situations, such as feeling joy when love conquers all, or despair when the bad guy looks certain to win. The cognitive component refers to how situations relevant to emotions are perceived and thought about. The conative component is related to expression of emotion, including facial expression, vocalizations, and gestures. The physiological component encompasses physical responses outside of regular conscious control, such as heart rate, opening and closing of sweat glands, and breathing. Finally, the motivational component refers to action readiness or behavioral intention—what we do after we feel what we feel. Let's turn to a close examination of the role of empathy in fiction to illustrate all these aspects.

conative
Dealing with behavior

physiological
Dealing with bodily reactions that are usually involuntary (heart rate, skin conductance, respiration, pupil dilation)

motivational
Dealing with psychological forces that lead to behavior

Empathy
The act of understanding and "feeling with" another person

The Three-Factor Model of Empathy

Empathy has been central to understanding emotions experienced while engaging with media. Empathy is traditionally defined as feeling *with* someone else. Empathy is different from sympathy, which is typically described as feeling *for* someone. For example, if someone you didn't know experienced a tragedy and you felt sorry for them without feeling sad yourself, you would be experiencing sympathy. However, if your friend experienced a tragedy and you felt sad along with them, you would be demonstrating empathy. Thus, empathy is an affective response from witnessing or imagining the emotions of others. How does empathy occur and what is its relationship to entertainment?

Zillmann (1991) explicated a three-factor theory of empathy that describes the elements of an empathic experience. The three components of the theory are (1) the dispositional component, (2) the excitatory component, and (3) the experiential component, which is subdivided into (a) the experience proper, (b) the correction and redirection of affect, and (c) the generation of affect.

The dispositional component of empathy. The dispositional component of empathy is conceptualized as a largely involuntary response. Humans will often reflexively replicate the emotions of others. For example, babies in nurseries cry when other babies cry. You might have also seen the "Try Not to Laugh" videos on YouTube that challenge a viewer to make it through without laughing. Many of these videos are simply footage of other people laughing. **Emotional contagion** is the phenomenon by which the emotions of others spread like a cold. Emotional contagion is a normal adaptive response, and it partially underlies the dispositional component of empathy. When we witness the emotions of others, we naturally and reflexively have similar emotional reactions activated in us. This reflexive element of empathy includes those responses that we didn't need to learn (e.g., babies crying at the cries of other babies; no one taught them to do that) and those responses that we have learn through conditioning.

The excitatory component of empathy. Like the dispositional component, the excitatory component is also categorized as an involuntary response. As described earlier, emotional responses have an arousal component. Witnessing emotions in others activates not only the affective component of an emotion, but also the arousal component. Situations that lead to strong emotions will elicit more arousal in the observer than situations that lead to weaker emotions. The strength of the arousal will then determine how much of the emotion the viewer feels when seeing the emotions of another person.

The experiential component of empathy. The experiential component of empathy is the cognitive component of the empathic process. Whereas the dispositional and excitatory components are under the control of the autonomic nervous system (the part of the nervous system responsible for nonconscious processes, such as

Emotional contagion

A phenomenon by which one person's emotions are experienced by others, even if those others did not experience the root cause of the original person's emotional state breathing), the experiential component is largely under the control of the cerebral cortex (the part of the nervous system responsible for higher order cognitive processes, such as thought, language, and learning). The first subcomponent of the experiential component of empathy is the **experience proper**. This refers to the cognitive interpretation related to witnessing the event. Zillmann argues that the experience proper is primarily the result of the dispositional and excitatory components, and as such, we would expect it to be similar to the emotional response of the person being witnessed. In other words, if we see someone crying, we're likely to feel some sadness as well, thanks to processes such as emotional contagion.

However, we don't always cry when we see someone crying. Sometimes we might even feel happy. When a Red Sox fan sees a Yankees fan crying after a loss, she probably doesn't feel sad with the Yankees fan. She probably feels happy. This is a process that Zillmann described as **counter-empathic**—feeling a dissimilar usually opposing emotion as compared to the observed other. Zillmann argued that this component of empathy was determined by cognition and fell under **correction and redirection of affect**, the second subcomponent of the experiential component. We don't feel empathy with everyone. Our empathy only extends to those we deem worthy of it. Think of how bad movies would be if you felt the same emotions as the villain as they were vanquished (**Sidebar: Always feeling empathy**).

experience proper
The perception and interpretation of a witnessed event

counter-empathic
When a person feels good about another person's suffering or feels bad about another person's happiness

correction and redirection of affect
The ability to shift one's feelings of empathy from one character to another

Sidebar   Always Feeling Empathy

Because cognitive processing is slightly slower than the dispositional and excitatory components, Zillmann argued that counter-empathic responses occur after the initial empathic response and that counter-empathy is the result of cognitive processing. When watching a villain suffering physical pain, we might initially have an initial empathic reaction to their suffering. However, we very quickly remind ourselves that the same person currently suffering on-screen was only moments ago trying to inflict great physical harm on innocent victims. Once we remember this, we're a lot less empathetic.

There is some evidence from studies on children with intellectual disabilities that suggest cognitive processing is responsible for correction and redirection leading to counter-empathy. Zillmann and Cantor, (1977)

(Continued)

showed two versions of a narrative to groups of children. One version had a very nice child as the main character and the other had a very mean child as the main character. The researchers also created two endings: In one ending, the main character is rewarded by receiving a bike and rides off having fun; in the other, the main character receives a bike too, but when he rides off he falls and hurts himself. Disposition theory would predict that children watching the narrative would enjoy the one where the good child rides off having fun or when the bad child fell and hurt himself. The other two narratives—the good child falling and hurting himself and the bad child riding off having fun—should have been less enjoyable. The predictions for empathy are somewhat distinct. Children should feel empathy with the good child and counter-empathy with the bad child. When the good child is happy the viewers should feel happy and when the good child is sad the viewers should feel sad. When the bad child is happy the viewers should feel sad, and when the bad child is sad, the viewers should feel happy. These predictions were generally upheld for most children. However, children with an intellectual disability always experienced empathy. They were happy when either child was happy and sad when either child was sad. Zillmann argued that these patterns indicate that the correction and redirection process is under the control of cognitive systems and influenced by the cognitive development of viewers.

The final subcomponent of the experiential component of empathy is described as the **generation of affect**. So far, the processes we've described require some observation of emotion. However, we know that empathy can occur even without observing another person. In fact, sometimes we can make ourselves feel strong emotions simply by imagining an emotion-inducing event. Zillmann categorizes this as an empathic response even though the observed emotions remain "unobserved" and only imagined. The generation of affect is perhaps the most cognitively based form of empathy.

generation of affect
When a person anticipates or imagines the hypothetical emotions of another person and feels empathy toward that person as a result

The Time Course of Emotions in Media Entertainment

When we experience media entertainment, we often feel emotions. Emotions are central to (1) why we seek out content, (2) what we experience when we are immersed in the content, and (3) how we feel after the experience is over. We can think about these three different aspects of media exposure as before, during, after, and long after the media entertainment experience.

Before selection. Emotions have several important effects when it comes to selection of content. For example, our current mood state might drive us toward specific types of content as compared to others. If we're feeling incompetent after a bad day at work or school, we might be less likely to watch a challenging quiz show, such as *JEOPARDY!*. We might also actively want to feel a certain way, and therefore we seek out content that we think will make us feel that way. For example, we might want to feel afraid and excited, and so we flip through Netflix looking for that perfect horror film. Given the fact that most of us have a well-developed history of media entertainment exposure, we can usually anticipate how a piece of media entertainment will make us feel.

Anticipatory emotions are those emotions that we predict we will feel before they occur. We know that we will likely feel fear if we go see a horror film, and we know we will likely feel sad if we go see a tear-jerker. Anticipatory emotions have a strong part to play in what we select. But there are some types of content that prevent precise prediction. If your university is in the Final Four (national college basketball championship), you can anticipate that you'll likely feel distress during the game if your team is trailing and elation during the game if your team is winning, but you wouldn't be able to predict exactly which of these two emotions you'll ultimately feel until the game is over.

During exposure. The previous paragraph gives two definitions of anticipatory emotions: the emotions we expect to occur and the emotions we feel toward possible outcomes. The second definition relates to the emotions we feel while we are experiencing the content. Some forms of content lead us to feel emotions vicariously, or in the place of another person. When we're playing a video game, we are often feeling emotions that we would feel if we were the character. When Nathan Drake from the popular video game series *Uncharted* is in peril, we feel in peril with him. Of course, these emotions are likely far less severe that they would be if we were really jumping over falling boulders or climbing out of a crashed airplane, but they are emotions we feel with the character. The emotional experiences of video game play are different than the emotional experiences of watching a drama. During video game play, we are controlling the character and a virtual part of

Anticipatory emotions
The emotions that people predict they will feel before actually feeling any emotions at all

the action. During narrative drama, we aren't the character, but rather witnesses to the actions that are happening to the character. A simple example to illustrate the difference can be seen in viewer's responses to similar actions. When the masked killer is sneaking up on the helpless and hapless victims in a movie, no one yells, "Look out behind me!" (although we might shout for the movie character to look out behind themselves). Yet, when we fall off a cliff in a video game, almost everyone says, "I died."

After exposure. The final way emotions relate to media entertainment is how we feel after the media entertainment experience is over. Sometimes media entertainment can cause us to ruminate and think about what we've just seen long after the experience is over. For example, *The Sopranos* ended in 2007, but people are still writing and analyzing the finale trying to figure out what happened **Sidebar: The End of the Sopranos**.

Sidebar	The End of the Sopranos

HBO's *The Sopranos* aired from 1999 to 2007. The show was a cultural phenomenon with catchy music, compelling characters, subtle plot, and gritty cinematography. *The Sopranos* was the brainchild of David Chase, a writer, director, and producer who had previously been involved with the TV series *The Rockford Files* and *Northern Exposure*, but *The Sopranos* was his biggest critical and commercial success. As the show's primary creative director (also known as the **showrunner**), Chase was in charge of how the show developed and where the stories would go and end.

showrunner
The person in charge of the creative and management aspects of a television show

On June 10, 2007, "Made in America," the final episode of *The Sopranos*, aired to 11.9 million viewers. The show's plot seemed to wrap up some final threads that had been unwinding throughout the season: A mob war between New Jersey and New York's crime families was averted; several prominent mafiosos had been "whacked" by their rivals; and Tony, the show's lead character, was learning that he might be the subject of a federal indictment. The final scene featured Tony waiting in a restaurant for his family. First his wife, Carmella, shows up, and they chat. Then their son Anthony Jr. (AJ) arrives. Meadow, the daughter, is outside trying to parallel park her new car. Just when she walks into the restaurant, the camera cuts to Tony's face. Then, the screen turns black. After a few seconds, the credits start running over a black, quiet screen. The show was over.

(Continued)

Many viewers were confused at what happened, with some even thinking that their cable signal had cut out on them. Some were angry that they didn't get to see any kind of final moment. Was Tony killed? Was he still alive? Is there more to the story that we simply won't see? Chase was asked many times about the ending but never really explained why he ended his show the way he did. Matthew Weiner, the creator and showrunner of *Mad Men*, was also involved with *The Sopranos* as a writer and executive producer. He described the ending as David Chase "smashing his guitar" as a rockstar would do at the end of an epic concert. Regardless, the ending still generates passionate discussion, perhaps because of the intense emotions experienced by viewers at this unconventional ending.

Long after exposure. Sometimes we feel emotions about our emotions, for example we may feel scared during a horror movie, and then later ashamed of that fear when speaking of the experience to friends. Or, we may feel sad during a tragic love story, but later feel grateful for our own loved ones. This type of emotion about another emotion is called a **meta-emotion**. Media psychologists Mary Beth Oliver and Anne Bartsch adapted the concept of meta-experiences to explain how media entertainment can not only make us feel certain emotions but make us feel emotions about the emotions we're feeling. Oliver and Bartsch originally proposed the concept of meta-emotions to explain why a movie can make us cry, and yet we still say we enjoyed it. Many people watch sad movies knowing that they will feel sad afterward, yet they still expose themselves to these negative feelings and say they enjoy it.

meta-emotions
Emotions that we feel about our own felt emotions, as well as the emotions of others

Why would we choose to watch stories about others' suffering? This apparent paradox has been deemed the **empathy paradox**. Meta-emotions might provide one solution to the paradox. Perhaps feeling sad can make us feel good. After watching a tragedy, we might feel sad because of what happened to the characters on the screen. At the same time, feeling sad might make us feel happy: "I'm happy that I'm sad because it tells me that I am empathetic person." Still, if meta-emotions can partially explain why we can enjoy sad films, there is still the question about why we feel emotions at all when we watch, read, or listen to entirely fictional events.

empathy paradox
A problem in media theory that asks how can audiences enjoy sad or scary movies if the movie makes them feel negative instead of positive

Can we have chronic emotions? Moods are similar to emotions in that they are about feeling. However, moods are distinct in several ways from emotions. Moods tend to be longer-lived. That is, a mood is something that lasts from moment to moment or even day to day.

It's a chronic state, whereas emotions are an acute state. In addition, emotions tend to be linked to specific objects or events, so individuals can attribute why they feel the way they feel to some specific thing. It is *this specific* scene in the movie that made me sad. Moods on the other hand are less specific. You might feel down or depressed for a day or several days and you might not know why.

The Lingering State of Arousal

Two final emotion-relevant processes have also been explored in relation to media entertainment. Both of these processes have to do with arousal and excitation, and their persistence over time. The first is the **arousal boost/arousal jag hypothesis** (Berlyne, 1972). The arousal boost hypothesis argues that sudden jolts in arousal can be pleasant. Riding a roller coaster is a good example of the arousal boost hypothesis. The sudden drop from the first hill creates a lot of arousal, which can be pleasurable. At the same time, the relief from an extremely arousing stimulus can also be pleasant—this is the arousal jag hypothesis. Picture this: You go to see a horror movie. Scene after scene is full of jump-scares and terrifying imagery. Your arousal is off the charts over and over and over again. Finally, you leave the theater and the things that were making you nervous are now resolved and you are released and separated from the thing that was scaring you. This can lead to feelings of pleasure—phew! You survived!

Building off arousal boost/jag logic, **excitation transfer theory** argues that excitement and arousal created by one event can be transferred to another. We discussed this theory in Chapter 5 as well. Remember that arousal comes on fast but decreases slowly. Importantly, we often times think we've returned to baseline, but we actually haven't; our arousal is still higher than normal. Because of this lag and lack of full awareness, arousal can transfer from one event to another. For example, if the first scene of a movie is exciting and tense, you'll likely build some arousal from that scene. The next scene might not be as intense, but if the arousal from the first scene doesn't have time to entirely resolve, you will enter scene three with some left over (or residual) arousal from the first scene. Excitation transfer theory argues that this residual arousal gets added to and confused with whatever arousal is elicited by the third scene, leading to a more intense response to the third scene than if you had watched it in isolation. The third scene elicits stronger emotions in you because of the things that happened earlier in the movie. This is excitation transfer theory in action.

arousal boost and **arousal jag hypothesis**
An argument that proposes that both sudden bursts of arousal (arousal boost) and relief of arousal (arousal jag) can be pleasant experiences

excitation transfer theory
A theory that argues that arousal created by one stimulus can be carried over to another event, which can result in higher-than-expected levels of arousal

New Directions in Emotional Media Entertainment Research

Researchers have begun to explore several new avenues to understand emotions and entertainment. One area that has garnered quite a bit of attention in the literature is the role of **moral emotions**. Moral emotions are typically defined as emotions that relate to the well-being of others or that are activated by behavior that adheres to or violates one's moral code. For example, when we do something bad, we might feel guilt, whereas if we do something nice, like help an old lady with her groceries, we might feel pride. Moral emotions are complex emotional responses because they originate from cognition; in order to experience a moral emotion, we have to recognize that a moral precept has been either upheld or violated. Other cognitively complex emotions—for example, awe, an emotion we feel when we observe massive and expansive environments, or nostalgia, an emotion that makes us remember times gone by—are also being explored as they relate to media entertainment content. Video games may be especially good at eliciting these complex emotions. They provide players agency over their character's actions and can simulate realistic consequences due to player actions.

Another area that researchers are looking into is the role of **mixed affect** as it relates to entertainment. Some films, such as horror films, focus on eliciting one family of emotions, like fear. Other media entertainment can elicit a range of emotions that may not be related. For example, some movies like *Silver Linings Playbook*, *Birdman*, and even *Inside Out* attempt to elicit a range of emotions, sometimes simultaneously. Mixed affect is the combination of various emotions, with a focus on incongruent emotions. Feeling both happy and sad at the same time is an example of mixed affect, and many movies can elicit such emotional states. Mixed affect is often associated with eudaimonia—which we discussed back in chapter one. We began the chapter by discussing entertainments role in delighting and enlightening us. We can think of hedonic entertainment as being more relevant to *delighting* us, and eudaimonic entertainment as *enlightening* us.

Conclusion

Emotion is always central to entertainment. We select media entertainment because we desire some emotional experience. Media entertainment provides us a safe space to experience a range of emotions that we typically don't have access to on a regular basis, such as intense fear, sadness, grief,

---

moral emotions

Emotions that are activated when witnessing violation or reinforcement of an individual's own moral concerns, such as guilt or elevation

mixed affect

An emotional state brought about when an individual experiences more than one conflicting emotions at the same time and joy. These are all emotions that are somewhat rare in our daily lives. Yet, media entertainment gives us the opportunity to feel them with very little risk to ourselves. Understanding the full experience of emotion, from selection to immersion to deliberation and meta-emotion after entertainment consumption, can allow us to better understand how the entertainment experience as a whole can affect viewers.

 # Key Terms

Paradox of fiction   The idea that feeling emotions in response to fictional narratives is irrational because the events and characters are not real

Dimensional model (of emotion)   An argument proposing that emotions can be defined through a combinations of psychological factors, namely arousal and valence

Discrete model (of emotion)   An argument proposing that discrete emotional states can be identified by independent appraisals and neural architecture underlying these basic emotions

Circumplex model of affect   A dimensional model of emotion that understand emotions as a combination of positive or negative affect and high or low arousal

Discrete emotion(s)   A small group of unique, distinct, and universally felt emotions (based on a discrete model of emotions) that include including anger, disgust, fear, happiness, sadness, and surprise

Conative   Dealing with behavior

Physiological   Dealing with bodily reactions that are usually involuntary (heart rate, skin conductance, respiration, pupil dilation)

Motivational   Dealing with psychological forces that lead to behavior

Empathy   The act of understanding and "feeling with" another person

Emotional contagion   A phenomenon by which one person's emotions are experienced by others, even if those others did not

experience the root cause of the original person's emotional state

Experience proper   The perception and interpretation of a witnessed event

Counter-empathic   When a person feels good about another person's suffering or feels bad about another person's happiness

Correction and redirection of affect   The ability to shift one's feelings of empathy from one character to another

Generation of affect   When a person anticipates or imagines the hypothetical emotions of another person and feels empathy toward that person as a result

Anticipatory emotions   The emotions that people predict they will feel before actually feeling any emotions at all

Showrunner   The person in charge of the creative and management aspects of a television show

Meta-emotions   Emotions that we feel about our own felt emotions, as well as the emotions of others

Empathy paradox   A problem in media theory that asks how can audiences enjoy sad or scary movies if the movie makes them feel negative instead of positive

Arousal boost and **arousal jag hypothesis**   An argument that proposes that both sudden bursts of arousal (arousal boost) and relief of arousal (arousal jag) can be pleasant experiences

Excitation transfer theory   A theory that argues that arousal created by one stimulus can be carried over to another event, which can result in higher-than-expected levels of arousal

Moral emotions   Emotions that are activated when witnessing violation or reinforcement of

an individual's own moral concerns, such as guilt or elevation

Mixed affect   An emotional state brought about when an individual experiences more than one conflicting emotions at the same time

 # References

Berlyne, D. E. (1972). Humor and its kin. In J. H. Goldstein & P. E. McGhee (Eds.), *The psychology of humor: Theoretical perspectives and empirical issues* (pp. 43–60). New York, : Academic Press.

Cantril, H., & Allport, G. W. (1935). *The psychology of radio*. Oxford, England: Harper.

Ford, T. E., & Ferguson, M. A. (2004). Social consequences of disparagement humor: A prejudiced norm theory. *Personality and Social Psychology Review, 8*(1), 79–94. doi: 10.1207/S15327957PSPR0801_4

Hovland, C. I., Janis, I. L., & Kelley, H. H. (1953). *Communication and persuasion; psychological studies of opinion change*. New Haven, CT, US: Yale University Press.

Lin, J.-H. (2017). Fear in virtual reality (VR): Fear elements, coping reactions, immediate and next-day fright responses toward a survival horror zombie virtual reality game. *Computers in Human Behavior, 72*, 350–361. doi:10.1016/j.chb.2017.02.057

Lynch, T., & Martins, N. (2015). Nothing to fear? An analysis of college students' fear experiences with video games. *Journal of Broadcasting & Electronic Media, 59*, 298–317. doi:10.1080/08838151.2015.1029128

Münsterberg, H. (1916). *The photoplay: A psychological study*. Retrieved from Project Gutenberg: https://www.gutenberg.org/files/15383/15383-h/15383-h.htm

Nabi, R. L., & Wirth, W. (2008). Exploring the role of emotion in media effects: An introduction to the special issue Media and Emotion. *Media Psychology, 11*(1), 1–6. doi: 10.1080/15213260701852940

Russell, J. A. (1980). A circumplex model of affect. *Journal of Personality and Social Psychology, 39*(6), 1161–1176. doi: 10.1037/h0077714

Zillmann, D. (1991). Empathy: Affect from bearing witness to the emotions of others. In J. Bryant & D. Zillmann (Eds.) *Responding to the screen: Reception and reaction processes* (pp. 135–167).

Zillmann, D., & Cantor, J. R. (1977). Affective responses to the emotions of a protagonist. *Journal of Experimental Social Psychology, 13*(2), 155–165. doi: 10.1016/s0022-1031(77)80008-5

Suggested readings

Coleridge, S. T. (1817). *Biographia Literaria.* In H. J. Jackson (Ed.), Samuel Taylor Coleridge. Oxford

Ekman, P. (1993). Facial expression and emotion. *American Psychologist, 48*(4), 384–392. doi: 10.1037/0003-066X.48.4.384

Freud, S. (1916). *Wit and its relation to the unconscious* (A. A. Brill, trans.). Bartleby.com. Retrieved from https://www.bartleby.com/279/

Hemenover, S. H., & Bowman, N. D. (2018). Video games, emotion, and emotion regulation: Expanding the scope. *Annals of the International Communication Association, 42*(2). 125–143. doi: 10.1080/23808985.2018.1442239

Zajonc, R. B. (1965). Social facilitation. *Science, 149,* 269–274. doi: 10.1126/science.149.3681.269

CHAPTER 7

Narratives and Characters

"Without thinking, I made two cups."

—Alistair Daniel

"For sale: Baby shoes, never worn."

—Anonymous

What do you think about when you read the stories above? Each story is only six words, but did they create images in your mind? Perhaps the first story made you think of a widower who mistakenly made two cups of coffee the day after his wife passed away. Or perhaps it was a divorcee waking up after her husband left her or maybe, just a tired college student trying to get through their morning. The second, which is commonly but erroneously attributed to Ernest Hemingway, might make you think of a bereaved mother and father who are selling shoes who belonged to their late child, shoes that were never worn. These are incredibly vivid images conjured out of just six words, and illustrate how good humans are at creating stories to better explain their worlds. Jonathan Gottschall in his 2012 book dubbed humans "the storytelling animal." We seem to be preoccupied with stories and characters from an extremely young age. We see patterns and attribute cause-and-effect relationships to all sorts of events that may be entirely unconnected. Stories certainly play an important role in media entertainment. Songs often tell stories (e.g., "A Boy Named Sue" by Johnny Cash or "How Much a Dollar Cost" by Kendrick Lamar). Stories guide video games. Film and TV shows feature narratives and compelling characters. And of course, literature and books are filled with stories.

What is a story, how do we experience them, and can social scientific theories make predictions about what makes a story enjoyable? These are just some of the questions that we will explore in this chapter.

Objectives

After student read this chapter, they will:

➤ Understand the core structures of narrative in entertainment media.

➤ Be able to identify the different types of relationships that entertainment media audiences engage with in terms of on-screen characters.

➤ Discuss the role that audience dispositions toward the characters have toward the product and outcome.

What is a Narrative?

plot

The major events within a story

We listen to narratives and stories from a young age. They are all around us. Yet, coming up with a definition for what makes a narrative a narrative is surprisingly difficult. Dutch cultural theorist Mieke Bal proposed one definition. She said that a narrative is "a series of logically and chronologically related events" (p. 5, 1985). This definition outlines some of the major aspects of narratives and tells us some elements of what is important in a story. It points us to the **plot**, or major events, within the story (see **Sidebar: Seven Basic Plots**). The plot of a narrative is the events that happen that motivate the characters. But where are the characters within Bal's definition? Rudrum (2005) argued that Bal's definition wasn't enough. Rudrum and others have pointed out four essential components of narratives: characters, events, temporal progression, and telling.

Sidebar   Seven Basic Plots

With all the different variables in play—chronological versus nonchronological, first-person omniscient versus third-person unreliable—it may seem like there are a nearly infinite number of narratives. In fact, many narrative scholars argue that there are very few narrative types. For example, Joseph Campbell documented and examined ancient myths and stories from around the globe in his best-known work, *Hero with a Thousand Faces* (1949), and found stark similarities between the myths and stories of diverse civilizations. Christopher Booker argues in

(Continued)

his book *The Seven Basic Plots* (2004) that narratives can be broken down into seven basic plots, from which all other narrative plots are derived. The seven plots identified by Booker are:

- Overcoming the Monster: The protagonist must vanquish an evil force.
  - Examples: *Star Wars, Justice League*
- Rags to Riches: A poor person gains wealth/status/etc., loses it, and then regains it having learned something along the way.
  - Examples: *Cinderella, The Great Gatsby*
- The Quest: The protagonist sets out on a quest to acquire or deliver an object while facing temptation along the way.
  - Examples: *The Lord of the Rings, Pirates of the Caribbean*
- Voyage and Return: The protagonist goes to a strange place and after overcoming challenges there returns
  - Examples: *Alice in Wonderland, Back to the Future*
- Comedy: A cheerful story with a happy conclusion. Not just "funny" but rather a light-hearted story about a character.
  - Examples: *The 40-Year-Old Virgin, My Big Fat Greek Wedding*
- Tragedy: A sad story with an unhappy conclusion, typically brought about by some character flaw within the protagonist.
  - Examples: *Romeo and Juliet, Gone Girl*
- Rebirth: Story about a transition where a bad character is forced to confront themselves and they emerge changed.
  - Examples: *A Christmas Carol, Beauty and the Beast*

Whether these plots represent all plots is a point of debate. However, most stories can be categorized as one of these seven or a combination of them. How we experience these various plot structures though can keep them fresh even if we have an idea about how they'll end.

You try it! *What popular entertainment media can you identify that includes these seven basic plots that we've not included up above? Can you think of any movies or books or video games that might fit into more than one of these plots?*

characters

The first component is **characters**. Characters are the beings within a story. They don't need to be human (Bambi and the shark from *Jaws* are both characters). They don't even need to be an animal;

The person, animals, or entities within a story, play, novel, or movie there's a cult 2010 movie called *Rubber* about a homicidal tire that goes on a killing spree. In fact, people can imbue human characteristics in almost anything. For example, a famous experiment showed that people attributed motives, personalities, and feelings to simple shapes based solely on how the shapes moved in a short animation (Heider & Simmel, 1944). In addition, viewers of media narratives often confuse actors with their characters. The power of characters is so strong, we devote the second half of this chapter to characters alone.

events
Associated occurrences within a story

The second component of narratives is **events**. Events are things that occur with some sort of causal or associative relationship. A narrative isn't a series of unrelated events happening to different people. Rather it is a series of events where the events are related to each other, to the characters involved in them, or both.

temporal progression
The time-ordering of associated events in a story

The third component of narrative is that events are presented in some kind of **temporal progression**, which means over the course of time. Narratives can be chronological, so that the events happen in order from oldest to newest, such as *Up* (2009) or *Harry Potter and the Sorcerer's Stone* (2001); nonchronological with events out of order (e.g., flashbacks can occur that show something in the past), such as *Memento* (2000) or *Pulp Fiction* (1994); or even in reverse order, from conclusion to beginning such as *Irreversible* (2002) or *Eternal Sunshine of the Spotless Mind* (2004). The key isn't the order for temporal progression; rather the focus of the concept is that the narrative is not revealed in an orderly schematic, but the audience must be carried along with the storyteller to find out the entirety of the story.

telling
The way and manner in which the events of a story are communicated to the audience

The fourth and final component of a narrative is **"telling."** The root word for narrative is narro (-are), from Latin for "to tell." Telling refers to who communicates the events in the story to the reader and how those events are communicated. They could be communicated by a disembodied omniscient or semiomniscient **narrator** (someone who knows all or most events related to the story both in the past and into future) or one of the characters (e.g., a first-person narrative). How narratives are communicated could vary between accurate or inaccurate (known as unreliable narration). The unreliable narrator presents an interesting twist to this concept. An unreliable narrator compromises the accuracy of the narrative. As a result, the audience can no longer trust in their version of the "telling" because we find out that they are lying to us, or that they might not actually know all of the facts of a story. Movies such as *Inception* (2010, with Leonardo

narrator
A character who tells the story to the audience

DiCaprio) or *Memento* (2000, with Guy Pearce) are good examples of these kinds of narratives.

How We Experience Narratives

Have you ever been "lost" in a book, or felt that you were transported to another world when playing a video game or watching a movie? The idea of being "immersed" or "transported" into the world of a story is a topic that has garnered scholarly interest over the last several decades. Originating in the work of Nell (1988) and Gerrig (1993), the concept of **transportation** was re-introduced to social psychology and communication by narrative researcher Melanie Green and Timothy Brock. Green and Brock (2000) argue that feeling transported into a narrative is a melding of attention and emotion, which results in less awareness of our actual physical surroundings and an acute sense of being within the story. Feeling transported can make a narrative seem more interesting and enjoyable . . . and if the narrative has some sort of persuasive message, feeling transported can even increase an individual's susceptibility to persuasion.

transportation
The feeling of "being there" in a story, that is, attentionally and emotionally absorbed into a narrative world

For these reasons, narratives are often used by public service organizations to persuade an audience. Some of these public service narratives can be as short as a 30- or 60-second commercials (The Real Cost's "Little Lungs in a Great Big World" tells the story of a pair of lungs that are diminished in size due to their owner smoking as a teenager: and others might be embedded in popular media (such as when the Netflix animated show *Big Mouth* partnered up with Planned Parenthood to use the show's characters to promote and start discussions around Planned Parenthood's services). We can also think of narratives such as *Uncle Tom's Cabin*, which was instrumental in telling a compelling narrative about the life of a slave in the US to a wider population, and helped change public attitudes about slavery.

presence and/or **telepresence**
A psychological perception in which a technologically mediated interaction is experienced as being nonmediated, i.e., "being there" even when one is seeing an environment on a computer monitor

Of course, transportation is not the only term used to describe the phenomenon of feeling as though one is within a story world. Other terms, such as **presence** and **telepresence** (i.e., the feeling or illusion that the mediated environment is nonmediated), **immersion**, and **engagement** have also been used. We will discuss presence and telepresence more thoroughly in Chapter 13, but all of these terms seem to relate to a process whereby a reader or viewer's attention is captured so fully by a narrative that their psychological processing is responding more to the narrative than to their actual environment.

immersion
The feeling of being perceptually absorbed into a mediated experience

Parasocial Interactions and Relationships

parasocial interaction

The perceived interpersonal interaction between a media user and a mediated character or persona

consistency (behavior)

When a character acts in a manner that is expected based on previous knowledge of the character

direct involvement

When character addresses the audience members as if they were actually present

fourth wall

A hypothetical boundary between the fictional narrative and the audience; the fourth wall is often considered the television screen or other screen through which the characters are observed

eye contact

When a character looks directly at the audience

spontaneous (behavior)

When a character acts unexpectedly within the frame of a larger story

Have you ever caught yourself thinking about a character at some moment in the day? Maybe you've remembered a character from a show you used to watch and "missed" them? Have you ever bought something because you were influenced by a character (or maybe a celebrity)? If so, it is likely you instinctively know what we mean when we say you have had a **parasocial interaction [PSI]** —that is, the simulated conversation that takes place between users and mass media performers, particularly television performers (Horton & Wohl, 1956). We call these interactions *parasocial*, because they resemble social relationships, but they are primarily one-sided, and take place inside the head of the viewer. Schramm and Hartmann (2008) highlight this aspect of PSI when he calls them "an (illusionary) experience of the viewer who feels as if he or she is interacting with a television performer, despite the nonreciprocal nature of the exposure."

Media characters have specific characteristics which make us more or less likely to experience PSI. First, characters tend to be **consistent** in their behavior and actions. Unlike real-life people who may be unpredictable or act unexpectedly, in narrative characters often play a role that remains consistent over the course of the narrative. This makes it easy for viewers to predict what the character might say or do in imagined situations or conversations. Next, characters or media personae may engage in **direct involvement** with viewers (think of Deadpool or Fleabag breaking the **fourth wall** and addressing the audience). Even characters who don't specifically pause to address the audience may engage in **eye contact** with the audience (think of newscasters or talk show hosts staring into the camera). Characters may show a conversational give-and-take, for example by acting **spontaneous**—here, think of Ellen's trademarked dance moves to start her show. Audiences may also experience PSI because of **indirect involvement**, for example when the audience **overhears** conversations between two characters. While *The Office* and other mockumentaries (scripted shows presented as documentaries or found footage) are the classic example, we can also think of morning talk shows featuring a panel of hosts who banter before the show actually starts or as part of the show. One particularly interesting formal feature of such interactions is the gentle pause newscasters or talk show hosts give for the audience to react and respond to their comments. This allows for **audience acceptance**, which is when the audience feels the newscaster is listening to them. If done well, these brief pauses can help us feel like they *are* responding to us, even though the screen and thousands of miles may be between us and them.

If PSI exists for some time, we may develop a **parasocial relationship** with a character. Like real relationships, parasocial relationships include **relational schema**, where we can predict what the character will do, and how it will make us feel. Relational schemata (or relational schemes) are based on an image of yourself, your image of the media character, and an idea of how you would get along together.

Sidebar   PSI/PSR

You try it!   *Think of your favorite TV or movie character. Picture that person in your mind, and then answer the questions below with a "yes" or a "no:"*

- My favorite character makes me feel comfortable, as if I am with a friend.
- If my favorite character appeared on another TV program, I would watch that program.
- I would like to meet my favorite character in person.

If you are able to answer "yes" to these items, you likely have a PSR going on with your favorite character. Now, imagine if your favorite television personality would be taken off the air. Would you:

- miss your favorite personality
- feel like you lost a close friend
- feel angry
- feel lonely?

If so, you may be prone to experiencing what is called a "parasocial breakup." Just like a real breakup, the end of a parasocial relationship can cause distress, negative affect, and feelings of loneliness and isolation.

Parasocial relationships function much like real-world relationships (nonparasocial). For example, we may vary our attachment to media characters based on the type of relationship we are

indirect involvement
When character addresses other characters within a story, without acknowledging the audience's presence as witnesses to the events

overhears
A storytelling convention by which audiences are able to observed characters interacting without those characters being aware of the audience's presence

audience acceptance
Relevant to programs that use direct address, brief pauses in storytelling that provide time for the audience to process and understand events within a narrative

parasocial relationship (PSR)
The perceived relationship between an individual and media characters, usually a consequence of parasocial interactions with that character

relational schema
The internalized mental model of how a person experiencing a parasocial relationship understands that they would interact with the mediated character

attachment styles
Refer to the different types of interpersonal relationships that an individual is most comfortable forming, based on how they view themselves and other people.

parasocial contact hypothesis (PSC)
A hypothesis that predicts parasocial interactions with minority characters through media exposure can reduce prejudices that an individual holds toward the social groups that those characters represent

surrogate
A media character that acts as a representative of a larger social group; a stand in for a particular viewpoint or group of people

comfortable with. Cohen (2004) looked at three **attachment styles**: Secure, or those who believe that real love exists, have a positive self-other perception, and hold optimistic expectations for a relationship; Anxious-ambivalent, who believe that falling in love is easy, but worry "does the other want me?," and may have a negative self and idealized-other viewpoint; and Avoidant, who believe that love is transitory, have difficulties in trusting others, and hold pessimistic self-other views. Cohen (2004) found that people who were anxious-ambivalent were more likely to form PSRs with media characters, whereas people who were avoidant were less likely to form PSRs. Parasocial relationships also buffer the effects of social exclusion. Twenge et al. (2007) found that thinking of a favorite media character can help you suffer less if you are having a bad day, and make you less likely to take out your isolation in the form of aggression toward others. Some research has even shown that audiences might grieve over lost characters, just as they would real people. In analyzing Twitter following the death of a very prominent character in *Game of Thrones*, Daniel and Westerman (2017), found that audience members engaged in denial, anger, bargaining, depression, and acceptance critical to the Kübler-Ross stages of grief processing. In short, we treat media characters as if they were not simply characters, but real people engaging in our lives.

Characters that we see and form relationships with could even affect how we see those same people (or similar people) in our daily lives. Research into the **parasocial contact hypothesis** has found compelling evidence that when we are exposed to diverse characters in television shows that we tend to drop our prejudices against some of those groups. For some people, the presence of diverse characters in entertainment might serve as a **surrogate** for social interaction. For example, Schiappa, Gregg, and Hewes (2005) found that audiences who watched two popular television shows that featured gay male characters, *Six Feet Under* and *Queer Eye for the Straight Guy*, had less prejudiced attitudes toward gay men in general after viewing. In a series of studies, Vezzali et al. (2015) found that with children of all ages (from elementary school to high school, to university students), readers of the *Harry Potter* books tended to have more positive attitudes toward stigmatized groups, including immigrants and refugees. In other words, simply seeing a diversity of characters in our favorite media programs can be enough to change our attitudes about any number of minority groups that we might not actually encounter in our daily lives.

Identification

When we're watching or reading a narrative, questions arise as to what the relationship is between the reader/viewer and the characters in the narrative. This relationship likely varies quite a bit by medium. For example, in video games or narratives written in the second-person (e.g., "You walk into a bookstore and you keep your hand on the door to make sure it doesn't slam," The opening line to Caroline Kepnes' novel *You*), the reader could be said to "be" a character. This idea of being a part of the narrative is defined as **identification**. When we **identify** with a character, we engage in a form of **ego-confusion**—that is, confusing ourselves as the character—as described by Freud and later described in relation to narrative drama by Zillmann.

Ego-confusion and identification are things that are more likely with some forms of media than others. For example, when we're watching a film, we might root for some characters and root against others, but this doesn't mean that we think we are the character. Instead, Zillmann argues in his broad theory of the processing of narratives that we are witnesses to the action. We have no ability to alter the events as they unfold; we can't make a beloved character safer from the villain. Rather we must watch—sometimes in dread, sometimes in anticipation—as the characters succeed or fail. This processes of observing fates befall liked and disliked characters is the crux of Zillmann's **affective disposition theory**.

Affective Disposition Theory

As has been mentioned in other chapters in the book, Dolf Zillmann was a social science researcher interested in how popular entertainment, particularly narratives, could elicit strong responses from viewers. Some of his most early works examined arousal and its relationship to emotions and the nature of humor. Building on this work, Zillmann began to examine whether or not social science could make predictions about why narratives would delight and enlighten their viewers.

identify/Identification
A process by which one sees oneself as similar to or like a media character

ego-confusion
When someone confuses himself or herself as the character within a story

affective disposition theory
A theory that predicts that audiences will enjoy stories in which liked characters triumph and disliked characters are foiled

---

Sidebar | Disposition in Joke Work

As we noted in the chapter on emotion, humor from jokes is often derived from the disparagement of someone or some social group. In an early study, Zillmann and Cantor (1972) created two versions of a

(Continued)

cartoon where a pie was being thrown into someone's face. In one version, a professor was throwing the pie into a student's face after giving the student his diploma; in the other, the student was throwing the pie into the professor's face after receiving his diploma. The caption read: "Over, and. . . POW!"

Zillmann and Cantor showed the cartoon to college students as well as nonstudent, adult professionals. Which cartoon do you think each preferred? The results showed that college students thought the cartoon where the professor was getting hit with the pie was funnier, while professionals thought the cartoon where the student was getting hit with the pie was funnier. These findings led Zillmann to the conclusion that humor is dependent upon people being able to regulate their own emotions based on which person in the joke they were similar to. College students could likely identify with the student graduating and taking "revenge" on their strict-but-compassionate professor, while the working professionals could likely identify with the professor exacting revenge on an ambitious-yet-tiresome youth.

For a contemporary take on disposition theory in humor, watch the first third of the Netflix special *Nannette,* in which the comedian Hannah Gadsby eviscerates the practice of joke-work disparaging the target of the joke. How does her thesis on humor fit into Zillmann's ideas about disposition theory in comedy?

Zillmann and Bryant (1975) extended the findings on humor to drama. They reasoned that how much we like characters and the fates that befall them in the narrative should predict whether we like or dislike the narrative as a whole. This proposition relates to an "interaction" between character liking and character outcome. Affective disposition theory predicts that narratives where (a) liked characters experience positive outcomes and (b) disliked characters experience negative outcomes should be enjoyed more than narratives where (c) disliked characters experience positive outcomes and (d) liked characters experience negative outcomes. In other words, we hope that liked characters will succeed and disliked characters will fail, while we fear that liked characters will fail and disliked characters will succeed.

If character liking and narrative outcome determine enjoyment of a narrative, where does character liking come from? The earliest disposition theory applications argued that similarity determined who we were rooting for in a joke. If the target of the joke was similar to us, we wouldn't find it funny. However, similarity isn't a very important determinant for drama. You might be rooting against someone very similar to you and rooting for someone very dissimilar to you. Zillmann and Bryant therefore looked for another variable that might explain liking of characters. They argued that moral judgments of characters and their behaviors was a likely candidate. After all, heroes are moral and villains are not. Zillmann conceptualized viewers of narratives as **untiring moral monitors** who constantly render judgments about the morality of a character's actions. When characters behave morally, liking increases, but when they behave immorally, liking decreases. This basic proposition was explicated formally in Zillmann's moral sanction theory of delight and repugnance. The model describes a process whereby viewers watch a character behave and make judgments about the morality or immorality of that behavior with liking or disliking developing.

untiring moral monitors
The notion that entertainment media audiences are constantly making moral judgments about events, characters, and narratives

The previous two paragraphs describe the nuts and bolts of disposition theory, but there are other processes that also come into play. For example, recall our discussion of empathy in Chapter 6. Empathy is traditionally defined as feeling *with* someone else. Empathy is different from sympathy, which is typically described as feeling *for* someone. For example, if someone you didn't know experienced a tragedy and you felt sorry for them without feeling sad yourself, you would be experiencing sympathy. However, if your friend experienced a tragedy and you felt sad with them, you would be experiencing empathy. In this way and in Zillmann's words, empathy is an affective response from witnessing the emotions of others. How does empathy occur and what is its relationship to narrative?

Empathy and Narrative

Empathy and narratives are intricately related. Disposition theory argues that we hope for some outcomes (liked characters being rewarded, and disliked characters being punished) and we fear others (liked characters being punished and disliked characters being rewarded). As we watch a narrative, empathic and counter-empathic responses are constantly being stoked in us. When Thor drives his axe "Stormbreaker" into the heart of Thanos at the climax of *Avengers: Infinity War*, many in the audience cheered—probably feeling empathy with Thor (he seemed to finally exact his revenge on Thanos for the death of his brother) and feeling counter-empathy with Thanos (he seemed to be finally receiving his just deserts). In fact, the pain felt by Thanos might have increased one's joyful response to the scene. The viewers' hopes seemed to be realized and their fears seemed to be allayed. Yet, moments later, there is a dramatic twist we will not reveal, which dashed audiences' hopes for a happy ending. Yet, this disappointment also sets up the possibility of a sequel to resolve the lingering disappointment.

Sidebar   Micro- and Macro-Plots

micro-plots
Smaller plots within a larger narrative that are resolved within the scope of the larger narrative

macro-plot
The overall plot of a narrative

When we go see a Batman movie—really, pick any *Batman* movie, going all the way back to 1966 to the most recent 2017 *The Lego Batman Movie*—we are fairly certain that Batman won't die at the hands of the Joker in the final act. Yet, when Batman and the Joker are fighting midway through the picture and the Joker pulls out a knife to stab Batman as he lays on the ground, we might feel fear. Why do we feel fear in this scene when we know what the end is likely to be? Empathic responses are constantly occurring and the fears we feel in some events relate to something call **micro-plots**.

Micro-plots in narratives are the mini-plots that occur, which drive the **macro-plot** forward. For example, in the film *The Dark Knight*, the macro-plot is that Batman must come to terms with the fact that he acts outside of the law, he won't always be around to save the city, and people like the Joker will constantly challenge him. Situated within this macro-plot are many micro-plots. For example, Batman must travel to China to retrieve a money launderer. The Joker interrupts Harvey Dent's fundraiser and Batman must save Rachel from a fall. Harvey Dent falsely confesses that he is Batman and Batman must defend him as the Joker attempts to capture Dent. All these events drive the major plot forward, and empathy occurs within the micro-plots. So although we know the Joker probably won't cut off Batman's head, he might hurt him in some way. We can feel fear in the moment (related to the micro-plot) even when we "know" the ending.

In addition to empathy, another key process important for disposition theory is the approval of what a character does by the viewer, known as **moral sanctioning**. Although viewers typically want "good guys" rewarded and "bad guys" punished, it is possible to dole out too much punishment. When the punishment fits the crime, viewers sanction it and it leads to enjoyment of the narrative. However, when the punishment is too lenient or too harsh, viewers are unlikely to sanction it and enjoyment is unlikely to result. In fact, for particularly harsh punishments, the counter-empathic responses that would typically be expected for disliked characters can reverse and lead to empathy. Such a perspective might explain why heroes never dole out more extreme punishment than the villains. In fact, this notion of moral sanctioning is what makes some entertainment media characters like Walter White (from *Breaking Bad*), Wolverine (of the Marvel Universe), and Severus Snape (*Harry Potter*) so complicated. These **antiheroes** seem to push the boundaries of moral sanction, while still possessing and espousing qualities that we cheer for.

Disposition theory is still a highly active area of research. One particular aspect of disposition theory that has garnered some interest as of late is the formation of character liking and disliking. Although evidence does suggest that morality of a character's behavior is an important contributor of liking, other formation processes may also exist. Arthur Raney pointed to these **schema** processes in 2004. He argued that because we have experienced narratives before and how they will unfold, we will sometimes accept bad behavior committed by protagonists. A further extension and testing of Raney's model by Grizzard et al. (2017) found that characters whose appearances were consistent with heroic or villainous visuals can activate moral judgments that reflect those schemata. Characters who look heroic are judged to be heroic even if no behavior is observed.

A related question that is beginning to drive research is how we can like characters who engage in objectively immoral behavior. Serial killers (Hannibal Lecter, Dexter), drug dealers (Walter White), and mobsters (Tony Soprano) have all been the protagonist of popular television series. Even movies (e.g., *Deadpool*, *Venom*) have featured morally questionable characters as their lead. How viewers accept their behavior—which would be abhorrent to most standards of acceptable behavior—and maintain positive dispositions toward them is a question that still challenges researchers.

moral sanctioning
Judging a character's action as morally acceptable

antiheroes
A protagonist who engages in morally questionable behavior

schema
A mental network of related concepts

Conclusion

Narratives are ever present in our lives. We tell stories and listen to stories almost constantly. Media entertainment is no exception. The stories in media entertainment are filled with virtuous heroes, despicable villains, and everything in between. Although past research has identified key aspects of stories that make them more or less enjoyable, there is still much work to be done to fully understand how humans respond to stories and narrative characters. Future research, in addition to exploring the appeal of antiheroes and the development of dispositions, might further examine whether new modalities of storytelling are providing unique and novel forms of contact with characters. Do interactive narratives where the viewer is an actor alter disposition theory's predictions? Is disposition theory capable of explaining the appeal of interactive narratives? The future of research on narratives is bright.

 # Key Terms

Plot   The major events within a story

Characters   The person, animals, or entities within a story, play, novel, or movie

Events   Associated occurrences within a story

Temporal progression   The time-ordering of associated events in a story

Telling   The way and manner in which the events of a story are communicated to the audience

Narrator   A character who tells the story to the audience

Transportation   The feeling of "being there" in a story, that is, attentionally and emotionally absorbed into a narrative world

Presence and/or **Telepresence**   A psychological perception in which a technologically mediated interaction is experienced as being nonmediated, i.e., "being there" even when one is seeing an environment on a computer monitor

Immersion   The feeling of being perceptually absorbed into a mediated experience

Parasocial interaction   The perceived interpersonal interaction between a media user and a mediated character or persona

Consistency (behavior)   When a character acts in a manner that is expected based on previous knowledge of the character

Direct involvement   When character addresses the audience members as if they were actually present

Fourth wall   A hypothetical boundary between the fictional narrative and the audience; the fourth wall is often considered the television screen or other screen through which the characters are observed

Eye contact   When a character looks directly at the audience

Spontaneous (behavior)   When a character acts unexpectedly within the frame of a larger story

Indirect involvement   When character addresses other characters within a story, without acknowledging the audience's presence as witnesses to the events

Overhears   A storytelling convention by which audiences are able to observed characters interacting without those characters being aware of the audience's presence

Audience acceptance   Relevant to programs that use direct address, brief pauses in storytelling that provide time for the audience to process and understand events within a narrative

Parasocial relationship (PSR)   The perceived relationship between an individual and media characters, usually a consequence of parasocial interactions with that character

Relational schema   The internalized mental model of how a person experiencing a parasocial relationship understands that they would interact with the mediated character

Attachment styles   Refer to the different types of interpersonal relationships that an individual is most comfortable forming, based on how they view themselves and other people.

Parasocial contact hypothesis (PSC)   A hypothesis that predicts parasocial interactions with minority characters through media exposure can reduce prejudices that an individual holds toward the social groups that those characters represent

Surrogate   A media character that acts as a representative of a larger social group; a stand in for a particular viewpoint or group of people

Identify/Identification   A process by which one sees oneself as similar to or like a media character

Ego-confusion   When someone confuses himself or herself as the character within a story

Affective disposition theory   A theory that predicts that audiences will enjoy stories in which liked characters triumph and disliked characters are foiled

Untiring moral monitors   The notion that entertainment media audiences are constantly making moral judgments about events, characters, and narratives

Micro-plots   Smaller plots within a larger narrative that are resolved within the scope of the larger narrative

Macro-plot   The overall plot of a narrative

Moral sanctioning   Judging a character's action as morally acceptable

Antiheroes   A protagonist who engages in morally questionable behavior

Schema   A mental network of related concepts

References

Bal, M. (1985). *Narratology: Introduction to the theory of narrative.* Toronto: University of Toronto Press.

Campbell, J. (1949). *The hero with a thousand faces.* New York: MJF Books.

Cohen, J. (2004). Parasocial break-up from favorite television characters: The role of attachment styles and relationship intensity. *Journal of Social and Personal Relationships, 21*(2), 187–202. doi: 10.1177/0265407504041374

Daniel, E. S., & Westerman, D. K. (2017). Valar Morghulis (All parasoical men must die): Having nonfictional responses to a fictional character. *Communication Research Reports, 34*(2), 143–152. doi: 10.1080/08824096.2017.1285757

Gerrig, R. (1993). *Experiencing narrative worlds: On the psychological aspects of reading.* New Haven, CT: Yale University Press.

Green, M. C., & Brock, T. C. (2000). The role of transportation in the persuasiveness of public narratives. *Journal of Personality and Social Psychology, 79*(5), 701–721. doi: 10.1037//0022-3514.79.5.701

Grizzard, M., Huang, J., Fitzgerald, K., Ahn, C., & Chu, H. (2017). Sensing heroes and villains: Character-schema and the disposition formation process. *Communication Research, 45*(4), 479–501. doi: 10.1177/0093650217699934

Heider F. & Simmel M. (1944). An Experimental Study of Apparent Behavior, *The American Journal of Psychology, 57* (2) 243. DOI: 10.2307/1416950

Horton, D., & Wohl, R. (1956). Mass communication and para-social interaction: Observations on intimacy at a distance. *Psychiatry, 19*(3), 215–229. doi: 10.1080/00332747.1956.11023049

Nell, V. (1988). *Lost in a book: The psychology of reading for pleasure.* New Haven, CT: Yale University Press.

Rudrum, D. (2005). From narrative representation to narrative use: Towards the limits of definition. *Narrative, 13*(2), 195–204.

Schiappa, E., Gregg, P. B., & Hewes, D. E. (2005). The parasocial contact hypothesis. *Communication Monographs, 72*(1), 92–115. doi: 10.1080/0363775052000342544

Schramm, H., & Hartmann, T. (2008). The PSI-Process Scales. A new measure to assess the intensity and breadth of parasocial processes. *Communications, 33*(4), 385–401. doi 10.1515/comm.2008.025

Twenge, J. M., Zhang, L., Catanese, K. R., Dolan"Pascoe, B., Lyche, L. F., & Baumeister, R. F. (2007). Replenishing connectedness: Reminders of social activity reduce aggression after social exclusion. *British Journal of Social Psychology, 46*(1), 205–224. doi: 10.1348/014466605x90793

Vezzali, L., Stathi, S., Giovannini, D., Capozza, D., & Trifiletti, E. (2015). The greatest magic of Harry Potter: Reducing prejudice. *Journal of Applied Social Psychology, 45*(2), 105–121. doi: 10.1111/jasp.12279

Zillmann, D., & Bryant, J. (1975). Viewer's moral sanction of retribution in the appreciation of dramatic presentations. *Journal of Experimental Social Psychology, 11,* 572–582. doi:10.1016/0022-1031(75)90008-6

Zillmann, D., & Cantor, J. R. (1972) Directionality of transitory dominance as a communication variable affecting humor appreciation. *Journal of Personality and Social Psychology, 24*(2), 191–198. doi: 10.1037/h0033384

 # Suggested Readings

Booker, C. (2004). *The seven basic plots: Why we tell stories.* A&C Black.

Gottschall, J. (2012). *The storytelling animal: How stories make us human.* Boston: Houghton Mifflin Harcourt.

Kübler-Ross, E., & Kessler, D. (2005). *On grief and grieving: Finding the meaning of grief through the five stages of loss.* New York: Simon and Schuster.

Raney, A. A. (2004). Expanding disposition theory: Reconsidering character liking, moral evaluations, and enjoyment. *Communication Theory, 14*(4), 348–369. Doi: 10.1111/j.1468-2885.2004.tb00319.x

Chapter 8

Understanding Genres

"Tous les genres sont bons, Hors le genre ennuyeux."
(All genres are good, Except the boring one."

—Voltaire, 1736

How a story is told is often as important as the story itself. A story about a young girl held captive in a castle by a hideous beast could easily be a horror film or a children's film, depending on how the story is told. There are many notable genres of media entertainment that have garnered interest from scholars. These include drama, comedy, horror, mystery/suspense, and sports. Individuals are drawn to these different genres for many different reasons, yet there are also commonalities across them that might not appear obvious at first glance. One goal of this chapter is to describe and delineate the unique features of various media entertainment genres. What makes a comedy a comedy rather than a drama? The other goal of this chapter is to describe how viewers process and respond to different genres.

Objectives

After reading this chapter students will be able to:

➤ Define and describe the various genres that have garnered the interest of media entertainment researchers.

➤ Understand how viewers respond to the various genres.

➤ Discuss the features within genres that elicit specific responses in viewers.

Defining Genre

genre
A group of conventions or styles that categorize an entertainment product

The word **genre** is derived from the Latin word *genus (generis)*, meaning thing or kind. Genres for media entertainment relate to conventions that are employed in the creation of their content. For example, country music as a genre of music has specific elements and conventions that help listeners to classify and identify a song as country; these might include a singer with a "twangy" accent; the inclusion of fiddles, banjos, and steel guitars; and songs about specific subjects (e.g., rural life, patriotism, nostalgia). Other forms of media entertainment also have specific features and conventions. For example, laugh tracks in comedies, the soft visual style of soap operas, the muted colors of horror films, and the futuristic settings of science fiction.

Conventions help to define genres and viewers seem to quickly adapt to these conventions. A viewer probably wouldn't notice an audience laughing at a joke during a TV sitcom, but such laughter might seem out of place in the middle of a serious drama. Although familiarity and consistency help to define genres, some forms of media entertainment deliberately play with and mix two or more genres together, creating what are called **cross genres** or **hybrid genres**. For example, the film *Tucker and Dale vs. Evil* mixes horror, comedy, and the classic buddy movie together for hilarious results. The film is about mistaken identity: Local teenagers assume two rural guys who are cleaning up their cabin in the woods are actually backwoods killers who kidnapped their friend; in reality, they rescued her from drowning while they were fishing at night. Of course these types of films rely on a strong adherence to the features of both genres in order for the hybridization to work. In the film, a teen accidentally falls into a wood chipper while he is attacking the two fishing buddies who have no idea why teenagers are "killing themselves all over their property." The scene, which would be horrific in a pure horror film, is rendered amusing when it is mixed with witty banter and play face joke telling (more on this later).

cross genre or **hybrid genre**
When an entertainment product mixes two or more genre conventions together

To review, genres are types or kinds of media entertainment. They have conventions that relate to how they are created and how viewers respond to them. In the next sections, we'll dive more into the specific conventions and responses related to various genres.

Drama

Drama is perhaps the most basic genre of storytelling. Dramas focus on one or more characters' journeys and development over time.

The characters typically include a **protagonist** (the leading character of the story), an **antagonist** (the major character who creates obstacles and barriers for the protagonist), and supporting characters, sometimes called helpers. In hero versus villain dramas, the protagonist is typically the hero and the antagonist, the villain. Dramas tend to feature one key conflict that the protagonist is trying to overcome.

Any story that contains characters is a drama. However, drama as a term is commonly used to refer to more serious stories rather than comedies. Dramas are also often seen as focusing primarily on a character's transitions and changes rather than the events or actions within in a narrative. For example, a horror film, even though it contains characters and it is about a serious subject, would not often be referred to as a drama because of the focus on the horrific events that are occuring. Because dramatic content and thus, the drama genre, is so heavily focused on narrative progression, we have already discussed many of the core features of drama in Chapter 7.

protagonist
The main character of a narrative

antagonist
The character that works against the protagonist in a narrative

Comedy

Comedy is perhaps the most popular of all media entertainment. Comedy is the highest grossing genre, with comedies accounting for almost one half of the top films and TV programs of all time. What makes something funny, though, is a question that is difficult to answer. Of course, an individual's taste matters: What is funny to some is entirely unfunny to others. But despite this fact, there are some patterns that make something funny, which we detail in this section.

Play face joke telling is one way that humor is communicated. After saying something, a comedian might make a funny face or an exaggerated expression to let the audience know that what they said was a joke. The winks and nods of a comedian like Mr. Bean would be considered play face jokes. Chris Pratt often did this on *Parks and Rec*, and John Krasinski perfected it with his "Jim Face" on *The Office*. Other similar behaviors by an actor, like the exaggerated movements and silly voices of Adam DeVine from *Workaholics*, can also be used to signify humor and are an example of play face jokes. A similar genre convention for comedy is **deadpan**, where a comedian will say something ludicrous but do so with a straight face. Comedians Steven Wright ("I spilled spot remover on my dog and now he's gone") and Mitch Hedberg ("Rice is great when you're hungry and want 2,000 of something") were famous for their deadpan joke delivery. The one-liners of Captain Raymond Holt on *Brooklyn Nine-Nine* are a good current example of deadpan.

Play face joke telling
When a comedian uses exaggerated expressions or funny faces to indicate a joke is being told

deadpan
When a comedian says or does something humorous, but without showing any reaction to the joke work

Canned laughter or laugh track

An audio recording of laughter that is played during an entertaining media program to signal a funny moment or joke in a program

situation comedies (sitcoms)

Comedy programs that have a set of recurring characters from one episode to the next

sweetening

An industry term for the use of canned laughter or laugh tracks when broadcasting or producing comedy programs

copresence

The feeling that a person is using entertainment media at the same time as others or with others

mere presence

The phenomenon when an individual feels an increased sense of arousal when in the presence of other people

social presence

The degree to which a person feels that they are in the presence of other people, even when no other people are physically present

"**Canned laughter**" or the "**laugh track**" is another genre convention that helps to identify humor. Early comedy shows on radio and television were filmed in front of live studio audiences, and so listeners and viewers at home often heard the audience's response to the jokes. Later **situation comedies** (a.k.a., sitcoms) were filmed on sets with a laugh track added after the fact (e.g., *M*A*S*H*). The laugh track is still used in some comedic content, such as *The Big Bang Theory*, to indicate when the joke should land (**Sidebar: "...before a live studio audience"**).

Sidebar	*"...Before a Live Studio Audience"*

For most anyone who has watched a sitcom before, the laugh track is something that is all-too-common. Whether a show is actually filmed before a live audience or not, producers will often add canned laughter to those parts of the show that are meant to be funny—adding additional canned laughter to the live audience's laughter is known as **sweetening.** As we said above, the laughter cues are a signal to the viewer that the actions on-screen are meant to be funny.

Besides, signalling for the audience that a certain event is supposed to be funny, canned laughter and other similar audio cues (such as audiences who might react in shock at a major plot twist, or hoot and holler if characters on-screen show affection toward each other) serve to stimulate a sense of **copresence** in viewer. That is, they might give the psychological illusion that a particular program is being enjoyed by (or otherwise reacted to similarly by) lots of different viewers. It turns out that even the very presence of other people can be a psycholgically arousing experience, an effect that psychologist Robert Zajonc studied as the **mere presence** effect. Although Zajonc and his colleagues were studying the influence of mere presence on how people perform at different tasks when being watched by others, the arousal that is caused from the (even perceived) presence of others can be applied to explain why laugh tracks might make us laugh harder at a joke, or report enjoying it more. If we hear those laugh tracks and they cause us to be psychologically aroused by the perceived presence of others (in media psychology research, this feeling is referred to as **social presence**), the resulting arousal could intensify our own emotional experiences. In fact, Cohen, Bowman, and Lancaster (2015) demonstrated that

(Continued)

when people watch television with others, the positive emotions that they experience are much stronger than those same positive emotions when viewing alone. Do laugh tracks have a similar effect? We think so. Lawson, Downing, and Cetola (2010) found that when viewers thought that canned laughter was actually from a live audience, they felt that the show content was funnier. In fact, besides increasing the arousal levels in audiences, canned laughter (and other social cues) could also be thought to be an emotional contagion—as we hear others' emotions, we might begin to experience them for ourselves.

In these ways, canned laughter is more than just a cue to tell us when to laugh. It's also a social cue that gets us thinking about other viewers and how they might respond to something . . . and as a result, we get a bit more caught up in the joke than we would otherwise.

But what are we laughing at? Much comedy revolves around what is known as **disparagement humor**. Often times, when we are laughing at a humorous scenario or situation, we are laughing at someone, even if we don't think of it this way. Freud's analysis of humor argued that some jokes are a form of **tendentious humor**, or humor with a purpose. According to Freud's analysis, the purpose of tendentious humor can be hostility and superiority or expressing a sexual taboo in a "more socially acceptable" setting. **Joke work**, the cues that tell us something is not meant to be taken seriously, allow for the expression of socially taboo ideas with an easy exit for the performer (i.e., "It was just a joke").

Much of the humor we see in media entertainment is hostile tendentious humor, particularly in sitcoms. Michael and Dwight on *The Office* and Phil Dunphy on *Modern Family* are two recent examples of the **buffoon**, a character who is the butt of others' jokes. The more deserving we think the character is of derision, the more we enjoy the joke. YouTube Fail videos and celebrity roasts are other forms of tendentious humor based on **schadenfreude**. Normally, pain (in the case of the fail video) and public disparagement (in the case of the roast) are not things that are socially acceptable to laugh at. But, the joke work and humor cues present in this sort of entertainment media—the snickers from onlookers in a YouTube Fail video or the laughs and playful banter between members of a roast—provide audiences with the necessary social sanctions to laugh.

disparagement humor
Humor that puts down or demeans another character or person

Schadenfreude
A German word meaning the pleasure one feels from observing others' suffering

tendentious humor
Humor in which there is a purpose, such as disparaging a person/group or in which a taboo opinion/topic is described; disparagement humor would be a form of tendentious humor

nontendentious humor
Humor in which there is no target being disparaged or mocked

Joke work
Any cue that tells the audience that something is not meant to be taken seriously

buffoon
A character who is the victim of another's jokes; key to tendentious humor

nonsense humor
Humor that presents a puzzle or incongruous situation and then refuses to solve it; a form of nontendentious humor

supernatural horror or **horror of the demonic**
Horror that deals with supernatural forces that disrupts the natural world

science-fiction horror/ horror of the Armageddon
Horror that deals with supernatural forces that threaten life and existence

psychological horror or **horror of the personality**
Horror that deals with threats from a nonsupernatural person or thing that results in terrible consequences

Of course, not everyone finds hostile or painful humor funny, and if the ridicule of the target is too harsh, humor and laughter can turn into anger. Additionally, some forms of hostile humor include racist, sexist, homophobic, and transphobic statements or attitudes which rely on disparaging minority or outgroup members. There is research to suggest that when the targets of tendentious humor are minority groups, the end result can be the development of normalized prejudices and negative attitudes against those groups.

However, not all humor is based on pain. **Nontendentious** humor also had a prominent place in Freud's theory of humor. Nontendentious jokes are those that have an air of suspense and surprise, or present a puzzle for the listener to solve. Some nontendentious jokes pose a question and then answer it in a surprising way (e.g., "Why was the teacher cross-eyed? Because she couldn't control her pupils."). Other nontendentious jokes require the reader to discover why the joke is funny ("I bought a new thesaurus, but it's terrible. Not only that, it's also terrible."). One of the keys to nontendentious jokes for Freud relates to the "saving of psychic energy." Freud argued that nontendentious jokes create confusion and then resolve the confusion. The resolution moves the listener from a conflicted unresolved state to a more resolved state. Such resolution, according to Freud, is pleasurable.

What happens if the puzzle cannot be solved? Then you have **nonsense humor**. Nonsense humor presents a puzzle or incongruous situation, and then refuses to solve it. Much meme humor on the Internet is built on nonsense premises. For example, why is it funny that a cat would like a cheeseburger, or that a dog surrounded by pidgin English could be used to express admiration and awe (a dog exclaiming "So humor. Much laugh. Many funny.")?

Horror

Horror is another popular genre. According to Tamborini and Weaver (1996), drawing from Derry (1977), horror can be subdivided into sub-genres such as **supernatural horror** (or **horror of the demonic**), **science/quasi-science fiction horror** (or **horror of the Armageddon**), and **psychological horror** (or **horror of the personality**). Horror of the demonic usually focuses on some supernatural force that disrupts the natural world: *Dracula*, *The Exorcist*, and *The Conjuring* series are all examples of supernatural horror. Horror of the Armageddon is horror whereby a natural force or presumably natural event has occurred that threatens life and existence. Zombie films such as *28 Days Later, The Birds,* and *Annihilation* all represent examples of the horror of the Armageddon. Finally, horror of the personality is horror where the threat is from a non-supernatural person or thing that results in terrible consequences. *Silence of the Lambs* and *The Human Centipede* both feature killers who are simply humans doing terrible things. Regardless of the sub-genre, horror entertainment typically features content intended to frighten, gross out, disturb, or exhilarate the viewer, but what frightens and grosses us out?

Fear and disgust in horror relate back to the Media Equation discussed in Chapter 6. The things that induce fear in us or that gross us out in the real world, tend to elicit fear in us in media content. Dangerous things elicit fear whether mediated or not. Gross things elicit disgust whether mediated or not. The monsters in films represent evolutionarily dangerous things; they have sharp teeth and fangs, and they could (if they were real) kill you, much like the cave bears that our distant ancestors lived alongside. When you see a character being stalked on screen by the monstrous killer, you can almost feel your heart pounding out of your chest. Imagine how it would feel if you felt like you were the one being stalked! (**Sidebar: Oh the (Virtual) horror!**).

Sidebar   Oh the (Virtual) Horror!

One video game genre that has grown in popularity in recent years is that of the horror genre. Horror video games can vary quite a bit from one system to the next, but they have a few common elements: they feature a very weak or vulnerable protagonist that the player has to control in the face of numerous on-screen dangers—monsters, mazes, and other entrapments. In most horror games, the player has to navigate their way out of a near-impossible situation, such as being trapped in a shopping mall with waves of zombies in *Dead Rising*, solving the mysteries of an abandoned mental hospital (armed only with a camera and a notepad) in *Outlast,* or acting as a night security guard in a haunted arcade at *Five Nights at Freddy's*.

(Continued)

Just as horror movies and television shows tend to frame protagonists as being hopelessly outnumbered by gruesome and often supernatural monsters, horror games take this a step further by requiring the player to take control of the main character and thus be directly responsible for their survival. Likewise, when the main character dies, so virtually does the player . . . and this can be quite gruesome and memorable, and very emotional. Lynch and Martins (2015) found that over half of a sample of college-aged video game players reported feeling high levels of fear when playing video games, and that these emotions were particularly high when the games were highly interactive and presented as realistic (such as using high-quality graphics and authentic storylines). These intense fear emotions can be even higher when players are wearing virtual reality gear when playing games, with Lin (2017) finding evidence of very high levels of fear not only while playing a video game, but even some lingering and residual fear (such as a moderate concern of being attacked from behind) as much as 24 hours later. Of course in both studies—and with the countless others who play horror games every day—the genre is considered both delightfully fun and remarkably scary.

The appeal of horror is another component of the empathy paradox discussed in Chapter 6. Since being afraid and grossed out aren't particularly pleasant feelings, you might be wondering why on earth would anyone want to feel this way or watch movies that they know, or hope, will make them feel that way? There are several explanations for the appeal of horror.

morbid curiosity

Fascination with death and destruction

One explanation relates to **morbid curiosity**, or a fascination with death and destruction. Why might we be interested in death and destruction? Evolutionary psychology suggests that stimuli in our environment that relate to our survival and procreation should be particularly strong attention grabbers. Knowing the sources of death and destruction can help us avoid them. So we might not watch horror for any conscious reason; we might simply be drawn to it by very old psychological programming that causes us to attend to images of death and destruction.

mastery of affective disturbances

The ability to control one's emotions during a tragic, horrific, or dangerous event

Another reason we might expose ourselves to horror relates to **mastery of affective disturbances**. In our lives, we will all have situations that require us to control our emotions. If your child busts his or her head open on the playground, the best action isn't to become distraught and freak out. You must control your emotional reactions and get him or her to the doctor. By exposing ourselves to emotional disturbances in media, we vicariously experience strong emotions and learn how to cope with them through desensitization (the cons of which are discussed in Chapter 5). When we repeatedly expose ourselves to the same stimulus, the ability of that stimulus to elicit the response decreases over time. Medical doctors and paramedics react very differently to blood than the ordinary person on the street. This is because they have desensitized themselves to the presence of blood through repeated exposure.

Another reason that viewers might enjoy horror is **sanctioning of the ultimate outcome**. When we go see a horror film, we know deep down that the villain will not win the day. There will likely be at least one survivor who manages to kill the killer. Some people enjoy horror films because they sanction this ultimately "just" ending. Still, this explanation doesn't always work. There are some horror films that end in an utterly hopeless manner. For example, *Invasion of the Body Snatchers* ends with the entire world being taken over by alien invaders; in *Halloween*, Michael Myer's body is not found and he is left wandering the town of Haddonfield when the credits roll. Such endings aren't really consistent with the sanctioning of the ultimate outcome theory, unless viewers ultimately were rooting for the bad guy the entire time.

sanctioning the ultimate outcome
The idea that people enjoy horror because the threat will be stopped and the lead character will be safe at the end

A final explanation relates to the arousal jag hypothesis that we discussed in Chapter 6. Recall from Chapter 6 that fear fits into Ekman's model of basic emotions, which are often bottom-up reactions to content—they are nearly instantaneous and subconscious reactions to content over which we have very little cognitive control. Essentially, there is no evolutionary benefit for our bodies and minds treating "mediated horror" as fake, and as a result, we react very strongly to horrifying content. Some researchers, such as Mundorf, Weaver, and Zillmann (1989) have even discussed these strong arousal reactions to horror as one reason why the genre is so appealing to teenagers. Younger teens often go to horror movies together, in order to both experience the exhileration of high arousal and to demonstrate their ability to tolerate this highly arousing content to their peers.

Mystery and Suspense

Mystery and suspense are two other genres that have gained substantial interest from media entertainment researchers. Although often thought of together as "two sides of the same coin," mystery and suspense are actually quite different: Suspense is about *certainty* whereas mystery is about *uncertainty*; suspense is about *what will happen* whereas mystery is about *what did happen*.

Mystery
A genre in which something has happened and the plot is focused on solving a puzzle

uncertainty model of mystery enjoyment
An explanation of the appeal of mystery genre suggesting that enjoyment is highest when the mystery resolves following complete uncertainty regarding the narrative outcome

surprise model of mystery enjoyment
An explanation of the appeal of mystery genre suggesting that enjoyment is highest when the mystery resolves in an unexpected manner usually due to misdirection built into the narrative

confirmation model of mystery enjoyment
An explanation of the appeal of mystery genre suggesting that enjoyment is highest when the mystery resolves in a way that the viewer expected it to

"Who dun it?!" **Mystery** as a genre is focused on solving a puzzle. Usually a crime has been committed and the reader along with characters within the story are trying to ascertain the who, the why, and the how of the crime. Mysteries typically end with the details of the crime being understood, but there is less focus on punishment for the person responsible. Usually, the perpetrator's punishment for the crime isn't a key feature; simply learning the details is enough.

Zillmann (1991) outlined three main models for explaining the enjoyment of mysteries. The first is the **uncertainty model of mystery enjoyment**. According to this model, uncertainty converts to joy when the mystery is solved. Thus, enjoyment of mysteries is highest when there is a lot of uncertainty revolving around the who, why, and how questions. For example, if there are four main suspects (a common number for mysteries), the uncertainty model would predict enjoyment to be highest when each suspect had a 25% probability of being the perpetrator before the reveal.

The second model of mystery enjoyment is the **surprise model of mystery enjoyment**. According to this model, enjoyment is high when evidence points strongly to one suspect, but in the end, the real perpetrator is someone else who was not suspected very highly. The film, *The Usual Suspects*, is a good example of the surprise model. Gabriel Byrne's character is suspected with evidence mounting throughout; however, in the end Keyser Soze turns out to be perhaps the least suspected character in the film.

The final model is the **confirmation model of mystery enjoyment**. According to this model, enjoyment comes from guessing correctly. TV mysteries such as *Scooby Doo*, *Murder She Wrote*, and the *Law & Order* series all present viewers with mysteries that have limited suspects and are easily solvable. Solving these mysteries can provide feelings of enjoyment for guessing correctly.

Notably, the three models apply differently depending on the when enjoyment is measured during the narrative. During viewing, the uncertainty model likely predicts enjoyment, as the solution is not yet known. However, following the ending of the narrative when the solution becomes apparent, the confirmation and surprise models likely predict enjoyment more accurately. Research from Knobloch-Westerwick and Keplinger (2006) shows that the surprise model is more predictive for individuals higher in self-esteem, whereas the confirmation model is more predictive for individuals lower in self-esteem. A person who feels confident is more comfortable being wrong than a person who is less confident, leading to higher enjoyment for surprising endings for high self-esteem.

If mystery is about what *did* happen, **suspense** is about what *will* happen. Suspense is defined as an affective reaction due to the perceived likelihood of outcomes to observed others Zillmann, 1991. Suspense is the emotional response we feel when it appears something bad will happen. Suspense typically relates to liked characters being in dangerous situations. For example, the most suspenseful scenes in the Netflix series *Stranger Things* are when the liked protagonists seem to be in imminent danger due to the big bad monster (the demogorgon). Unlike mystery (which benefits from low certainty; "I'm not sure who the killer is"), suspense is highest when (a) there are only two possible outcomes (e.g., the demogorgon will kill the kids or they will get away) and (b) there is high certainty of harm (i.e., it seems *very* probable that the bad thing will happen). Suspense often accompanies horror films, but it is the emotional backbone of drama as well. In horror films, writers will often kill an attractive young person who viewers instinctively find appealing first. This type of death generates high levels of suspense for later: "If that likeable character can be killed, no one is safe!" Suspense is usually more appealing to individuals high in sensation seeking.

suspense

An affective response to narrative that results from the perceived likelihood that something bad will happen to a liked character

Sports

Sports is the final genre we will discuss in this chapter. Sports viewers often develop strong allegiances toward specific teams and players. Their affiliations toward these players can be interpreted in conjunction with disposition theory discussed in Chapter 7. Individuals come to like some teams and players and dislike others. While morality is the primary determinant of liking of characters, **geographical location** and **past success** are the two largest predictors of team fandom. Local teams have fans in local areas, but teams that were successful in the past (e.g., the Yankees, UNC and Duke, the Lakers) have large fan-bases outside of their immediate geography (**Sidebar: KMOX and Cardinals Nation**).

Sidebar | KMOX and Cardinals Nation

"As a kid growing up, I listened to KMOX down in the state of Louisiana late at night. So I knew a lot about [St. Louis Cardinals Hall of Famer Stan] Musial; never knew what he looked like, but I knew a lot about him."

—Former St. Louis Cardinals pitcher Lou Brock, on growing up as a fan of the team.

(Continued)

How does a small-market baseball team in the midwestern United States end up with fans in 44 states, much of Western Europe, East Africa, and Micronesia? The St. Louis Cardinals of Major League Baseball accomplished this feat in part due to their success (with 11 World Series titles, they are second only to the New York Yankees in terms of historical success) but mainly due to the 50,000-watt broadcast signal from KMOX.

In a project for *The New York Times,* David Waldstein drive from Busch Stadium in St. Louis, to Horn Lake, Mississippi and back—a 600-mile, 12-hour road trip in which Waldstein was able to maintain the broadcast signal for nearly his entire trip. Waldstein chronicled his trip online: https://www.nytimes.com/2013/10/30/sports/baseball/trying-to-out-run-the-long-reach-of-cardinals-baseball.html.

In 2005, the Cardinals dissolved their exclusive broadcast relationship with KMOX, opting instead for partial ownership of a local 5,000-watt station KTRS. However, Waldstein's broadcast experience on October 29, 2013, was an exception, as KMOX had the St. Louis broadcast rights to that year's World Series. The Boston Red Sox won the series that year.

> **You try it!**   *Are you a fan of a particular sports team that is nowhere near your hometown, or a team that is located in city or country that doesn't have any particular personal importance to your life? If so, what do you think caused you to become such a fan of the team? Do you find yourself following the team through the media? Does newer entertainment technology make it easier to be a fan of this team?*

It's important to note that responses to sports are not so different from other genres. The drama that unfolds on the field of play can be seen as an example of suspense. Viewers witness liked and disliked others in potential perilous situations (e.g., losing). Will my team win, or will they lose?! Like horror, sports fans often revel in the misfortunes of a disliked foe. The only thing as sweet to a University of North Carolina basketball fan as UNC winning a game, is Duke losing a game. Sports has some unique features related to fandom and social relationships outside of media. We will discuss these in further detail in Chapter 11.

Conclusion

Media entertainment content often can be divided and distinguished based on its genre. There are many kinds of stories and content that we can expose ourselves to, and we have expectations about what those genres are. Knowing that a TV show is a horror show rather than a comedy will create certain expectations in your mind before you view it. Although genres have unique characteristics (after all they wouldn't be distinguishable if they weren't slightly unique), our responses are often similar regardless of genre: We feel suspense in horror, sports, and mystery. Understanding the commonalities as well as the differences is an important step in understanding media entertainment.

Key Terms

Genre   A group of conventions or styles that categorize an entertainment product

Cross genre or **hybrid genre**   When an entertainment product mixes two or more genre conventions together

Protagonist   The main character of a narrative

Antagonist   The character that works against the protagonist in a narrative

Play face joke telling   When a comedian uses exaggerated expressions or funny faces to indicate a joke is being told

Deadpan   When a comedian says or does something humorous, but without showing any reaction to the joke work

Canned laughter or laugh track   An audio recording of laughter that is played during an entertaining media program to signal a funny moment or joke in a program

Situation comedies (sitcoms)   Comedy programs that have a set of recurring characters from one episode to the next

Sweetening   An industry term for the use of canned laughter or laugh tracks when broadcasting or producing comedy programs

Copresence   The feeling that a person is using entertainment media at the same time as others or with others

Mere presence   The phenomenon when an individual feels an increased sense of arousal when in the presence of other people

Social presence   The degree to which a person feels that they are in the presence of other people, even when no other people are physically present

Disparagement humor   Humor that puts down or demeans another character or person

Schadenfreude   A German word meaning the pleasure one feels from observing others' suffering

Tendentious humor   Humor in which there is a purpose, such as disparaging a person/group or in which a taboo opinion/topic is described; disparagement humor would be a form of tendentious humor

Nontendentious humor   Humor in which there is no target being disparaged or mocked

Joke work   Any cue that tells the audience that something is not meant to be taken seriously

Buffoon   A character who is the victim of another's jokes; key to tendentious humor

Nonsense humor   Humor that presents a puzzle or incongruous situation and then refuses to solve it; a form of nontendentious humor

Supernatural horror or **Horror of the demonic**   Horror that deals with supernatural forces that disrupts the natural world

Science-fiction horror/ Horror of the Armageddon   Horror that deals with supernatural forces that threaten life and existence

Psychological horror or **Horror of the personality**   Horror that deals with threats from a nonsupernatural person or thing that results in terrible consequences

Morbid curiosity   Fascination with death and destruction

Mastery of affective disturbances   The ability to control one's emotions during a tragic, horrific, or dangerous event

Sanctioning the ultimate outcome   The idea that people enjoy horror because the threat will be stopped and the lead character will be safe at the end

Mystery   A genre in which something has happened and the plot is focused on solving a puzzle

Uncertainty model of mystery enjoyment   An explanation of the appeal of mystery genre suggesting that enjoyment is highest when the mystery resolves following complete uncertainty regarding the narrative outcome

Surprise model of mystery enjoyment   An explanation of the appeal of mystery genre suggesting that enjoyment is highest when the mystery resolves in an unexpected manner usually due to misdirection built into the narrative

Confirmation model of mystery enjoyment   An explanation of the appeal of mystery genre suggesting that enjoyment is highest when the mystery resolves in a way that the viewer expected it to

Suspense   An affective response to narrative that results from the perceived likelihood that something bad will happen to a liked character

■ References

Cohen, E. L., Bowman, N. D., & Lancaster, A. L. (2015). R U with Some1? Using text message experience sampling to examine television coviewing as a moderator of emotional contagion effects on enjoyment. *Mass Communication and Society*, 19(2), 149–172. doi: 10.1080/15205436.2015.1071400

Knobloch-Westerwick, S., & Keplinger, C. (2006). Mystery appeal: Effects of uncertainty and resolution on the enjoyment of mystery. *Media Psychology*, 8, 193–212.

Lawson, T. J., Downing, B., & Celota, H. (1998). An attributional explanation for the effect of audience laughter on perceived funniness. *Basic and Applied Social Psychology*, 20(4), 243–249. doi: 10.1207/s15324834basp2004_1

Lin, J.-H. (2017). Fear in virtual reality (VR): Fear elements, coping reactions, immediate and next-day fright responses toward a survival horror zombie virtual reality game. *Computers in Human Behavior, 72*, 350–361. doi:10.1016/j.chb.2017.02.057

Lynch, T., & Martins, N. (2015). Nothing to fear? An analysis of college students' fear experiences with video games. *Journal of Broadcasting & Electronic Media*, 59, 298–317. doi:10.1080/08838151.2015.1029128

Mundorf, N., Weaver, J., & Zillman, D (1989). Effects of gender roles and self perceptions of affective reactions to horror films. *Sex Roles, 20*(11-12), 655–673. doi: 10.1007/BF00288078

Voltaire, *(1736). L'Enfant prodigue: comédie en vers dissillabes (1736),* Preface

Zillmann, D. (1991). The logic of suspense and mystery. In J. Bryant & D. Zillmann (Eds.), *Responding to the screen. Reception and reaction processes* (pp. 281–303). Hillsdale, NJ: Lawrence Erlbaum Associates, Inc.

 # Further readings

Berlyne, D. E. (1972). Humor and its kin. In J. H. Goldstein & P. E. McGhee (Eds.), *The psychology of humor: Theoretical perspectives and empirical issues* (pp. 43–60). New York, : Academic Press.

Ford, T. E., & Ferguson, M. A. (2004). Social consequences of disparagement humor: A prejudiced norm theory. *Personality and Social Psychology Review, 8*(1), 79–94. doi: 10.1207/S15327957PSPR0801_4

Freud, S. (1916). *Wit and its relation to the unconscious* (A. A. Brill, trans.). Bartleby.com. Retrieved from https://www.bartleby.com/279/

Hemenover, S. H., & Bowman, N. D. (2018). Video games, emotion, and emotion regulation: Expanding the scope. *Annals of the International Communication Association, 42*(2). 125–143. doi: 10.1080/23808985.2018.1442239

Zajonc, R. B. (1965). Social facilitation. *Science, 149,* 269–274. doi:10.1126/science.149.3681.269

CHAPTER 9

Children's Entertainment

"And shall we just carelessly allow children to hear any casual tales which may be devised by casual persons, and to receive into their minds ideas for the most part the very opposite of those which we should wish them to have when they are grown up?"

—*Plato*

Introduction

Before we start this chapter, think back to your childhood. In particular, try to think of your favorite books, television shows, movies, video games, and other forms of entertainment media. Ask yourself, do you think that the content of those media was **developmentally appropriate** for you as a child? If your younger siblings were using those media today, would you feel comfortable?

Entertainment media is particularly attractive to children and adolescents. Media entertainment, such as cartoons, movies, comic books, and other texts, provides a low effort means to fill the abundance of leisure time children have. In addition, media producers often make products specifically aimed at children, and do so with very wide profit margins and perhaps not deep consideration into the how that content might impact children's development. Media entertainment, like other forms of socialization, has the power to help shape childhood development by offering engaging programs for learning and emotional development, but there may be other unintended effects that are coupled with these processes. Children's content is often developed and produced with the end goal of selling toys

developmentally appropriate
Media content that matches the mental and emotional competencies of (usually, younger) audiences

141

rather than helping children grow. Moreover, although children are often exposed to content produced for more mature audiences, they may lack the cognitive ability to understand the nuance. Because of these reasons, children's entertainment media often faces stricter regulations and restrictions than other types of content. This chapter will offer insights into each of these dimensions, while also demonstrating the role that media technologies—from the earliest radio to the latest smartphones—play in how children use entertainment media, and how it impacts them.

Objectives

After reading and studying the concepts in this chapter, students should be able to:

➤ Understand why children are a unique market for media entertainment.

➤ Recognize milestones in the history of media entertainment that are particularly relevant to children.

➤ Distinguish between the different types of intended and unintended effects of children's media.

➤ Describe and critique the formal and informal regulation of children's media, in terms of access and content.

A History of Concern

On October 1, 2017, Matt Groening's animated series *The Simpsons* entered its 29th season of broadcast, making it not only the longest-running cartoon, but also the longest-running prime time program in US television history. One of the recurring characters on this show is Helen Lovejoy, the wife of Reverend Lovejoy, who's classic line in the face of any struggles facing Springfield is, "Won't somebody please think of the children?" To be sure, some of the very earliest concerns about media content inspired Mrs. Lovejoy's question. In this section we examine historical attempts to understand the effects of specific media on children.

Cinema. In the 1930s, noted education professor W. W. Charters was among a group of researchers interested in the influence of movies on children, writing:

No one in this country up to the present time has known in any general and impersonal manner just what effect motion pictures have upon children. Meanwhile children clamor to attend the movies as often as they are allowed to go. (1933, v.)

Charters was the chairperson of perhaps the very first set of scientific research studies on how media entertainment influences children, funded by wealthy Ohio philanthropist Frances Bolton Payne. The **Payne Fund Studies** gathered **social scientists** from several different areas of study (such as education, sociology, psychology, and what would become the discipline of communication) to study the effect of movies on children.

The 1920s and 1930s were the **golden age** of Hollywood movies (Paulz, 2002). At that time, nearly 70% of Americans went to at least one movie per week—by far, the highest level of attendance at any point in the history of cinema. A large portion of this audience was comprised of children. While most adults generally knew *where* children (here, preadolescents and elementary school-aged children) were spending their time, less was known about (a) what sort of content was in the movies that these children were watching and (b) if any of that content actually influenced their thoughts, emotions, or behaviors. The Payne Fund Studies attempted to answer both questions. As explained by Lowery and DeFleur (1995), researchers with the Payne Fund found a number of common themes featured in Hollywood movies, including crime, sex, love, mystery, war, children, history, travel, comedy, and social propaganda. Payne Fund researchers also found a number of effects of that movie content on children, including anxiety and loss of sleep as well as a desire to imitate the content, such as sexual behaviors (kissing and petting) as well as substance use (smoking). The general conclusion drawn from the Payne Fund were that (a) movies contained adult themes that were probably not appropriate for children and (b) children endorsed the themes presented and mimicked the behavior of the actors and actresses. At the time, the Payne Fund data were interpreted as supportive of the **magic bullet model** of media effects, a perspective that argued media messages struck every eye and every ear creating uniform and powerful effects.

In the same era, other social forces were pushing against a perceived moral decay in Hollywood. The Motion Picture Producers and Distributors of America, under the leadership of Presbyterian

Payne Fund Studies

A series of privately funded studies in the early 20th century that investigated how cinema affected children and adolescents

social scientist

Someone who studies human behavior using the scientific method

golden age

In reference to film history, The period in cinema history after the invention of synchronized sound that lasted to the 1960s

magic bullet theory

A paradigm in media psychology research in which it was assumed that media had a direct, powerful, and uniform effects on audiences thoughts, actions, and behaviors

Will H. Hays

The president of the The Motion Picture Producers and Distributors of America (MPPDA) between 1922 and 1945 who created the Hays Code

Hays Code

A set of rules used by the MPPDA to restrict certain content in films that was deemed inappropriate

the "Don'ts" and "Be Carefuls"

A list of behaviors and features from the Hays Code that were not allowed (the "Don'ts") or should rarely occur ("Be Carefuls") in movies

ratings system

In reference to entertainment media, a set of labels sanctioned by a given media industry designed to inform audiences about specific types of content such as sexual or violent behavior or language

Comics Code Authority

A ratings system used by the Association of Comics Magazine Publishers

Church elder **Will H. Hays**, was facing mounting public pressure from concerned parents and politicians who also invoked Mrs. Lovejoy's question and were curious about the potential dangers of a nascent film industry on audiences, including children. It did not help that several high-profile scandals involving Hollywood stars sent Hollywood into its own panic: Either sanitize the movie industry to quell public fears or risk legal and political actions. In the absence of any data that could help him argue with critics, Hays worked with other filmmakers to draft the **Hays Code** as an early draft of **the "Don'ts" and "Be Carefuls"** of Hollywood. Among the "Don'ts" were using any profanity (especially use of the word "God"), showing childbirth, ridiculing priests, or discussing sex hygiene; among the "Be Carefuls" were discussions of weapons, depictions of crime, sympathy for criminals, or showing men and women sharing a bed. By the end of the 1960s thanks to pressure from directors and the popularity of films produced in Europe where the Hays Code was not followed, the Motion Picture Association of America (MPAA) abandoned the Hays Code in favor of a voluntary **ratings system**. Movie studios had their films rated along a continuum that indicated approximate ages where the content would be considered appropriate.

Comic Books. Similar to films, comic books also enjoyed a "golden age" of sorts in the late 1930s, with some of the more famous characters of entertainment media today being introduced for the first time—Superman (1938), Batman (1939), Captain America (1941), and Wonder Woman (1941). The popularity of these heroes led to a boom in the publication of comic books on any number of topics, including stories on crime, horror, and romance—the same themes both found in the Payne Fund Studies as well as those feared by Hayes and other Hollywood producers. Critics of the medium were quick to seize on this more adult-themed content, including psychiatrist Fredric Wertham, whose 1953 article in *Ladies Home Journal* "What Parents Don't Know About Comics" sparked national concern over children and comic books that eventually lead to the **Comics Code Authority**. As with the Hays Code, the Comics Code was eventually abandoned (the last comic publisher to follow the code was Archie Comics, breaking with it 2011 as their editorial focus became increasingly progressive; **Sidebar: Kevin Keller Comes Out**), but not without having an indelible impact on an entire entertainment medium.

Sidebar	Kevin Keller Comes Out

In 1942, American comic book audiences were introduced to four students from fictitious Riverdale High: Archie Andrews, Betty Cooper, Veronica Lodge, and Jughead Jones. Set in a nondescript small town, the comic featured storylines that might be familiar with many high school students: schoolwork, sports, dating, part-time jobs, car problems, and the occasional big adventure. For most of Archie's comic book career, he and the hijinks of most of the Riverdale High game were rather wholesome—the comics adhered very strictly to the Comics Code Authority and avoided any discussions that might be seen as unsavory or inappropriate for children.

Given the rather conservative and noncontroversial themes of most Archie storylines, the content of Veronica #202 (published in September 2010) was surprising to many readers, as it featured the series' first openly gay character in Kevin Keller. In that issue, Kevin Keller—a chiseled blonde teenage boy—was featured on the front cover, with text reading "Meet the hot new guy!" and one of the female characters, Veronica, telling Archie, "Sorry Archie! We're over!" Throughout the issue, Veronica pursues Kevin's attention, but he shows no interest in her advances—confiding in Jughead that he's not interested: "It's nothing against her! I'm gay!" By all reports, Keller's character was well-received by audiences, as the character was eventually given his own series. The writer of Veronica #202, Dan Parent, was acknowledged with a Gay and Lesbian Alliance Against Defamation Media Award in 2011 for creating Kevin. Kevin's character has been retained in other Archie properties as well, including the popular live-action television show *Riverdale*.

Television. Television followed a similar path as the movie industries. In 1951, the **National Association of Broadcasters (NAB)** adopted the **Code of Practices for Television Content** (or the **Television Code**). Like the Hays Code for films, the Television Code forbade the presence of some types of content (e.g., profanity, explicit sex) and encouraged programming that "should enlarge the horizons of the viewer, provide him with wholesome entertainment, afford helpful stimulation, and remind him of the responsibilities which the citizen has toward his society." In 1976, the Television Code was ruled unconstitutional by a Los Angeles Federal Judge and it was

National Association of Broadcasters (NAB)

An industry organization that represents television and radio broadcasters in the United States

Code of Practices for Television Content or **Television Code**

A set of rules used by the NAB to restrict certain content in television revised. However, the NAB eventually scrapped the code altogether when in 1983 it faced additional legal threats posed by Reagan's Justice Department. The current **TV Parental Guidelines** represent a rating system similar to the MPAA's rating system with ratings like TV-G for general audiences and TV-MA for adult audiences. However, whereas the MPAA switched to a rating system immediately upon abandoning its code, TV operated under vague rules (and in many ways still does). For example, today there are vastly different standards for broadcast channels (e.g., ABC, NBC) as compared to cable channels (e.g., FX). You could air programs that included the f-word on FX without fear of fines from the Federal Communications Commission.

TV Parental Guidelines

A rating system used in broadcast television to inform audiences about specific types of sexual and violent content in a television show

Children as an Audience of Concern

Many countries will consider anyone under the age of 18 as a "minor"—generally suggesting that they're incapable of making legal decisions for themselves or being solely responsible for their actions. Many researchers will further distinguish between younger children and **adolescents**, usually making distinctions based on the cognitive capacities and developmental differences of the audience. Three approaches to developmental psychology are useful here: the cognitive development stages proposed by Jean Piaget, the moral development stages proposed by Lawrence Kohlberg, and theory of mind concepts proposed by David Premack and Guy Woodruff. We'll describe each of these briefly, below.

adolescence

The stage in development between childhood and adulthood

Piaget's (1936) perspective provides a basic explanation for how children at different ages understand the world around them in very different ways. At the youngest ages (up to 2 years old), he argues that children are really just focused on basic sensory perception—trying to make sense of the sights and sounds of the world around them. As they age to 7 years old, children begin to engage in basic **symbolic thinking** where they can use words and phrases to express their thoughts, as well as understand other people's conversations. Up to age 11, more abstract concepts that are often **intangible,** such as space, time, and even basic mathematics begin to make sense—at the same age, children can start to understand relationships even if they cannot necessarily make predictions or know why relationships exist. Finally, as they progress through adolescence, they are able to understand abstract logic and reasoning and can critically process messages.

symbolic thinking

The ability to understand abstract concepts, such as language, math, and social relationships

intangible

Something that is not physically represented or able to be sensed

Kohlberg (1974) expanded on Piaget and proposed a somewhat-analogous set of moral development stages where he described how children's abilities to engage in **moral reasoning** change as they grow. The youngest children (up to the age of five or six) are not often capable of anything more complex than reward and punishment. In this stage called "preconventional moral reasoning" children interpret good and moral things as those that are rewarded, whereas bad and immoral things are those things that result in punishment. As children age, morality shifts to the conventional stage (around age 11 or 12) in which understandings of right and wrong are based more on considerations of how a child might be perceived—a so-called "good boy/good girl" attitude in which children recognize that there are social sanctions that come with engaging in immoral behavior. As they grow through to adolescence, children are thought to grow into a postconventional moral reasoning stage in which they realize the differences between what is legally right and what is morally right are not always the same; some refer this as the debate between the "letter of the law" and the "spirit of the law."

Finally, Premack and Woodruff (1978) took a look at trying to understand how people are able to understand the mental state of others—that is, how children might develop a **theory of mind**, or the ability to infer what another person is thinking. A classic way of testing this is the **Sally-Anne Test** in which a child is shown a story about two other children, one who hides an object from the other (**Sidebar: Sally has lost her marbles!**). Children with a developed sense of theory of mind are able to distinguish between what they know about a story (as the reader, who often knows even more than the characters) and the characters themselves, and this is a skill that usually happens around age four or five.

moral reasoning
The ability to rationalize why a behavior in a particular context is right or wrong

theory of mind
The ability to infer what other people are thinking

Sally-Anne Test
A psychological test of the theory of mind, often used to test theory of mind development in young children

Sidebar   Sally has Lost Her Marbles!

Sally and Anne are playing in room. Sally has a basket, and Anne has a box. While they're playing, Sally finds a marble and decides to place it in the basket. Sally then leaves the room, and this is when Anne gets mischievous: she decides to take Sally's marble out of the basket, and place it inside of her box. Later, Sally comes back to the room.

(Continued)

Where will she look for her marble?

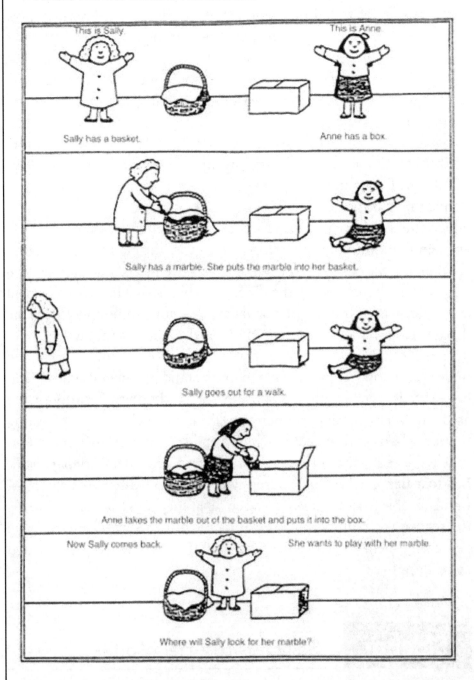

Children (or adults, of course) who answer "the basket" are demonstrating that they are able to understand the perspective of other people, independent from their own perspective—they have developed a theory of mind. After all, if Sally wasn't in the room when Anne misplaced the marble, then how would she have known that the marble was moved. Likewise, children who answer "the box" are confusing their own knowledge (as the reader of the story) with Sally's perspective (as a character in the story).

The concepts above are somewhat older and have since been extended on by other scholars. However, they do provide a basic framework for why media entertainment effects could be unique to children. Children at very low cognitive stages (from Piaget) and moral reasoning levels (from Kohlberg) and who don't have a well-developed theory of mind (from Premack and Woodruff) likely struggle with understanding that much of what happens in a movie, or a comic book, or any other entertainment medium is fantasy, and they probably do not understand even basic levels of humor, satire, or other messages embedded in entertainment programming.

(How) Do Children Process Entertainment Media?

When a child is watching television or playing a video game, how do they understand the on-screen content? Some of the largest associations for communication research (such as the National Communication Association and International Communication Association) have entire research divisions devoted to this topic. In the subsections that follow, we discuss some of the mechanisms and processes that are thought to be particularly relevant.

Equilibrium and disequilibrium. About the same time that Piaget was writing about children's' cognitive development, pediatrician and psychologist Arnold Gesell argued that children seem to move back and forth between periods of **equilibrium** (in which they are more or less well-behaved and content) and **disequilibrium** (in which they might act out more and seem generally troubled or disturbed). Shifts toward disequilibrium are thought to occur when a child is learning new things and developing new abilities. Shifts back toward equilibrium are thought to occur when the child is demonstrating mastery of what they have already learned. For Gesell, these stages are predictable and a natural byproduct of what most people would call "growing up." Applied to entertainment media, we might expect that new content could spur periods of disequilibrium if there are new concepts and new skills developed by the content. In addition, some forms of media entertainment might be difficult to understand during periods of disequilibrium—although scholars such as Labouvie-Vief (2015) suggest that the stress induced during these phases might actually activate **neurons** and facilitate learning. Notably, these stages of equilibrium/disequilibrium tend to progress much more quickly at very young ages.

equilibrium

A period in child development where a child is typically calm and predictable and practices mastery over known skills

disequilibrium

A period in child development where a child is quickly developing new skills and is uneasy and unpredictable

neurons

Cells in the brain that transmit information to other cells

stimulus

In media psychology, the content that one is exposed to such as a specific image or piece of content

moderate discrepancy hypothesis

A prediction of human learning that suggests individuals need to be exposed to a challenge that is slightly more difficult than their current skill set; challenges that are too difficult will not be effective in increasing learning

curvilinear

A relationship between two variables in which an effect increases before decreasing; also called a "U-shaped" curve. Curvilinear effects can also work in reverse, in which an effect decreases before increasing (a "reverse U-shaped" curve)

channel-surfing

When a viewer browses through different television shows in order to select one to watch, usually spending very little time on any given show (or channel)

Moderate discrepancy hypothesis. For any entertainment media to have any sort of effect (positive or negative), audiences have to actually pay attention to the content. Most of us do not pay attention to every single **stimulus** in our environment, because it would completely overload our senses (imagine how hard it would be to focus on reading this chapter while trying to touch, taste, see, hear, and smell every single object on your desk at the same time!). As explained by McCall and McGhee (1977, p. 179):

> Typically, adults are not very likely to approach and spend time examining stimuli that are thoroughly familiar or stimuli that are so deviant from their experience that they do not understand them. We are bored on the one hand and stupefied on the other.

The bored and stupefied experience described above is essentially the **moderate discrepancy hypothesis**. To advance and learn, something must be discrepant from our current skill set (e.g., harder), but not so hard that it would be impossible to learn. Applied to attention, there is a **curvilinear** relationship between any new stimulus and the degree to which we pay attention to it. In a comprehensive test of the moderate discrepancy hypothesis, Valkenburg and Vroone (2004) found that in four age groups (6 to 18 months, 19 to 35 months, 36 to 48 months, and 49 to 58 months), the youngest children were most likely to pay attention programs such as *Sesame Street* and *Teletubbies*, while the oldest children were most likely to pay attention to *Lion King II*—all four groups tended to ignore news programming as well as commercials aimed at adults. Those patterns made sense, given that *Sesame Street* and *Teletubbies* are both aimed at very young audiences and *Lion King II* would have been made for older children. This study was particularly robust in that it presented all of the children in the study with the same 38-minute video recording that had sort segments of the programs above, somewhat simulating an individual (such as an older sibling or parent) **channel-surfing** through different television stations.

Fantasy-reality distinction. One of the early assumptions about children's inability to understand media entertainment is that they would confuse on-screen fantasy as a reality. Piaget talks about this extensively in his writings, and many cite common beliefs that children have in fictitious entities—Santa Claus, the Easter Bunny, and the Tooth Fairy might be common myths in many parts of the United States, for example. However, more recent research, such as that by psychologist Jacqueline

Woolley and her colleagues, has somewhat challenged this critique of children. For example, she would classify the belief that "Santa Claus is real" as less about children confusing fantasy and reality but instead believing in a common cultural myth. Woolley and Ghossainy (2013) offer a more granular distinction between four different types of fantasy–reality judgments that children might make:

- A "hit" refers to a correct assessment of something as real as being, in fact, real. Believing that dinosaurs existed would be a "hit" as we have empirical evidence for the existence of dinosaurs.

- A "false alarm" refers to children judging something as real that is not, such as believing in Santa Claus.

- A "miss" refers to a scenario in which a child rejects the reality of something that is actually real, such as refusing to believe that the moon and the sun are different interstellar objects.

- A "correct rejection" is when a child rejects the reality of something that is not real; Woolley uses the example of a child doubting the existence of dancing carrots.

Applied to entertainment media broadly, both "false alarms" and "misses" can be equally important. For example, "false alarms" would correspond with children believing that on-screen characters such as Big Bird are real, or believing that when a superhero such as Batman or Wonder Woman is injured during an on-screen fight, that they are actually suffering. Likewise, "misses" might happen when a child sees something in a news broadcast or some other realistic entertainment portrayal, and is quick to dismiss it as pretend. For Woolley, that children would engage in enough skepticism to make several "misses" in their judgements of reality is evidence that they are not so naïve as we might assume.

Sidebar   Toys, Made-for-TV

G. I. Joe, He-Man, and *Transformers.* Some of the most popular toys for children in the 1980s had something very interesting in common: Entertainment media tie-ins. In fact, while *G. I. Joe* was already based on a successful toy line from the 1960s, both *He-Man* and *Transformers* were completely new franchises for children, with no currently existing

(Continued)

backstory or other reason for children to know or understand the characters—something very different from toys based on *Star Wars* for example, in which children already knew the toy characters from the popular movie franchise of the same name.

How do you encourage children to play with toys without any existing backstory? You create one. Toy manufacturers in the 1980s turned to creating comic books and **Saturday morning cartoons** as a way to provide children with a narrative and context for their toys, and such efforts were remarkably successful. In a 2017 Netflix documentary series called "The Toys That Made Us," toy manufacturers talk extensively about the strategy of using children's media as a way to sell toys and the incredibly profitable results: *G. I. Joe* earned toy maker Kenner over $50 million in 1982 alone, *He-Man* earned Mattel nearly $1 billion from 1982 to 1986, and *Transformers* earned Hasbro $50 million in 1984 alone. Today, many of the original toys from these franchises are highly sought after, with some toys selling for hundreds or even thousands of dollars online (an original Snake-Eyes *G. I. Joe* action figure sells for upward of $1,000). Some of the franchises still exist as popular cartoons and movies today—five *Transformers* movies released between 2009 and 2017 have earned over $4 billion in gross box office sales worldwide.

You try it!   *Think of some of the toys that you played with as a child. How many of them had direct tie-ins with a popular entertainment media franchise, such as a television show, video game, or comic book series? If you have to estimate, about how much money do you think that you (or your family) spent on those toys? Was it worth, in the end?*

Saturday morning cartoons

For most of the middle to late 20th Century, US television networks would broadcast cartoons from early morning until early afternoon, referred to colloquially as "Saturday morning cartoons."

Perceptual boundedness and centration.   Another area of research into how children understand entertainment media has to do with the types of things that are displayed on-screen. Media psychologist Patti Valkenburg (2004, also discussed earlier in the section on moderate discrepancy) explains that particularly young children—such as those under the age of five—pay much more attention to visual information. For example, they might pay attention to what a television or comic book character is wearing or the color of the character's hair, and ignore the behaviors of the character. One reason that children do this, which Valkenburg borrows from earlier writings by Piaget, is through a process called **centration**, or paying attention to one particularly unique or striking feature of a character. The children's books in the *Clifford* series (which feature a big red dog) or the *Despicable Me* movie series (the bean-shaped, one-eyed, and yellow minions) offer good examples of centration.

centration

Paying attention to one particularly unique or striking feature of a media character

These perceptual boundaries can also lead to children being confused about, or even scared by, different character transformations. Sparks and Cantor (1986) observed this by showing both younger-aged (3 to 5 years old) and older-aged (9 to 11 years old) children scenes from the television show *The Incredible Hulk* in which the character David Banner (called Bruce Banner in the comic books) transforms into the massive, green Hulk when he is angry. As predicted, older children expressed more fear pretransformation (when the human David Banner was in danger) and younger children expressed much greater fear during the transformation. The researchers explained that while the older children were more concerned with the perils befalling David Banner, the younger children were more scared by the character's visual transformation.

Social role-taking.   Another question of interest is how children come to understand various social roles through media entertainment exposure. As children grow older, their theory of mind gets stronger and as a result, they are able to understand other people's motivations and internal states better. For example, a very young toddler will assume that any rewarding social interaction with another person is evidence of a friendship, regardless of the person that they are interactive with. Likewise, as children age and develop a stronger **sense of self**, they also begin to distinguish between the different motivations and interests of other people—over time, using this knowledge to assume different social roles (being more or less friendly with some people over others depending on shared or dissimilar interests). As we have seen elsewhere in this chapter, children adopt a similar stance toward entertainment media characters. Older children tend to engage characters that they feel very similar toward, or characters that they dream of being like, such as when they grow up. (**Sidebar: What does a scientist look like?**)

sense of self
One's self-awareness that they are a unique individual

Sidebar   What does a Scientist Look Like?

If somebody asked you to draw a scientist, what would you draw? Common things that most people draw would probably include a white lab coat, eyeglasses or safety goggles, and some sort of laboratory equipment such as glass beakers or Bunsen burners. These were mostly the things that researcher David Wade Chambers found in a 1983 study

(Continued)

draw-a-scientist-test (DAST)

A method of measuring an individual's cognitive biases associated with how they view scientists, such as the age, gender, ethnicity, and other personal attributes associated with the profession

self-report

In media psychology, measuring a person's attitude or belief by using survey questions, usually without researcher involvement

Children's Television Workshop (CTW)

A nonprofit organization that created several children educational television shows. Today, the organization is called Sesame Workshop.

Sesame Street

A television show created by CTW to teach children basic educational lessons and social skills

socioeconomic status (SES)

An estimation of an individual's social standing based on a number of factors such as income or occupation

of nearly 5,000 children living in Quebec, based on the results of the **draw-a-scientist test** method that he used. Although not the focus of his work, Chambers suggested that some of these stereotypes likely come from how scientists are portrayed in cartoons and other popular entertainment media.

Fast-forwarding to 2007, communication scholars Jocelyn Steinke and colleagues were curious to see not only how media might influence how children see scientists, but to look for a particularly troubling stereotype common to how scientists are often portrayed on television: as men. In their study, based on a sample of U.S. seventh-graders, they found that girls were more likely to draw a female scientist and boys were more likely to draw a male scientist. However, they also found that media portrayals played an important role in how children "saw" a scientist, in their mind. A few examples from the research included:

- "I got this from movies I have seen. This is what one character looked like." (girl, video group, drew male scientist)
- "It just popped into my head and I remember from the TV show I used to watch called like science guy or something." (girl, control group, drew male scientist)
- "My idea came from the movies and TV. I drew a woman because an obvious choice would have been men." (girl, discussion group, drew female scientist)

You try it! *How would you draw a scientist? What about a professor, manager, or banker? What about a homemaker or a babysitter? Compare your drawings to others, and discuss reasons why they might be similar or different.*

Fear and horror. Finally, we might discuss one of the most primal and basic human emotions: Fear. As far back as the Payne Fund studies, entertainment-induced fear was a common emotion observed in children. In those studies, as many as 93% of children (fourth-graders, to be precise) **self-reported** feeling frightened by a movie, and kids would often shield their eyes to avoid the content—some kids even reported having nightmares afterward. Given that most young children can have difficulty separating fantasy from reality, these findings are probably not very surprising. More recent research (cf. van den Bulck, 2004) found that among secondary school-aged children, the rate of nightmares from both television content to be just over 30%, and video games to be about 7.5% (slightly higher, 10%, for boys).

Effects of Children's Media

Cognitive Learning. Perhaps one of the best examples of learning through television can be found with the **Children's Television Workshop**, or **CTW**, the creators of *Sesame Street*. The program was created in association with Harvard University out of recognition that (a) there was a growing academic achievement gap between children from lower and higher **socioeconomic status (SES)** homes and (b) many children from lower SES backgrounds tended to watch more television. Researchers with CTW proposed a novel idea: If children are already watching television, why not bring educational content to them?

Sesame Street was first broadcast commercial-free on November 10, 1969. Ten years later, nearly nine million children watched the program daily, and research showed that watching *Sesame Street* improved academic performance for children from all backgrounds. However, rather than closing the achievement gap, the gap actually increased—a phenomenon often referred to as the **"rich-get-richer" hypothesis.** It turns out that children from higher SES backgrounds were more likely to watch the program with their parents, and thus, they could more often practice the lessons being taught.

Affective learning. Beyond the cognitive effects of television, society was also concerned with the **psychological well-being** of children. This is where affective learning programming can be helpful to teach self-control and positive self-esteem. The best example may be that found in *Mister Rogers' Neighborhood*. The eponymous Fred Rogers, a Presbyterian minister from Pittsburgh, felt that television could play an important role in inspiring and nurturing children's imaginations and **emotional intelligence**, and his show dealt often with a wide-ranging set of themes, from exploring creativity by visiting factories, to discussions of complex emotions such as jealousy, anger, and sadness, as well as coping with loss—such as when Mr. Rogers' fish died. Studies have demonstrated that children who regularly watched *Mister Rogers Neighborhood* tended to be more in control of impulses and emotions, and had fewer disciplinary problems in school.

Displacement. There are a fixed number of hours in any given day, time spent with media is time that cannot be spent on something else. Thus, media use displaces other activities. Recent estimates from **Common Sense Media** suggest that young children (those aged zero to eight years

"rich-get-richer" hypothesis

An argument that predicts individuals who already have a fair number of resources tend to acquire more resources more easily than individuals without resources

psychological well-being

A family of individual states that relate to one's quality of life apart from physical well-being. States that lead to high levels of psychological well-being include feelings of self-worth, connection with others, capability, and mastery.

emotional intelligence

A person's ability to understand his or her emotions and the emotions of others and to express their emotions during the appropriate settings

Common Sense Media

A nonprofit organization based in the United States that rates media products for their age-appropriateness, and supports research and education into media's impact on children

screen media
Media that involve visual information, such as televisions and computers

old) spend just over 2 hours per day using **screen media**. Because media use is typically sedentary, concerns abound that it might contribute to increased rates of childhood obesity (Robinson et al., 2017). Excessive media usage might also encourage children to spend more time alone, which could increase feelings of loneliness, and could even displace important activities such as homework (cf. Potter, 1987). As recently as 2018, the World Health Organization has classified gaming addiction as a mental health addiction, with symptoms that include excessive and compulsive play as well as impairment of other healthy activities.

Socialization. Children can be uncritical consumers of on-screen portrayals of minorities or persons with disabilities. The Payne Fund studies found that movies with positive or negative framing of a minority group (*Son of the Gods* as a film that framed Chinese in a positive manner, and *Birth of a Nation* as a film that framed African-Americans in a negative manner) led to children viewing the minority in a similar manner. Learning **stereotypes** can happen for any number of social constructs. For example, Steinke et al (2007) found that media portrayals of women in science, engineering, and technology careers, or STEM, influenced the ways in which younger boys and girls envisioned a scientist.

stereotypes
An generalized belief about a particular group of people

One explanation for these findings is that entertainment media content provides a source of parasocial contact for children to encounter people from backgrounds and cultures that they may not have direct contact with. Schiappa and colleagues (2005) argued that this vicarious contact is but one way that children (as well as adults) can understand different people and places, but such contact is a bit of a double-edged sword: If depictions are skewed and there is no direct experience to contextualize the portrayals, children might be even more susceptible to aligning their views with those portrayed on the screen.

effect sizes
A standardized measure of how much one variable affects another

Aggression. While the **effect sizes** of these effects are debatable, there is little debate that children are influenced by media violence. This was the conclusion of a comprehensive review of nearly 60 years of research into the topic, conducted by 17 experts on the topic (Anderson et al., 2017). In their meta-analysis, one of the media forms that they paid particular attention to was video games, arguing that the interactive and arousing nature of video game content might make them particularly well-adept at encouraging aggression elsewhere. However, Anderson et al (2017) are also careful to explain that no single risk factor (such as viewing or using violent media) could ever been seen as a root cause of aggression, but rather:

"... the research consistently supports the hypothesis that it is one of the risk factors and that it is not the smallest of them. Importantly, it is one of the few risk factors that can be modified with little cost to parents or to society in general (p. 5)."

Regulating Children's Media Use

When considering the influences of children on media, perhaps the bluntest way that one could protect against any potential negative influence would be to simply restrict children's access. However, such a strategy might be at best an over-correction and at worst it could potentially also take away from many of the positive effects that have been discussed throughout this chapter. To end our discussion of children and media however, we turn to two common and effective ways of engaging parents and policy makers to better understand children's media content so that they might become more informed consumers: by providing content ratings, as well as by engaging in mediation strategies.

Content ratings. Short of prohibiting content, one way in which media producers can assuage social concerns about the content of their entertainment offerings is by assigning ratings to the work. Unlike the earlier-mentioned examples, such as the Comics Code Authority and Television Code which actively regulated and censored content, organizations such as the **MPAA** and the **Entertainment Software Ratings Board** offer content ratings for films and video games, respectively. These ratings, as well as international systems such as the **Pan-European Game Information**, offer ratings based on the perceived age-appropriateness of content as a way to inform consumers about what they might expect to view or play.

Content ratings can be complicated, however. For example, video games can be very difficult to rate, given that the player has a lot of control over what content is viewed on-screen. Ratings systems are also very culturally dependent, which can be seen when comparing how ESRB (the American rating board) and PEGI (The European Rating board) rate the same games. The video game *The Sims* was rated as 7+ (for ages seven and older) with a descriptor of mild violence by PEGI, but the same game was rated as "Teen" (for ages 13 and up) by ESRB. Why such a stark difference? As a U.S.-based rating system, *ESRB* was concerned that themes of crude humor and sexual innuendos would be too much for younger players. Finally, some have argued

Motion Picture Association of America (MPAA)
An industry organization that represents film studios in the United States

Entertainment Software Ratings Board (ESRB)
An industry organization that rates video games for age-appropriateness in the United States

Pan-European Game Information (PEGI)
An industry organization that rates video games for age-appropriateness in Europe

that assigning ratings to media products in order to warn parents will make those same products even more attractive to children, an effect known as the **forbidden fruit hypothesis.**

forbidden fruit hypothesis
Predicts that people will desire more those things that are deemed inappropriate for them by others

Parental mediation. Even content ratings have their flaws, as descriptors used to explain media products might not always be as accurate as parents and policy makers would hope. To this end—and with a focus on parents as the core **gatekeepers** for their children's media exposure—one other way that parents can engage both media content and children during media consumption is through active parental mediation—or parents consuming media with their children. In one of the more comprehensive studies on how parents and children co-use media in the United States, Connell et al. (2015) found that in a sample of over 2,000 parents of very young children (under the age of eight), parents were most likely to use more traditional forms of media such as books and television with their children. Such active parental mediation strategies are thought to be particularly effective, because they allow parents to both understand the media content that their children are consuming and, if necessary, help contextualize and explain that content to their children.

gatekeepers
An individual who has the ability to either block or allow others to consume a media product

Conclusion

In many ways, the scientific study of media entertainment has been motivated by this concern for children as a special audience. Children can and do process information very differently throughout their developmental stages than adults. Understanding these processes is helpful, because we can use this knowledge to be sure that our children's media diets are healthy and productive, while still fun and entertaining. As we learned from *G.I. Joe*, "Knowing is half the battle."

 # Key Terms

Developmentally appropriate   Media content that matches the mental and emotional competencies of (usually, younger) audiences

Payne Fund Studies   A series of privately funded studies in the early 20th century that investigated how cinema affected children and adolescents

Social scientist   Someone who studies human behavior using the scientific method

Golden age   In reference to film history, The period in cinema history after the invention of synchronized sound that lasted to the 1960s

Magic bullet theory   A paradigm in media psychology research in which it was assumed that media had a direct, powerful, and uniform effects on audiences thoughts, actions, and behaviors

Will H. Hays   The president of the The Motion Picture Producers and Distributors of America (MPPDA) between 1922 and 1945 who created the Hays Code

Hays Code   A set of rules used by the MPPDA to restrict certain content in films that was deemed inappropriate

The "Don'ts" and "Be Carefuls"   A list of behaviors and features from the Hays Code that were not allowed (the "Don'ts") or should rarely occur ("Be Carefuls") in movies

Ratings system   In reference to entertainment media, a set of labels sanctioned by a given media industry designed to inform audiences about specific types of content such as sexual or violent behavior or language

Comics Code Authority   A ratings system used by the Association of Comics Magazine Publishers

National Association of Broadcasters (NAB)   An industry organization that represents television and radio broadcasters in the United States

Code of Practices for Television Content or **Television Code**   A set of rules used by the NAB to restrict certain content in television

TV Parental Guidelines   A rating system used in broadcast television to inform audiences about specific types of sexual and violent content in a television show

Adolescence   The stage in development between childhood and adulthood

Symbolic thinking   The ability to understand abstract concepts, such as language, math, and social relationships

Intangible   Something that is not physically represented or able to be sensed

Moral reasoning   The ability to rationalize why a behavior in a particular context is right or wrong

Theory of mind   The ability to infer what other people are thinking

Sally-Anne Test   A psychological test of the theory of mind, often used to test theory of mind development in young children

Equilibrium   A period in child development where a child is typically calm and predictable and practices mastery over known skills

Disequilibrium   A period in child development where a child is quickly developing new skills and is uneasy and unpredictable

Neurons   Cells in the brain that transmit information to other cells

Stimulus   In media psychology, the content that one is exposed to such as a specific image or piece of content

Moderate discrepancy hypothesis   A prediction of human learning that suggests individuals need to be exposed to a challenge that is slightly more difficult than their current skill set; challenges that are too difficult will not be effective in increasing learning

Curvilinear   A relationship between two variables in which an effect increases before decreasing; also called a "U-shaped" curve. Curvilinear effects can also work in reverse, in which an effect decreases before increasing (a "reverse U-shaped" curve)

Channel-surfing   When a viewer browses through different television shows in order to select one to watch, usually spending very little time on any given show (or channel)

Saturday morning cartoons For most of the middle to late 20th Century, US television networks would broadcast cartoons from early morning until early afternoon, referred to colloquially as "Saturday morning cartoons"

Centration Paying attention to one particularly unique or striking feature of a media character

Sense of self One's self-awareness that they are a unique individual

Self-report In media psychology, measuring a person's attitude or belief by using survey questions, usually without researcher involvement

Draw-a-scientist-test (DAST) A method of measuring an individual's cognitive biases associated with how they view scientists, such as the age, gender, ethnicity, and other personal attributes associated with the profession

Children's Television Workshop (CTW) A nonprofit organization that created several children educational television shows. Today, the organization is called Sesame Workshop

Sesame Street A television show created by CTW to teach children basic educational lessons and social skills

Socioeconomic status (SES) An estimation of an individual's social standing based on a number of factors such as income or occupation

"Rich-get-richer" hypothesis An argument that predicts individuals who already have a fair number of resources tend to acquire more resources more easily than individuals without resources

Psychological well-being A family of individual states that relate to one's quality of life apart from physical well-being. States that lead to high levels of psychological well-being include feelings of self-worth, connection with others, capability, and mastery

Emotional intelligence A person's ability to understand his or her emotions and the emotions of others and to express their emotions during the appropriate settings

Common Sense Media A nonprofit organization based in the United States that rates media products for their age-appropriateness, and supports research and education into media's impact on children

Screen media Media that involve visual information, such as televisions and computers

Stereotypes An generalized belief about a particular group of people

Effect sizes A standardized measure of how much one variable affects another

Motion Picture Association of America (MPAA) An industry organization that represents film studios in the United States

Entertainment Software Ratings Board (ESRB) An industry organization that rates video games for age-appropriateness in the United States

Pan-European Game Information (PEGI) An industry organization that rates video games for age-appropriateness in Europe

Forbidden fruit hypothesis Predicts that people will desire more those things that are deemed inappropriate for them by others

Gatekeepers An individual who has the ability to either block or allow others to consume a media product

References

Anderson, C. A., Bushman, B. J., Bartholow, B. D., Cantor, J., Christakis, D., Coyne, S. M., et al. (2017). Screen violence and youth behavior. *Pediatrics, 140*(2). Retrieved from http://pediatrics.aappublications.org/content/140/Supplement_2/S142

Charters W. W. (1933). Chairman's preface. In R. C. Petersen & L. L. Thurstone. (Eds.) *Motion pictures and the social attitudes of children: A Payne Fund study*. New York: Macmillan &

Connell, S. L., Lauricella, A. R., & Wartella, E. (2015). Parental co-use of media technology with their young children in the USA. *Journal of Children and Media, 9*(1), 5–21. doi: 10.1080/17482798.2015.997440

Kohlberg, L. (1971). *From is to ought: How to commit the naturalistic fallacy and get away with it in the study of moral development*. New York: Academic Press.

Labouvie-Vief, G. (2015). Equilibrium and disequilibrium in development. In *Integrating emotions and cognition throughout the lifespan*. New York: Springer.

Lowery, S., & M. DeFleur. (1995). *Milestones in mass communication research: Media effects. 3rd ed.* New York: Longman.

McCall, R. B., & McGhee, P. E. (1977). The discrepancy hypothesis of attention and affect in infants. In I. C. Užgiris & F. Weizmann (Eds.), *The structuring of experience*. Boston: Springer.

Pautz, M. C. (2002). The decline in average weekly cinema attendance: 1930–2000. *Issues in Political Economy, 11*, 54–65.

Piaget, J. (1936). *Origins of intelligence in the child*. London: Routledge & Kegan Paul.

Potter, W. J. (1987). Does television viewing hinder academic achievement among adolescents? *Human Communication Research, 14*(1), 27–46. doi: 10.1111/j/1468-2958.1987.tb00120.x

Premack, D. & Woodruff, G. (1978). Does the chimpanzee have a theory of mind? *The Behavioral and Brain Sciences, 4*, 515–526.

Robinson, T. N., Banda, J. A., Hale, L., Lu, A. S., Fleming-Milici, F., Calvert, S. L., & Wartella, E. (2017). Screen media exposure and obesity in children and adolescents. *Pediatrics, 140*(2). Retrieved from http://pediatrics.aappublications.org/content/140/Supplement_2/S97

Schiappa, E., Gregg, P. B., & Hewes, D. E., (2005). The parasocial contact hypothesis. *Communication Monographs, 72*(1), 92-115. doi: 10.1080/0363775052000342544

Sparks, G. G., & Cantor, J. (1986). Developmental differences in fright responses to a television program depicting a character transformation. *Journal of Broadcasting & Electronic Media, 30*(3), 309–323.

Steinke, J., Lapinski, M. K., Crocker, N., Zeitsman-Thomas, A., Williams, Y., Evergreen, S. H., et al. (2007). Assessing media influences on middle school-aged children's perceptions of women in science using the Draw-A-Scientist Test (DAST). *Science Communication, 29*(1), 35–64. doi: 10.1177/1075547007306508

Valkenburg, P. M. (2004). *Children's responses to the screen: A media psychological approach.* Mahwah, NJ: LEA

Valkenburg, P. M., & Vroone, M. (2004). Developmental changes in infants' and toddlers' attention to television entertainment. *Communication Research, 31*(1), 288–311. doi: 10.1177/0093650204263435

Van den Bulck, J. (2004). Media use and dreaming: The relationship among television viewing, computer game play, and nightmares of pleasant dreams. *Dreaming, 14*(1), 43–49. doi: 10.1037/1053-0797.14.1.43

Woolley, J. D., & Ghossainy, M. E. (2013). Revisiting the fantasy-reality distinction: Children as naïve skeptics. *Child Development, 84*(5), 1496–1510. doi: 10.1111/cdev.12081

▉ Suggested Readings

Allport, G. W. Davis, M. (2008). *Street gang: The complete history of Sesame Street.* New York: Viking Press.

Baron-Cohen, S., Leslie, A.M., & Frith, U. (1985) Does the autistic child have a 'theory of mind'? *Cognition, 21,* 37–46.

Chambers, D. W. (1983). Stereotypic images of the scientist; The Draw-A-Scientist Test. *Science Education, 67*(2). 255–265.

Doherty, T. P. (1999). *Pre-Code Hollywood: Sex, immorality, and insurrection in American Cinema 1930–1934.* New York: Columbia University Press.

Gesell, A. (1925). Monthly increments of development in infancy. *Journal of Genetic Psychology, 32,* 203–208

Wertham, F. (1954). *Seduction of the innocent.* New York: Holt, Rinehart, and Winston.

World Health Organization (2018, January). What is gaming disorder? Retrieved from: http://www.who.int/features/qa/gaming-disorder/en/

Chapter 10

News and Politics as Entertainment

"Entertainment has superseded the provision of information, human interest has supplanted the public interest; measured judgment has succumbed to sensationalism; the trivial has triumphed over the weighty; the intimate relationship of celebrities from soap operas, the world of sport, or the royal family are judged more 'newsworthy' than the reporting of significant issues and events of international consequence. Traditional news values have been undermined by the new values, 'infotainment' is rampant."

—(Franklin, 1997, p. 4)

Introduction

In early understandings of mass media, Lasswell (1948) suggested that users turn to mass media for three functions: to surveil the environment for possible risks or threats, to correlate society by selection of specific news and information, and to transmit cultural norms from one generation to the next. Entertainment, the function of mass media we have been focused on throughout this textbook, was added as a fourth function by Wright, but not until 1960 (see Chapter 1). This separation of news and entertainment continues, for the most part, in the separation of political science and entertainment studies today.

So what is a chapter on news and politics doing in an entertainment media textbook? The truth is that media coverage of news and politics can be very entertaining, and humor has been an important force in politics since ancient Greece and Rome. Today, programs such as John Oliver's *Last Week Tonight*, which blends current events, politics, and comedy, draw in around one million viewers per week. The size of the audiences of political and news-based satire and humor rival those for award-winning dramas and comedies, and news programs as a whole are not exempt from market forces and the need to capture viewers' attention. Therefore, when looking at the style and content of news and political coverage today, we may find it is not as separate from entertainment as we may think.

Objectives

After reading and studying the concepts in this chapter, students should be able to:

> ➤ Understand the relationship between entertainment media and more serious issues of news.

> ➤ Discuss the changing practices around news and political coverage that are most relevant to media entertainment.

> ➤ Examine how news is represented in entertainment media.

> ➤ Critique the effects that entertainment-based news and political content have on individuals and society.

infotainment or **soft news**

News coverage of information that is primarily focused on entertainment or leisure, or stories of personal interest without major consequences

hard news

News that cover stories related to current events and issues of great consequence

News as Entertainment

In the quote at the beginning of the chapter, British journalism professor Bob Franklin laments the state of a model of news production and distribution where content was becoming increasingly trivial—a style in-between entertainment and information known as "**infotainment**". The term **infotainment** is often used to refer to news content that seems to be more aimed at entertaining than informing audiences—others use the term **soft news** (to contrast more trivial content with **hard news**). Hard news represents Lasswell's (1948) traditional three functions of the media, in which news organizations accept the task of informing society about the most important issues of the day. Soft news in contrast focuses more on ensuring that audiences enjoy the news, focusing on humor and personal interest stories. Is soft news replacing hard news, as Franklin suggests? Perhaps.

Television today is very different from when it began. In the earliest days of television there were very few choices—**American Broadcasting Company** (**ABC**, which started broadcasting television in 1948), **Columbia Broadcasting System** (**CBS**, which began television broadcasts in 1941), and **National Broadcasting Company** (**NBC**, whose broadcast television content is the oldest beginning in 1939). This limited market led to high news consumption. In the 1970s, for example, researchers found that as many as 40% of television viewers watched news programming simply because it was included in the nightly program schedule of their favorite channel. However, the media landscape of the late 20th and early 21st century is very different. With the advent of the Cable News Network (better known as CNN) in 1980, the television market was introduced to channels covering nothing but news. Now, every major television market today has followed suit, with multiple news broadcasts, all airing at the same time, as well as all-day **cable news** stations, daily newspapers, and news-focused web pages. These news broadcasts and shows are now competing with each other, as well as entertainment for viewer's attention. These changes have led to what is known as a **high-choice media environment.** As stated by Prior (2005):

> ". . .in a high-choice environment, politics constantly competes with entertainment. . .Largely unexposed to entertainment competition, [mid-20th century] news had its place in the early evening and again before the late-night shows. Today, as both entertainment and news are available around the clock on numerous cable channels and websites, people's content preferences determine more of what those with cable or Internet access watch, read, and hear" (p. 577)

Content shifts. One of the ways in which traditional news sources compete with entertainment and each other is by blurring lines between what might be considered "news" and what might be considered "entertainment" by producing content framed as news broadcasts but more akin to emotionally charged editorials. Morning shows like *Good Morning America* and *Fox and Friends* are good examples. There is a marked change in the emotional tenor of modern mass mediated news compared to how news has been presented in the past. Peters (2011) explains that rather than the emotional content of the news per se, it is the emotional tenor that has changed. He offers three dimensions by which the role of emotions in modern news differs from the mid-20th

American Broadcasting Company (ABC)

A major television network established in the 1940s and currently owned by the Walt Disney Company

Columbia Broadcasting System (CBS)

A television network established in the 1940s and owned by the CBS Corporation

National Broadcasting Company (NBC)

A television network established in the late 1930s; currently owned by Comcast

cable news

News that is produced and distributed by cable stations that is usually delivered on a 24-hour rotation; this contrasts with network news, which is usually only shown at specific times in the morning, afternoon, and evening

high-choice media environment

A media marketplace that is characterized by numerous options and channels available to consumers century, including diversity of emotional style, acceptability of journalistic involvement, and attempts to involve the audience (Peters, 2011).

Diversity of emotional style. Historically, news deliveries were not "unemotional", rather they were an emotional posture that was a stylistic choice known as "**American Cool.**" Edward R. Murrow and Walter Cronkite both had broadcasts that were typified by the right balance of disengagement and nonchalance, without appearing disinterested in the topics at hand. Cronkite's American cool style of broadcast, coupled with his direct address to the audience on a regularly-scheduled basis, resulted in Cronkite being among the most trusted news anchors and people of his time (**Sidebar: The Most Trusted Man in America**).

American Cool

A vocal tone of news made popular in the middle 20th Century by American news anchors in which the news was delivered in a serious and emotionally neutral style

Sidebar   The Most Trusted Man in America

On the evening of March 6, 1981, Walter Cronkite ended his 12-year stint as the lead anchorperson of the *CBS Evening News*. During this time, Cronkite's version of the news was the most popular among U.S. news audiences. His broadcasts earned nearly half of the entire viewing audience. That final broadcast has been archived by *CBS Evening News'* official YouTube channel (https://www.youtube.com/watch?v=G5tdqo-jA26E) and a portion of the text of his farewell is included below:

> "This is my last broadcast as the anchorman of *The CBS Evening News*; for me, it's a moment for which I long have planned, but which, nevertheless, comes with some sadness. For almost 2 decades, after all, we've been meeting like this in the evenings, and I'll miss that. But those who have made anything of this departure, I'm afraid have made *too* much. This is but a transition, a passing of the baton . . . Old anchormen, you see, don't fade away; they just keep coming back for more. *And that's the way it is*: Friday, March 6, 1981. I'll be away on assignment, and Dan Rather will be sitting in here for the next few years. *Good night.*"

You try it!   *In watching this broadcast and/or reading the text of the broadcast above, what are some of the elements of news and entertainment that you see in the language? When Cronkite refers to "meeting like this in the evenings" do you think that this would encourage or discourage audience members from forming a parasocial relationship with him? Are there other elements that stand out to you?*

There is a noticeable diversity in the styles used in journalism today, from more somber or stoic style of reporting one might find on **National Public Radio (NPR)**, to a more bombastic style of commentary that one might find through digital media services. However, Grabe et al. (2000) found that while emotional and flamboyant portrayals of news content is better at increasing audience's arousal and attention toward the material, it has no effect on how much information that audiences recall from the material, and audiences were less likely to view the content as being credible. Therefore, modern newscasts must strike a balance between sensationalizing the news and being stoic about the news or they risk being viewed as not credible.

Journalistic Involvement. The second feature changing in news broadcasts is that the objective and uninvolved role of the journalist has shifted to a more partisan role. Whereas more traditional formats of journalism would usually call for a reporter to remain uninvolved in the stories that they are reporting on, modern journalists are more free to express their personal opinions, whether by offering slight editorial commentary during a story (such as using more biased adjectives to describe the people or events in a story) to actively arguing a **partisan** perspective when either reporting news or interviewing subjects (**Sidebar: All Sides of the News**).

National Public Radio (NPR)
A nonprofit radio membership organization that provides news and cultural content to radio stations across the United States

partisan
A type of bias which favors one particular cause or one particular political party over another

---

Sidebar   All Sides of the News

One of the problems with hypercompetitive news broadcasts is that they often become partisan to attract specific audiences. Online **news aggregators** have begun to gather up numerous news stories into a central location, so that audiences might be more likely to see other options. Sites such as www.popurls.com scrape other news sites to provide users with an array of information via listed headlines, so users can choose from a variety of options. These differ from sites like www.digg.com or www.reddit.com in that these online news aggregators simply present top stories from existing sites, rather than publishing user-submitted stories and information.

Such news aggregators might not help encourage partisan media sources to be more objective, but they do make an effort to give media consumers open and unfiltered comparisons between the many

news aggregators
Organizations or automated programs that gather news stories from multiple sources into one place for a person to read

(Continued)

echo chambers

A colloquial term used to critique news organizations for only exposing audiences to partisan news content that fits the audience's currently held political beliefs

syndicated column

Written content, such as a regularly scheduled newspaper editorial, that is distributed to multiple news outlet

No Spin Zone

A well-known syndicated column written by conservative commentator Bill O' Reilly

Fox News Channel

A cable news station established in 1996 and owned by the Fox Entertainment Group

Poynter Institute

A nonprofit institution for journalism research and professional education in the United States

Associated Press (AP)

A syndication agency based in the United States that is used by multiple newspapers and news stations to report national and international news

different options, online. Some are explicitly designed to combat **echo chambers** for readers. For example, the website www.allsides.com features summaries of various news events and directly below those summaries, presents a "From the Right," From the Center," and "From the Left" source. Users of the site can compare the headline language from all three sample sources, and from there, read each story.

> **You try it!** Make a visit to www.allsides.com and check out the many different perspectives that they aggregate on major U.S. and world events. Do you see clear differences in how media cover events? Do those differences line up with the "Left," "Center," and "Right" ratings that each source is given? How would you rate the sources, if you were in charge?

Actively encouraging a partisan perspective can be seen in the rhetoric of mainstream sources such as MSNBC and Fox News. For example, former Fox News anchor, Bill O'Reilly penned an infamous editorial in his then-nationally **syndicated column** (called the **"No-Spin Zone"**) in which he insisted that modern news audiences "want to know how the journalist they trust *feel* about things that are important to their lives. The news consumer is almost desperate for someone to define the truth of the matter" (O'Reilly, 2003).

Notably, O'Reilly went on to anchor *The O'Reilly Report* as part of the 1996 launch of **Fox News Channel** (renamed "The O'Reilly Factor" in 1998), and the program aired for 20 seasons. Personalities such as O'Reilly are remarkably popular with audiences. Indeed, it was not until sponsors canceled their ad buys following sexual harassment allegations surfaced against the host that his show was eventually cancelled on April 21, 2017 (the same day in which O'Reilly was fired from the network). However, a 2018 study by the **Poynter Institute** found that the majority of Americans believe that the more "Cronkite-esque" news outlets such as NPR, the **Associated Press**, and the **Public Broadcasting System (PBS)** are among the least biased and most accurate news sources.

Audience involvement. Finally, Peters argued that news agencies craft narratives that are aimed at generating emotional involvement in the audience, similar to how we might expect a good movie or book to cause us to feel angry or happy or any other range of emotions. This has been most researched in terms of the coverage of political and famous individuals in terms of **morality plays,** featuring the broadcasters as characters and news events as competitions.

News as morality play. One of the most powerful and effective ways to capture an audience's attention is through narrative. If individuals are not familiar with the specifics of a given event or story, framing them in terms of a protagonist to root for and an antagonist to root against is useful for engaging audiences. For Altheide (1997), these narratives take the form of **morality plays** in which content producers tap into the audience's' values and cultural heritage in order to frame conflicts along moral dimensions (after all, the content producers themselves are usually members of the same value and cultural set as the members of the audience). At least one way in which this is accomplished is through news stories that frame current events in terms of **problem frames** that emphasize the fears of the audience and the potential risks they may face if they do not weigh in. For example, in research analyzing two major news media outlets, *The Los Angeles Times* and *ABC News*, usage of problem framing (in this case, simply using the word "fear") had increased in a 10-year period (1985 to 1994) nearly 65% for the newspaper content and over 170% for the television content.

Broadcasters as characters. Another way in which news resembles entertainment is that that broadcasters may frame themselves as the lead character in their reports. Framed this way, audience often find themselves compelled toward the news reports of particular reporters whom they might feel a personal connection—referred to as having a parasocial relationship or parasocial interaction with the on-screen personality. Referring to Walter Cronkite earlier in this chapter, many public opinion polls during his time dubbed him as "The Most Trusted Man in America." Although he was simply reading the news, his role as a journalist and broadcaster led many viewers to trust him as they would a wise uncle or trusted friend.

News events as competitions. With respect to the coverage of politics, some journalists have turned to **horse race journalism** to cover political campaigns, often discussing political strategies of different candidates and their campaigns rather than the political positions of those same campaigns—such coverage can often feel like watching a nightly sports broadcast, framed in terms of winners and losers. Similarly, many broadcasts on news events will invite a "panel" to discuss the event, with some people representing one side and others a contrasting opinion or stance. Much the same as halftime shows at sporting events featuring discussion of the event by experts, this formatting often leads to shouting matches and personal insults

Public Broadcasting System (PBS)
A nonprofit television organization in the United States, founded in the mid-20th Century

morality plays
Used in reference to news coverage that is written to incorporate a conflict between different moral perspectives; for example, stories take on many of the conventions of traditional entertainment storytelling like having heroes versus villains

problem frames
News stories that emphasize public risks or dangers

The Los Angeles Times
A newspaper founded in 1881 based in southern California but focused on coverage of national and international news; it is routinely one of the largest newspapers in the United States by circulation

horse race journalism
When news coverage of political elections resemble coverage of a sport competition

between the participants. Entertaining? Surely. But it makes it difficult to separate substance from style.

Another way in which politics are often framed as competitions is through the use of highly publicized **debates** between political candidates, which are intended to provide the voting public an opportunity to see unfiltered political positions—debate questions are rarely (if ever) shared with candidates and thus, they cannot really prepare for any specific conversation. Yet, while the debates themselves should serve as objective spaces to assess a candidate's political positions, often times a mix of **confirmation bias** on behalf of news audiences (who typically engage their favorite candidate and disengage other candidates), and extensive coverage of debates by many in the news media as competitions (with analysis both predicting who will win or lose a debate, as well as analyzing footage of debates afterward to proclaim winners and losers), the competitive framing of politics tends to encourage fandom for politicians rather than understanding of political issues.

debates

Formal and organized discussions and arguments about topics between candidates for political office, usually held for public benefit

confirmation bias

The tendency for a person to seek out and pay attention to information that is consistent with their pre-existing beliefs

Entertainment as News

Our discussions to this point have focused on news programming that borrows elements of entertainment programming to attract audience attention. In other words, the news as entertainment. Yet, often entertainment can borrow the language of news, namely in the form of satire.

Satire. Satire takes entertainment and inserts news to make it more informative, which might be best described as entertainment as news. The roots of modern entertainment as news can perhaps be found in the *Weekend Update* segments on *Saturday Night Live*. Beginning in 1975, it is the longest-running sketch on the popular broadcast. The sketch is a fictional news broadcast that presents headlines of real news in a humorous format or parodies figures who were the subject of news stories during the week. In a rather famous blunder during the 2012 U.S. Presidential campaign, Fox News Network ran stock footage of Tina Fey impersonating former Alaska governor and Republican Vice-Presidential candidate Sarah Palin during a live news broadcast, rather than actual footage of Palin!

Eventually, *Weekend Update* inspired full-length broadcasts, such as *Politically Incorrect with Bill Maher*, *The Daily Show with Jon Stewart* (now hosted by comedian Trevor Noah), *Real Time with Bill Maher*, *The Colbert Report*, and *Last Week Tonight*. The success of early satire news shows led to more being produced, as they were seen as a fairly profitable venture: They cost little money to produce, and younger adult audience is a very attractive demographic for advertisers. The content of these programs is typically comedic, with interviews, "on location" reporting, and special coverage of important events, such as Presidential Elections. Of late, shows such as *Last Week Tonight* have focused attention on specific issues that may be ignored by other news outlets. Segments have included cash bail and its impact on poorer individuals accused of crime (who likely cannot afford to post bail without taking out expensive cash loans) and Sinclair Broadcasting Group's policy of requiring local network affiliates to run propaganda spots (in which the Group's news outlets were caught broadcasting simultaneous editorial statements).

In terms of what audiences actually take away form satire news, LaMarre and colleagues (2009) found that many of the same shortcomings that cause individuals to selectively perceive traditional media content also plague satire news as well. In their study, an individual's own **political ideology** was an important factor in how they perceived Stephen Colbert's own politics: conservatives tended to think that Colbert (who, on *The Colbert Report*, played the character of a staunch conservative talk show host, inspired by Bill O'Reilly's style from *The O'Reilly Factor*) is only pretending to be joking and really does endorse more conservative policies, while liberals were more likely to interpret the show as satirical. In actuality, Colbert tends to be more moderate-to-progressive with respect to his personal political beliefs. The fact that both groups found the show as equally entertaining—and both reported Colbert to be equally humorous—suggests that one's own political ideology has a major influence over the extent to which satire, as a form of social critique, has any effect on viewers (**Sidebar: The Archie Bunker Effect**).

political ideology
An individual's own beliefs about social and ethical issues related to law and government

Sidebar   The Archie Bunker effect

In the 1960s and 1970s, the United States was experiencing a great deal of political and social turmoil. Americans were heavily divided over the nation's involvement in the Vietnam War, while also facing a roaring debate over civil rights and the legal and social equality of African-Americans and other minority Americans. Inspired by a British show *Till Death Do Us Part*, television producer Norman Lear developed a program with the goal of showcasing the shortcomings and stupidity of

(Continued)

bigotry. The show contrasted Archie Bunker, a cigar-chomping middle-class American who fears social integration, with Michael Stivic, a Polish-American married to Bunker's daughter who represents the intellectual counterculture of the 60s and 70s pushing for social justice. Often, the show would feature a lesson in which Archie learned to be more progressive.

Despite this partisan perspective, the show was remarkably well-received. *All in the Family* was the highest-rated show on television for five straight years (from 1971 to 1976), and the show, its actors, and its writers and producers won numerous Emmys and Golden Globe awards. In 2013, the Television Critics Association honored the show with a prestigious Heritage Award for the "cultural and social impact the program has had on society."

It seems odd that a show with such a pointedly partisan political view could be so popular, doesn't it? The answer lies in the **selective perception bias.** This bias, discovered by psychologists Neil Vidmar and Milton Rokeach, demonstrated that progressive viewers tended to identify heavily with "Meathead Mike's" character whereas conservative viewers tended to identify heavily with Archie Bunker. Through identification with polarized characters, viewers on both sides of the political spectrum could watch and enjoy the show.

selective perception bias

The tendency for a person to pay attention to information he or she agrees with while ignoring information they disagree with or even reinterpreting it to support their beliefs

In terms of their impact on viewers, satire news can be engaging and informative for disinterested individuals who would otherwise avoid news broadcasts. At the same time, the critical depictions of other news organizations presented within satire news broadcasts can decrease perceived credibility for more mainstream news programs. This increased distrust is particularly concerning as it relates to other factors that decrease the credibility of news.

Fake news. It is important to differentiate satire and infotainment from false information, or what is popularly known as **fake news**—news articles that are intentionally and verifiably false, with the intent to mislead readers. Some fake news content is false content portrayed as legitimate news through imposter news sites that appear real. Fake news can also be stories that utilize real material out of context as a way to create disinformation. Fake news can be entertaining, but also can have severe political consequences when readers believe and share fake news. In a study by Allcott and Gentzkow (2017) on the 2016 U.S. election, fake news was widely shared by both Democrats

fake news

News articles that are intentionally misleading and verifiably false and Republicans (38 million times, to be exact), and a list of fake news websites received 159 million visits during the month of the election. After the election, survey data show that the average adult saw and remembered 1.14 fake news stories from the months before the election.

Why is fake news so popular? Fake news often appeals to an audience's emotions. **Clickbait** are headlines that attempt to draw an individual's attention in order to accumulate pageviews which translate into real dollars based on the advertisements on the clickbait page. Content that appeals to emotions is likely to draw attention and result in clicks. Essentially, purveyors of fake news are remarkably skilled scriptwriters and storytellers who understand the deepest hopes and fears of their target audiences, and they are able to craft realistic-sounding stories to play off of those hopes and fears.

News versus Entertainment: Does It Matter?

To this point, we have been seemingly critical of the notion of news content becoming increasingly entertaining in nature. However, Michael X. Delli Carpini, a professor in the **Annenberg School for Communication** at the University of Pennsylvania, argues that the distinction between news and entertainment is an arbitrary one for three reasons.

First, he argues that there is no real functional or theoretical distinction between the two. For example, even newsworthy content can be diversionary or amusing, such as the soft news content mentioned earlier in this chapter. A second reason given by Delli Carpini (2009) is that the news and entertainment distinction is often based on the context of the media system itself. For example, earlier debates about the role of broadcast news (either radio or television) often assumed a **centralized mass media** system in which the clear majority of content was produced by industry professionals. In this perspective, there was an implicit agreement between news producers and audience members that certain times of day and certain types of content were "news" and that other times of day and other types of content were "entertainment"—we might think about the **5 o'clock news** as an example of this. However, the modern media ecology is one that

Clickbait

A thumbnail or social media post that entices users with extravagant claims or images, but offers little to no substantive content

Annenberg School for Communication

A school at the University of Pennsylvania, founded in 1958, where the Cultural Indicators Project was conducted

centralized mass media system

A media system in which a handful of media companies create content for the majority of the available audience

5 o'clock news

A colloquial name for news broadcast in the United States that took place when most adults were arriving home from work, but before a traditional family dinnertime features both news and entertainment available to audiences whenever they choose.

Finally, in Delli Carpini's view, distinguishing entertainment from news does not really serve a useful function. To the extent that the distinction was an ideological one to begin with—working from the assumption that news is meant to be informational, while entertainment is meant to be titillating—he argued that the mechanics of 21st century media blur these lines in daily practice. If we consider the shifts away from objectivity mentioned above, the increased and varied emotional content within the news, and the fact that in a **Web 2.0** media system audiences are increasingly becoming both consumers and producers of media content, then we might challenge the idea that there is a rationale for distinguishing entertainment from news.

Web 2.0

An Internet architecture marked by audience participation, such as the ability to create content and directly share that content with others

Conclusion

As stated at the start of this chapter, we might not normally think of news as related to entertainment media, but we should. Although a more traditional perspective on news media would suggest a rather serious and straightforward telling of the day's events, news broadcasts are often full of emotional language, compelling characters, and dramatic narratives. Some are concerned that this "repackaging" of the news is a bit like chocolate-covered broccoli: It might look appealing and enjoyable, but the results might be an audience that is entertained but not necessarily informed. Others argue that narratives and dramatic stores are a useful way to capture an audience's attention, to orient them to the important news and events of the day. These issues are further complicated with an increasingly diverse media landscape, in which thousands of storytellers—many with their own political and economic agendas—can craft their version of news and events, in order to sway audiences toward a shared viewpoint. To this end, being aware of entertainment media conventions in news and politics is a useful way for audiences to be more critical of the underlying intentions of some programs, be they simply for attention, subtle persuasion, or other ulterior motive.

Key Terms

Infotainment or **soft news**   News coverage of information that is primarily focused on entertainment or leisure, or stories of personal interest without major consequences

Hard news   News that cover stories related to current events and issues of great consequence

American Broadcasting Company (ABC)   A major television network established in the 1940s and currently owned by the Walt Disney Company

Columbia Broadcasting System (CBS)   A television network established in the 1940s and owned by the CBS Corporation

National Broadcasting Company (NBC)   A television network established in the late 1930s; currently owned by Comcast

Cable news   News that is produced and distributed by cable stations that is usually delivered on a 24-hour rotation; this contrasts with network news, which is usually only shown at specific times in the morning, afternoon, and evening

High-choice media environment   A media marketplace that is characterized by numerous options and channels available to consumers

American Cool   A vocal tone of news made popular in the middle 20th Century by American news anchors in which the news was delivered in a serious and emotionally neutral style

National Public Radio (NPR)   A nonprofit radio membership organization that provides news and cultural content to radio stations across the United States

Partisan   A type of bias which favors one particular cause or one particular political party over another

News aggregators   Organizations or automated programs that gather news stories from multiple sources into one place for a person to read

Echo chambers   A colloquial term used to critique news organizations for only exposing audiences to partisan news content that fits the audience's currently held political beliefs

Syndicated column   Written content, such as a regularly scheduled newspaper editorial, that is distributed to multiple news outlet

No Spin Zone   A well-known syndicated column written by conservative commentator Bill O' Reilly

Fox News Channel   A cable news station established in 1996 and owned by the Fox Entertainment Group

Poynter Institute   A nonprofit institution for journalism research and professional education in the United States

Associated Press (AP)   A syndication agency based in the United States that is used by multiple newspapers and news stations to report national and international news

Public Broadcasting System (PBS)   A nonprofit television organization in the United States, founded in the mid-20th Century

Morality plays   Used in reference to news coverage that is written to incorporate a conflict between different moral perspectives; for example, stories take on many of the conventions of traditional entertainment storytelling like having heroes versus villains

Problem frames   News stories that emphasize public risks or dangers

The Los Angeles Times A newspaper founded in 1881 based in southern California but focused on coverage of national and international news; it is routinely one of the largest newspapers in the United States by circulation

Horse race journalism When news coverage of political elections resemble coverage of a sport competition

Debates Formal and organized discussions and arguments about topics between candidates for political office, usually held for public benefit

Confirmation bias The tendency for a person to seek out and pay attention to information that is consistent with their pre-existing beliefs

Political ideology An individual's own beliefs about social and ethical issues related to law and government

Selective perception bias The tendency for a person to pay attention to information he or she agrees with while ignoring information they disagree with or even reinterpreting it to support their beliefs

Fake news News articles that are intentionally misleading and verifiably false

Clickbait A thumbnail or social media post that entices users with extravagant claims or images, but offers little to no substantive content

Annenberg School for Communication A school at the University of Pennsylvania, founded in 1958, where the Cultural Indicators Project was conducted

Centralized mass media system A media system in which a handful of media companies create content for the majority of the available audience

5 o'clock news A colloquial name for news broadcast in the United States that took place when most adults were arriving home from work, but before a traditional family dinnertime

Web 2.0 An Internet architecture marked by audience participation, such as the ability to create content and directly share that content with others

References

Allcott, H., & Gentzkow, M. (2017). Social media and fake news in the 2016 election. *Journal of Economic Perspectives, 31*(2), 211–236. doi: 10.1257/jep.31.2.211

Altheide, D. L. (1997). The news media, the problem frame, and the production of fear. *The Sociological Quarterly, 38*(4), 647–668.

Delli Carpini, M. X. (2009). The inherent arbitrariness of the 'News' versus 'Entertainment' distinction. *Transformations in the Public Sphere*. Retrieved from http://publicsphere.ssrc.org/delli-carpini-the-inherent-arbitrariness-of-the-news-versus-entertainment-distinction/

Franklin, B. (1997). *Newszak and news media*. London: Arnold.

Grabe, M. E., Zhou, S., Lang, A., & Bolls, P. (2000). Packaging television news: The effects of tabloid on information processing and evaluative responses. *Journal of Broadcasting & Electronic Media, 44*(4), 581–598. doi: 10.1207/s15506878jobem4404_4

LaMarre, H. L. Landreville, K. D., & Beam, M. A. (2009). The irony of satire: Political ideology and the motivation to see what you want to see in The Colbert Report. *The International Journal of Press/Politics, 14*(2), 212–231. doi: 10.1177/1940161208330904

Lasswell, H. (1948). The structure and function of communication in society. In L. Bryson (Ed.), *The communication of ideas* (pp. 37–51). New York: Institute for Religious and Social Sciences.

O'Reilly, B. (2003). The old journalism is dead. *Creators Syndicate.*

Peters, C. (2011). Emotion aside or emotional side? Crafting an 'experience of involvement' in the news. *Journalism, 12*(3), 297–316. doi: 10.1177/1464884910388224

Prior, M. (2005). News vs. entertainment: How increasing medai choice widens gaps in political knowledge and turnout. *American Journal of Political Science, 49*(3), 557–592.

Suggested Readings

Bowman, N. D., & Cohen, E. L. (2019). Detecting and resisting fake news: A skill beyond our heuristics. In M. Zimdars & K. McLeod (Eds.), *Fake news: Understanding media and misinformation in the digital age.* Cambridge, MA: MIT Press.

Davis, E. H. (1921). *History of The New York Times, 1851–1921.* New York: The New York Times.

Vidmar, N., & Rokeach, M. (1974). Archie Bunker's bigotry: A study in selective perception and exposure. *Journal of Communication, 24*(1), 36–47. doi: 10.1111/j.1460-2466.1974.tb00353.x

Williams, B., & Delli Carpini, M. X. (2011). *After broadcast news: Media regimes, democracy, and the new information environment.* New York: Cambridge.

CHAPTER 11

Social Functions of Entertainment Media

"No [person] is an island, completely onto themselves"

—John Dunne

Introduction

Entertainment brings people together and creates shared experiences. Media entertainment allows for these experiences to be shared by millions. For example in the United States, the 20 most popular television broadcast of all time were watched by audiences ranging in size from 90 to 114 million people. 17 of those most-watched programs were the Super Bowl—an event known specifically for its associated social-viewing rituals such as team parties and mid-Winter cookouts. The shared experiences don't just end when the event ends either. We marvel, ponder, and talk about what we saw. According to the magazine *Entertainment Weekly*, the popular HBO series *Game of Thrones* was one of the top 10 Twitter Topics of 2016, with over 13.8 million tweets (The most popular emoji during this time? "a dragon emoji, of course!"). Even media that we tend to think of as being enjoyed in isolation, such as video games and mobile devices (smartphones, tablets, etc.) have surprisingly social functions. Media entertainment connects us with others and helps others connect with us. The following chapter will explore the many different social functions of entertainment media.

Objectives

After reading and studying the concepts in this chapter, students should be able to:

➤ Understand the social role that entertainment media plays for individuals and for society.

➤ Explain social science theories related to the social uses and effects of entertainment media.

➤ Unpack the concept of social capital, and how it relates to media entertainment.

➤ Discuss and critique the role of emerging communication technologies in the socializing that happens around entertainment media.

The Social Functions Of Narrative

The earliest forms of entertainment and symbolic storytelling that we know of date back to some 40,000 to 60,000 years ago. Cave paintings in Spain (Altamira Caves) and France (Chauvet Caves) have some of the earliest human art, and the surrounding areas have led archaeologists to discover bone flutes (early wind instruments made from the rib bones of animals) and Venus figurines (statues whose purpose is not entirely clear). Also discovered along with the cave paintings were small, semispherical impressions (i.e., impressions of human behinds) in the mud, usually dotting the base of the floors of the cave walls; in other caves, prints of dancing feet were found. These discoveries have suggested that the cave paintings were places of important social gatherings. (**Sidebar: Your Personal Cave Art**).

Zillmann (2000) provides an overview of some of the earliest historical entertainment gatherings. He documents invitations and announcements for events held in ancient Egypt and China which describe feasts, music, and dancing. This historical evidence, such as the cave paintings of Altamira and Chauvet, are not just valuable for their aesthetic and cultural importance, but also for what they can tell us about how early humans engaged with art.

Sidebar Your Personal Cave Art

As mentioned in this chapter, the Altamira Cave paintings are considered one of the oldest forms of human art, dating back nearly 40,000 years. For entertainment media research, we can think of these paintings as an early form of leisure. We can also consider these paintings some of the earliest examples of the social functions of media. Archeological evidence suggests that a primary purpose of these cave paintings was for storytelling. For example, similar caves in Chauvet France were built deep within the mountain where no natural light could reach. Fires and torches were used to illuminate the paintings and bring the static images to life—as documentarian filmmaker Werner Herzog describes them in his film *Cave of Forgotten Dreams*, the caves were a form of "proto-cinema."

EQRoy/Shutterstock.com

Some evolutionary psychologists have called humans "**the storytelling animal**" given our penchant to reframe and retell our own experiences to others, using narratives to entertain and enlighten (Gottschall, 2012). Given the strong social learning function of stories in our culture, several researchers have come up with different explanations for how narratives work as a social "glue" bonding us together. We review the most prominent and well-studied perspectives on the social functions of narrative below.

the storytelling animal

The idea that humans can be distinguished from other animals by their ability to think and communicate through the use of narratives

Social skill hypothesis or entertainment as play

An argument that narratives are useful as "safe spaces" for audiences to vicariously experience and learn practical social skills, and that individuals use entertainment as a form of simulation

morality sandbox

The ability for narratives to allow audience to play with what is right and what is wrong, safe from real-world consequences of those decisions

Social Identity Theory (SIT)

A theory that predicts how people identify with and function as members of various social groups

social categorization

The tendency for people to categorize themselves and others into social groups

social comparison

The tendency for people to compare and compete themselves with their social groups or their social groups against other social groups

The **social skills hypothesis** argues that exposure to narratives helps humans learn skills important for relationship maintenance, such as empathy (see Mar & Oatley, 2008; Oatley, 2009). This research suggests that narratives function as a "safe" (i.e., not physically harmful) arena in which humans may experience and practice social skills. Media entertainment can allow for individuals to experience rare and consequential events that they might now have much real-world experience with. For example, watching a soap opera or the film *Twilight* may allow viewers to experience what it would be like to be in a steamy and convoluted love triangle, without having to directly suffer the real-world relational consequences. Fiction, in this line of reasoning, acts as an *abstraction and simulation of social experience* that allows readers to learn via simulated experience, that is, through a movie or a novel.

This hypothesis is also known as **entertainment as play**—meaning that all entertainment allows participants to "play" with possible outcomes of social situations in ways that are not allowed in nonmediated settings (Vorderer, Steen, & Chan, 2006). Recently, researchers have discussed how morally-complex dramas such as *The Sopranos* and *Dexter* can function as a **morality sandbox**, that is, an area where we can play with what is right and what is wrong with no consequence. We can accept and enjoy the behavior of Tony Soprano and Dexter because the entertainment framework allows for us to "get in the sandbox" and mess around with our normal considerations of morality and the consequences for immoral behavior.

Social identity theory (**SIT**, Tajfel & Turner, 1979) is another theory applied to the selection and reception of media entertainment. SIT describes how we identify with and function as a part of groups we belong to (gender, race, university, sporting clubs, nationality). SIT begins with assumptions about the social group to which one belongs (like a sports club or university). Based on the social group you belong to, you will feel **social categorization** (feeling either more or less like part of a group), **social comparison** (comparing your group against other groups), **social identity** (feeling like a member of a group), and **self-esteem** (feeling valued for being part of the group). SIT suggests that we are motivated to attain positive self-esteem by making sure our group is perceived positively in regard to other out-groups.

Sabine Trepte (2006) applied SIT to entertainment and suggested that entertainment selection and consumption could be related to our social group memberships and social settings. For example, she provides a situation in which a young, single, urban woman wants to pick a television show to watch. The woman browses channels, social categories that apply to her become salient, and she may look for shows which positively portray members of young, single, urban, female groups (such as *Sex and the City* or *Broad City*). She has a motivation to attain positive self-esteem and social identity, so she will select shows portraying her social group in positive ways, and perhaps also portraying outgroups (men, married women) in less positive ways. Through these entertainment choices, her need for positive identification and self-esteem are met.

In line with propositions from SIT, the **narrative collective-assimilation hypothesis**, proposed by Gabriel and Young (2012), argues that individuals become more like the groups that they read about by adopting the psychological aspects of the characters in the narrative. In this study, readers read short stories about vampires (*Twilight*) or magicians (*Harry Potter*). Afterward, participants actually responded to survey items as if they were more like vampires or magicians—they were more likely to say they could "hide in shadows" or "move things with their minds" if they had read one of the fantasy texts. This theory can be applied to political narratives and sports as well as fictional worlds.

Finally, the **social surrogacy hypothesis** was proposed by Derrick, Gabriel, and Hugenberg (2009) and suggests that characters in shows can act like peers or friends. For example, many college students still start off their mornings watching the sitcom "Friends," even though the show has been off the air for 10 years. Joining these fictional 'friends' every morning helps students adjust to new circumstances and situations by acting as a social buffer against negative emotions. Bolstering this hypothesis, we can see the power of narratives in how we readily respond to characters in media (See Chapter 7). Some analyses of Twitter, such as that done by Daniel and Westerman (2017), found that audiences members engaged in public discussions of grief over the death of a very prominent character in *Game of Thrones*, including discussions of denial, anger, bargaining, depression, and acceptance—the same stages of grief that people go through when they lose someone close to them.

Despite the powerful evidence connecting social groups with entertainment selection and consumption, this is a relatively under-studied area of media entertainment. Social situations are complex and difficult to observe in the laboratory. Despite that, as we will see

social identity

The tendency for a people to create a self-identity based on the social groups that they see themselves as part of

self-esteem

How a person feels about their self-worth

narrative collective-assimilation hypothesis

Argues that people become more similar to the groups that they read about by adopting the psychological aspects of the characters in those groups

social surrogacy hypothesis

Argues that characters in entertainment media programming can serve as substitutes for a person's peers or friends throughout this chapter, social functions of entertainment are of paramount importance when understanding the appeal and selection of media. In the next section, we turn from social effects of narrative to understanding broader selection and effects of media from a social perspective.

Entertainment as Social Capital

Consider how regularly that discussions of entertainment media come up in your daily conversations with family and friends. This is known as the **watercooler effect**; an effect first explored by Charles Atkin (1972) to explain how we select television shows and mediated experiences in anticipation of discussions with our colleagues around the water cooler at the office the following day. Some of the shows we watch might not hold a lot of value for us outside of the social value that they bring when we are able to talk about them to our friends and colleagues.

Entertainment media is a source of **social capital** for many because it provides them with a common discussion point, especially with folks that they might not know very well. For example, you might recognize somebody on a train or at a mall with your college logo on their hat or short, and debate the most recent football game. Many of you have had the experience in which you find complete strangers debating whether or not Severus Snape (of *Harry Potter*) is a hero or a villain and likewise, you and your friends might have deep discussions about which of the four houses of Hogwarts you belong to.

Of course, many people are aware that others infer much about who we are by the entertainment media choices we make—and we might even try to actively influence these perceptions that others make of us. For example, Johnson and Ranzini (2018) looked at entertainment media sharing via Facebook, and found that when people were experimentally motivated to be concerned about how *others* saw them, they were more likely to share popular song and film titles (think pop music and blockbuster movies). However, when people were motivated to think more about *themselves*, they were more likely to share prestigious song and movie titles (think classical music and art house films). Both of these findings suggest a broad **social desirability** mechanic at play, but through slightly different mechanisms. For the former, people were likely trying to appeal to the tastes of others by showing common media tastes; for the latter, people were likely trying

---

watercooler effect

The time people spend talking about popular media entertainment in their break time from nonleisure activities, such as work or school; named after an observation that most office employees tend to socialize in break rooms where a watercooler is present

social capital

The benefits that social networks may offer among people in society

social desirability

The tendency for a person to behavior in ways that make themselves attractive to others to idealize themselves as being part of a more refined or aspirational taste culture.

Fandoms. Fandom, the word, comes from the Latin word *fanaticus*, meaning "of or belonging to the temple, a temple servant, a devotee" (Oxford Latin Dictionary). However, the term quickly assumed negative connotations, "of persons inspired by orgiastic rites and enthusiastic frenzy." Fandom refers to a subculture made up of fans, the state or attitude of being a fan, which essentially is a function of the social motivations for consuming and relating to entertainment.

One of the most prominent examples of the social capital that we find in entertainment media are large-scale fan-focused events, such as comic book conventions, cosplay conventions, and other fandom celebrations. These events can be massive—the annual San Diego Comic-Con (founded in 1970) now draws between 150,000 and 200,000 fans each year to celebrate comic books and other facets of **geek culture**, including fan-written books and scripts and **cosplay** competitions in which fans create and dress up as their own versions of famous pop culture characters. Jenkins (2012) refers to these events, and in particular the fan-driven activities at these events, as representative of **participatory cultures** by which fans both consume and produce media content, and do so across a variety of platforms and media: in-person annual conventions are buttressed by ongoing online discussion forums, fan-created **wikis**, and other unofficial printed publications.

Intra-audience effects. For most students reading this book, college campuses provide numerous social entertainment opportunities, between sports and concerts and other public parties and gatherings. For many of us, these events are enjoyable because we like the spectacle of the public event—we might enjoy football or pop music or slam poetry. However, advances in home entertainment technology probably provide much more intimate experiences. Sports fans can watch several different angles of their favorite broadcast and music fans can adjust stereo systems to deliver nearly perfect sound quality, and all of this can be done from the comfort of one's couch. So why do we get up and go join others as part of the audience? For researcher John Hocking (1982), the answer lies in a distinction between the event itself (the sport or the music) and the social situation around the event: he referred to these as the *game event* and the *stadium event*. He called the enjoyment we get when surrounded by a crowd the intra-audience effect. Individual responses to the entertainment event are amplified by the presence of others.

geek culture
The community and culture of fans of geek products or material

cosplay
The act of dressing up as a character from a media entertainment product

participatory cultures
When fans of an intellectual property both consume and produce media content

wikis
An online site where individuals can contribute information about a particular topic to build an online encyclopedia; based on the Hawaiian word for "fast" or "quick"

intra-audience effect
A phenomenon by which individual people in a larger audience are influenced by the emotions and behaviors of the other audience members

Some of this research is based on a basic psychological principle called the **mere presence** effect, by which humans as well as other animals tend to get psychologically and physically aroused when they are around others (Zajonc, 1968). Such arousal can magnify any of our reactions to our favorite content, such as a winning goal or an encore by our favorite band. However, Hocking and his team also found that the crowd's reactions and behaviors also had an impact on how individual people rated their own enjoyment. In a series of **field experiments**, his research assistants visited bars in the area surrounding Michigan State University and either *cheered* or *jeered* the same band; the band was in on the experiment and performed the same set each night. When crowds were surrounded by cheerers they responded more positively, individual concert-goers gave the show more positive reviews, and stayed at the concert longer!

field experiments
Experiments that occur in a real-world setting instead of in a laboratory

Genre and Media-Specific Social Functions

There are some unique social elements of specific type of mass entertainment media that have received a fair amount of theoretical and/or empirical attention: music, video games, and sports. We focus on specific aspects of those media below.

Music for social bonding and social conflict.
From a technological aspect, the creation and consumption of music is probably among the oldest forms of entertainment media. There is good archaeological evidence that music predates civilization by 30,000 years. Jake Harwood at the University of Arizona, writes about the centrality of music as a form of social identity. This identity can exist at an interpersonal level, such as sharing song recommendations with others as a way to facilitate friendships and interpersonal liking, but can also exist at the macro level, such as performing national anthems before major sporting events or in military contexts. Harwood suggests music has two functions: the first is **transmission**, where music is used to communicate some message using lyrics, emotion, beat, and content; and the second is **ritual**, where music is used as a form of signaling to ourselves and to others.

transmission
The purpose of music to communicate some message using lyrics, emotion, beat, or content

ritual use
A purpose of entertainment media to serve as a form of signaling and a form for social gathering

If we think about music as **transmission**, we can turn to research on tonality and rhythms, finding that specific music we find appealing depends on our social context and culture. For example, the pentatonic scales of many Chinese operas are often not as appealing to Western audiences, and the soaring sounds of German opera are not beautiful to all ears. With globalization, we see some of those cultural specifications reversing (think of the popularity of hybrid global pop styles such as Afro-Pop, K-Pop, and J-Pop). Harwood (2017) suggests music has another mechanism for improving social relations between different groups, by serving as a form of parasocial contact. From this perspective, it could be possible that listening to music from various cultural groups and peoples could help foster a better understanding of (or at least, respect for) those cultures and peoples.

If we think about music for **ritual** purposes, we mean traditional music often important for cultural activities and milestones (think of church music, the wedding march, national anthems, and fight songs for college sport teams; See **Sidebar, Kneeling at Attention**). This may be due to deep-seated roles of rhythm and harmony in facilitating group socialization. For example, Wiltermuth et al. (2012) showed that simply singing a song synchronously with others leads to more ingroup identification with the group and a greater willingness to share resources with members, versus singing asynchronously. Additionally, as Harwood points out, if we are busy singing a song together, we both have resources available for singing and dancing, and are likely not also engaging in warfare against each other. So the social bonds of music have deep roots that are still observable today in our everyday lives.

Sidebar   Kneeling at Attention

The 96th season of the U.S.-based National Football League began in August 2016 with the same general buzz that accompanies the start of any professional sport. August 2016 also came at politically unstable time in the U.S., between intensifying political rhetoric for an upcoming election between divisive candidates for the U.S. Presidency and a growing criminal justice concern in which African-Americans were twice as likely to be killed by U.S. police than nearly every other racial or ethnic group in the U.S. Census (Swaine & McCarthy, 2017).

These two events collided on the football field during the end of the 2016 NFL Preseason. High-profile football players, such as former San Francisco 49es Colin Kaepernick, began kneeling (rather than

(Continued)

Black Lives Matter
An activist movement in the early 21st century protesting against police brutality and systemic racism toward African Americans in the US.

standing) at attention during the playing of the U.S. national anthem. For Kaepernick and his kneeling colleagues, the act was a form of political protest to recognize social injustice—part of a larger U.S. political movement in **Black Lives Matter**. For detractors, angry fans saw Kaepernick and his colleagues being disrespectful toward the U.S. flag and by extension, toward the veterans and active military service personnel fighting for the very freedoms (such as the freedom of speech) being exercised by Kaepernick and others.

Regardless of how you might personally feel about these protests, they demonstrate the intense levels of social identity that can be communicated by a song, and the intense social identity threat that can be communicated by protesting it.

adolescent role moratorium
A period when adolescent break away from existing social structure of the family to form their own social groups

Music as developmental signal. Music can also act as a form of socialization in terms of our developmental trajectory from child to adult. When we are younger, we tend to listen to the music our parents like. However, during adolescence, we often break away from our parents' preferred music in a show of what psychologists call **adolescent role moratorium**. During this period, adolescents begin the process of breaking away from their family to form their own social groups. One effect of this process is that adolescents begin to seek out music very different from their parents', yet in line with their peer groups.

The music from adolescence is often central to one's identity for a lifetime. Studies of music preference find that we are most nostalgic for music we loved in our late teen/early adult years (18 to 25). This nostalgia is due to both the associations of becoming our own person, separate from the family group, but also due to neurological growth patterns. In late adolescence, our neural connections are being pruned and refined, so emotional experiences and social influences are strongly anchored during this phase. Because of these factors combined, we find that we can identify specific groups of musical tastes that were formed as large groups of people (i.e., generations) hit adolescence at the same time. This is where you sometimes hear generations referred to by the music of their era. For example, you might hear about The Beatles & The Rolling Stones generation versus The Smiths & Duran Duran versus Nirvana & Pearl Jam versus Brittany & Beyoncé generation. It is often easy to identify which generation a person is simply by checking out their playlist or record collection.

Video games as socialization. The stereotype of video games tends that they are isolating, and played by folks who are antisocial by nature. However, the history of video gaming technologies is very social in nature and in fact, the first video games usually required more than one person in order to be played. This was in large part because the technologies did not exist to create an opponent with an **artificial intelligence**. For this reason, early games such as MIT's *SpaceWar!* And Atari's *PONG* provided multiple players control of the action, the former placing two players in control over warring spaceships and the latter placing two players in control of on-screen table tennis paddles. Both games encouraged competition, and did so in public spaces such as an MIT computer lab for *SpaceWar!* and numerous California taverns and pubs for *PONG*. In fact, with the exception of purpose-made video games such as flight simulators, most arcade machines and home consoles have at least two controller ports so that people can play games side-by-side—even the Nintendo Wii system from the mid-2000s was meant to imply two players (the two "ii" in the name) standing next to each other. This was appropriate given the game's use of **motion sensor controllers** in which players bodies were used to control on-screen action.

Research consistently shows that many players enjoy socializing with video games broadly (Sherry, Lucas, Greenberg, & Lachlan, 2006) and with online video games in particular (Yee, 2006). In fact, people do not necessarily need to be playing the game with each other in order to socialize around the content, as even games that are meant to be played by a single person can be "played" socially: one person might control on-screen action but do so while consulting others who are co-located in the room (or more recently through online chat or **game streaming** services such as Twitch). This solo-to-social phenomenon of games is called **tandem play** Consalvo (2017; **Sidebar: Video games, now with less gaming!**).

artificial intelligence
The capacity for machines to possess and display original thoughts and decisions without input from a human operator or programmer

motion sensor controllers
Any sort of video game controller that uses body movement as inputs

game streaming
Playing video games while broadcasting or recording the gameplay for online audiences to watch

tandem play
A form of coplaying video games in which one person is in direct control of on-screen action and others are watching and providing input to the player controlling the game

| **Sidebar** | Video games, now with less gaming! |

One of the things that makes video games particularly appealing is that they are so active. Some people even argue that video games are different than other types of media because they are unfinished—the player is given the pieces of a potential story or activity, but has to actively coauthor the experience through their decisions on-screen. Noted video game designer Sid Meier describes a good video game as one that is full of "interesting decisions" to make.

(Continued)

So, if the fun of video games is in the active decision-making process . . . then how could it possibly be fun to watch somebody else play video games? For many people, watching video games is a way to enjoy the on-screen graphics and narratives without having to be stressed out by learning the complex controls or puzzles in a game. Consider that when watching a movie, the plot will progress from beginning to end no matter how skilled the audience is; with a video game, the plot will only progress from beginning to end if the player is good enough to make that happen. Sometimes it might be more fun to let somebody else deal with the hassle of making that one difficult jump or move, while you might sit back and just enjoy the action. Or, perhaps the "player" (the person holding the controller) might need an additional set of eyes to keep track of on-screen dangers or puzzles, or need help from others to take notes and help navigate the game-world. In this way, everyone in the room is playing the video game together—everyone is involved in the "interesting decision-making"—even if only one person is actually pressing the controller buttons.

Tandem play is becoming hugely popular. For example, game streaming is an incredibly popular leisure activity, with websites such as Twitch.tv broadcasting tens of millions of hours of video game play, every month. As of December 2018, Alexa.com ranks Twitch.tv as the 13th most popular website in the United States (31st in the world), and has over 2.2 million video game players broadcasting their video games for the world to see. Why so popular? First, it is cheaper than buying all the new games and playing through them yourself. But there are other reasons as well. For some people, services such as Twitch.tv operate similarly to professional sports in that they showcase the best players and thus, can be learning experiences for gamers who might try out new strategies in their own gameplay. For others, game streams are a way to be part of a larger gamer culture even if they might not have the skills required to be effective when playing difficult video games.

You try it! *Log on to twitch.tv or a similar site and watch one of the top player's feeds. What do you think? Does it compare to the fun of playing alone? What feels similar or different about the experience?*

Games too are yet another area in which players can be found socializing around a common media experience based on age. The same adolescence discussion from music plays a role here too—games experienced in late adolescence might trigger a sense of nostalgia and through that, a common bond with people that we've only met for the first time.

Finally, video game players can engage in social relationships not only with other human players, but also with their on-screen characters and avatars. Similar to how media audiences engage in parasocial relationships with media characters (discussed in Chapter 7), Banks (2015) demonstrated that video game players can actually engage in a wide variety of social relationships with their avatars, from an "object" void of any social consideration to an "other" in which the avatar is a completely separate social being, similar to how we might interact with a friend or family member.

Sports as social entertainment. It is probably no surprise that a major appeal of sports is social bonding and interaction. Zillmann identified two aspects of sports fandom: *the appeal of watching* and *the appeal of being part of a group*. We have covered his "appeal of watching" motivation when we discussed sports and disposition theory. We now turn to the appeal of being part of a group. According to Zillmann, Bryant, and Sapolsky (1989), sports fandom brings activities, such as football, to more sectors of society, including the very young, the very old, the ill, and those who simply lack the necessary athletic ability required for participation (think of the "armchair quarterback" who can call all the plays. . . from his or her couch.) Sports fandom allows individuals to be a part of the game without requiring any special skills and can offers social benefits including feelings of camaraderie, community and solidarity, as well as enhanced social prestige and self-esteem (Zillmann et al., 1989).

As discussed earlier, the social identities core to sports can also spark intense emotions on behalf of fans, especially after major competitions. Cialdini et al. (1976) observed that following victories, fans were far more likely to outwardly and socially express their fandom to others as a way of **basking in reflected glory** (or **BIRGing**). BIRGing, in practice, can look like attending games when the team is winning, wearing team colors, and speaking of the team as "we" instead of "they." Beyond the emotional benefits, BIRGing plays a social role as well, with fans seeking out others to BIRG with. When a team does poorly, in contrast, milder fans are prone to **cut off reflected failure** (or **CORF**). This may be seen in lack of attendance at matches, using "they" language instead of "we" language, or refusing to wear team colors (**Sidebar: Owen 16**). Notably, it's not only fickle fans who CORF. Still some hardcore fans are likely to **blast** (Winn, 1993), wherein they identify fans of competing teams to fight with. Blasting can restore self-esteem, despite the overall negative social connotations.

basking in reflected glory (BIRG)
When fans increase expressions of their fandom after a win

cut off reflected failure (CORF)
When fans decrease expressions of their fandom after a loss

blast
To verbally or physically fight against an opposing fan group

Sidebar   Owen 16

Imagine for a moment that it's 2008, and you're a fan of the National Football League's (NFL's) Detroit Lions (or perhaps, you are a fan of the Detroit Lions, both then and now). For Lions fans that year, one of the most popular team jerseys for sale had the surname "Owen" and the number "16." Yet, a quick check of the 2008 Lions roster will show only one player named "Owens" (a tight end, who wore the number 83) and a player named John Standeford who wore the jersey number 16.

Who was "Owen 16?" It wasn't a player on the team but rather, a clever play on words. The 2008 Detroit Lions were the first NFL team during the modern era to lose all 16 of their regular season football games, ending with a record of 0 wins and 16 losses, commonly written as "0-16." A common sight of Lions fans during this season was to still wear silver and blue Owen 16 jerseys (the team's colors), but to engage in perhaps the most obvious CORF of them all: wearing a paper bag over their heads, to hide their faces and thus, identities as Lions fans.

Of course, Lions fans would not be alone. In 2017 the Cleveland Browns also had a 0-16 season. However, Browns fans could rejoice in the fact that the 1948 team had a perfect 14-0 season, winning its third All-America Football Conference title.

Conclusion

hierarchy of needs
A theory that argues that humans have to fulfil fundamental needs like food and shelter before they can satisfy higher order needs and wants such as inclusion and self-actualization

Humans are good at forming social bonds. We feel a distinct need for social affiliation, and we may even become sick when denied the contact of others. From a psychological well-being perspective, Abraham Maslow spoke to the importance of feeling socially included as part of his **hierarchy of needs,** and more recent scholarship into self-determination theory (Deci & Ryan, 2012, discussed in Chapter 1) suggests that feeling a sense of relatedness with others is a strong motivational factor for any number of human leisure pursuits. We can see how socialization is a key function of entertainment, particularly narrative and music, and also has specific outcomes for fans, including sports and video games. The desire to share entertainment with others is relevant for understanding social identify and group identity, and will continue to be a powerful determinant of entertainment selection in the future.

Key Terms

The storytelling animal   The idea that humans can be distinguished from other animals by their ability to think and communicate through the use of narratives

Social skill hypothesis or Entertainment as play   An argument that narratives are useful as "safe spaces" for audiences to vicariously experience and learn practical social skills, and that individuals use entertainment as a form of simulation

Morality sandbox   The ability for narratives to allow audience to play with what is right and what is wrong, safe from real-world consequences of those decisions

Social Identity Theory (SIT)   A theory that predicts how people identify with and function as members of various social groups

Social categorization   The tendency for people to categorize themselves and others into social groups

Social comparison   The tendency for people to compare and compete themselves with their social groups or their social groups against other social groups

Social identity   The tendency for a people to create a self-identity based on the social groups that they see themselves as part of

Self-esteem   How a person feels about their self-worth

Narrative collective-assimilation hypothesis   Argues that people become more similar to the groups that they read about by adopting the psychological aspects of the characters in those groups

Social surrogacy hypothesis   Argues that characters in entertainment media programming can serve as substitutes for a person's peers or friends

Watercooler effect   The time people spend talking about popular media entertainment in their break time from nonleisure activities, such as work or school; named after an observation that most office employees tend to socialize in break rooms where a watercooler is present

Social capital   The benefits that social networks may offer among people in society

Social desirability   The tendency for a person to behavior in ways that make themselves attractive to others

Geek culture   The community and culture of fans of geek products or material

Cosplay   The act of dressing up as a character from a media entertainment product

Participatory cultures   When fans of an intellectual property both consume and produce media content

Wikis   An online site where individuals can contribute information about a particular topic to build an online encyclopedia; based on the Hawaiian word for "fast" or "quick"

Intra-audience effect   A phenomenon by which individual people in a larger audience are influenced by the emotions and behaviors of the other audience members

Field experiments   Experiments that occur in a real-world setting instead of in a laboratory

Transmission   The purpose of music to communicate some message using lyrics, emotion, beat, or content

Ritual use   A purpose of entertainment media to serve as a form of signaling and a form for social gathering

Black Lives Matter   An activist movement in the early 21st century protesting against police brutality and systemic racism toward African Americans in the US.

Adolescent role moratorium   A period when adolescent break away from existing social structure of the family to form their own social groups

Artificial intelligence   The capacity for machines to possess and display original thoughts and decisions without input from a human operator or programmer

Motion sensor controllers   Any sort of video game controller that uses body movement as inputs

Tandem play   A form of coplaying video games in which one person is in direct control of on-screen action and others are watching and providing input to the player controlling the game

Game streaming   Playing video games while broadcasting or recording the gameplay for online audiences to watch

Basking in reflected glory (BIRG)   When fans increase expressions of their fandom after a win

Cut off reflected failure (CORF)   When fans decrease expressions of their fandom after a loss

Blast   To verbally or physically fight against an opposing fan group

Hierarchy of needs   A theory that argues that humans have to fulfil fundamental needs like food and shelter before they can satisfy higher order needs and wants such as inclusion and self-actualization

■ References

Atkin, C. K. (1972). Anticipated communication and mass media information-seeking. *Public Opinion Quarterly, 36*, 188–199. doi: 10.1086/267991

Banks, J. (2015). Object, me, symbiote, other: A social typology of player-avatar relationships. *First Monday, 20*(2). doi: 10/5210/fm.v20i2.5433

Cialdini, R.B., Borden, R.J., Thorne, A., Walker, M.R., Freeman, S., & Sloan, L.R. (1976). Basking in reflected glory: Three (football) field studies. *Journal of Personality and Social Psychology, 34*(3), pp. 366–375. doi:10.1037/0022-3514.34.3.366.

Consalvo, M. (2007). *Cheating: Gaining advantage in video games.* Cambridge, MA: MIT Press.

Consalvo, M. (2017). Player one, playing with others virtually: What's next in game and player studies. *Critical Studies in Media Communication, 34*(1), 84–87. doi: 10.1080/15295036.2016.1266682

DeSarbo, W., & Madrigal, R. (2011). Examining the behavioral manifestations of fan avidity in sports marketing. *Journal of Modelling in Management, 6*(1), 79–99. doi: 10.1108/17465661111112511

Fox, J., & Tang, W.-Y. (2016). Women's experiences with general and sexual harassment in online video games: Rumination, organizational responsiveness, withdrawal, and coping strategies. *New Media & Society.* doi: 10.1177/1461444816635778

Gans, H. (1974). *Popular culture and high culture: An analysis of evaluation and taste.* New York: Basic Books.

Harwood, J. (2017). Music and intergroup relations: Exacerbating conflict and building harmony through music. *Review of Communication Research, 5,* 1-3-4. doi:10.12840/issn.2255-4165.2017.05.01.012

Hocking, J. E. (1982). Sports and spectators: Intra-audience effects. *Journal of Communication, 32*(1), 100–108. doi: 10.1111/j.1460-2466.1982.tb00481.x

Jenkins, H. (2012). *Textual poachers: Television fans and participatory culture.* New York: Routledge.

Johnson, B. K., & Ranzini, G. (2018). Click here to look clever: Self-presentation via selective sharing of music and film on social media. *Computers in Human Behavior, 82,*148–158. doi: 10.1016/j.chb.2018.01.008

Maher, B. (2016), Can a video game company tame toxic behavior? *Nature.* Retrieved from https://www.nature.com/news/can-a-video-game-company-tame-toxic-behaviour-1.19647

Sherry, J. L., Lucas, K., Greenberg, B., & Lachlan, K. (2006). Video game uses and gratifications as predicators of use and game preference. In J. Bryant & P. Vorderer (Eds.), *Playing video games: Motives responses, and consequences* (pp. 213–224). Mahwah, NJ: LEA.

Swaine, J., & McCarthy, C. (2017, January 8). Young black met again faced highest rate of US police killings in 2016. *The Guardian.* Retrieved from https://www.theguardian.com/us-news/2017/jan/08/the-counted-police-killings-2016-young-black-men

Trepte, S., & Krämer, N. (2008). *Expanding social identity theory for research in media effects: Two international studies and a theoretical model.* Hamburg: Universität Hamburg, Arbeitsbereich Sozialpsychologie.

Wann, D., & Branscombe, N. R. (1993). Sports fans: Measuring degree of identification with their team. *International Journal of Sport Psychology, 24,* 1–17.

Yee, N. (2006). Motivations for play in online games. *Cyberpsychology & Behavior, 9*(6), 772–775. doi: 10.1089/cpb.2006.9.772

Zillmann, D. (2000). The coming of media entertainment. In D. Zillmann & P. Vorderer (Eds.), *Media entertainment: The psychology of its appeal* (pp. 1–20). Mahwah, NJ: LEA.

Suggested Readings

Billings, A. C. (2008). *Olympic media: Inside the biggest show on television.* New York: Routledge.

Nathan, D. A. (1993). *Rooting for the home team: Sport, community, and identity.* Urbana-Champaign, IL: University of Illinois Press.

Schramm, W. (1988). *The story of human communication: Cave painting to microchip.* New York: Harper & Row.

Zajonc, R. B. (1968). Attitudinal effects of mere exposure. *Journal of Personality and Social Psychology, 9*(2), 1–27. Doi: 10.1037/h0025848.

CHAPTER 12

Entertainment Markets

"The essential is to excite the spectators. If that means playing Hamlet on a flying trapeze or in an aquarium, you do it."

—Orson Welles

Until this chapter, we have taken an approach to entertainment grounded in media psychology, by focusing on the effects of entertainment on the individual user, and on how individuals select and respond to different types of entertainment. However, to understand the broad appeal of media entertainment, and how media entertainment products are created and made available to users, we will shift to a slightly different approach in this chapter. We'll focus on groups of individuals, such as spectators or audiences. In this chapter, we examine entertainment markets in order to better understand the economics of today's entertainment environment.

Objectives

After reading this chapter students will be able to:

➤ Define audiences and the underlying features that delineate various audiences.

➤ Define what an entertainment market is.

➤ Identify how markets differ based on the producers and distribution of content.

➤ Understand changes in entertainment markets influenced by new technologies.

The Audience

The term audience originates from the Latin verb *audio* (-ire), meaning "to hear." It is interesting to note that the verb for hearing developed into the modern word representing a group of spectators attending or witnessing an event rather than the verb for seeing, *video* (-ere). Original audiences were those individuals within earshot of an event. They literally were the hearers.

In this original conception, audiences possessed some key attributes. First, they were localized in space. To be part of the audience, you had to physically be at the event. Second, there was also the physical co-presence of others; an audience was made up of a lot of individuals and so there was a shared experience that existed between the spectators. Third, the formation of the audience was temporary. The audience didn't exist across time but rather was situated within a specific moment in time.

You'll note that these attributes today are changing. Today, most of us carry a screen around with us, in our pocket, or have a screen in more than one room of our house, and many of us are not watching with others. A recent survey of television viewing habits by the U.S. Bureau of Labor Statistics found that television viewing was split between social (with others: 52.4%) and solo (47.6%) viewing (Krantz-Kent, 2018). On streaming platforms such as Netflix, 60% of customers are viewing alone (Truong, 2015).

In addition, viewers no longer need to be at an event to be part of the audience; the audience for the Olympics are all the spectators who are there in person as well as the media viewers from around the world. Physical copresence is also no longer inherent in the experience. One can be part of a large audience while being physically alone in their bedroom. The temporal nature of the audience is even more varied. Audiences before mass communication would have to travel distances to attend the event, so there were a lot of **sunk costs** associated with attending. You wouldn't spend time to get to the event to leave shortly after it began, and then return later and then leave again. Yet with so many channels available today, that's exactly what viewers do. You can be part of the audience for CBS, then switch over to TNT, then to NBC, then back to CBS all within a very short amount of time. Similarly with **time-shifted viewing** granted by video-on-demand and streaming services, audience trackers must account for audiences both on initial airing of a show, as well as the audience who watches the show several days, weeks, and sometimes even months later.

sunk costs
The time, energy, and money already put into pursuing a goal; in media entertainment, this might refer to investment into an experience or media product

time-shifted viewing
The ability for audiences to choose when to watch media programming that previously required life or scheduled viewing

That said, when we consider the mass audience for entertainment, we are still grouping large numbers of individuals who are similar in specific ways together. We describe some of the ways we can describe and define these audiences below.

Describing Audiences

Most entertainment media are produced with a target audience in mind. These audiences are often defined by attributes, such as the age, sex, race, education-level, and income level of the individuals. These factors are called **demographic** factors, and they weigh heavily on media producers' minds when they are deciding which content to create and how much to budget for them. Some types of content are geared toward extremely demographic groups that might seem very strange for some viewers, but are remarkably popular with specific audience segments (**Sidebar: Out of the pool, kids**).

demographics
Objective properties of an individual, such as their age, race, and biological sex

---

| **Sidebar** | Out of the Pool, Kids |

Consider the following program descriptions:

- Former heavyweight champion Mike Tyson solves mysteries with his adopted daughter Yung Hee Tyson, the ghost of the Marquess of Queensberry (in reality, the father of modern boxing), and a talking pigeon named Pigeon, voiced by deadpan comedian Norm Macdonald.
- A rotting ball of meat, a side order of French fries, and a half-empty milkshake fight crime while sparring with their blue-collar landlord and eternal New York Giants neighbor Carl, who "works from the home" (i.e., is unemployed).
- A family of squids from the northern Georgia mountains continually cause trouble for the local sheriff, including a pimply and confused teenager, a methamphetamine-addicted mother squid, a hypersexual and disabled grandmother, and a chauvinist and theme-hat wearing patriarch (hats such as "booty hunter" and "Cash is King") who consistently fails his family.

These shows, and others, can be found on Turner Broadcasting's [adult swim] lineup, a collection of mature-themed cartoons that airs

(Continued)

late-night time slot
Usually considered the time of day between 11:30 p.m. and 2 a.m., a television programming period in which stations and channels may broadcast more adult themed or mature content

during the **late-night time slot** on the Cartoon Network, along with streaming online content.

Launched on September 2, 2001, the [adult swim] programming block airs from 9 pm until 6 am, targeting young adult and adult audiences, and often pulling in relatively large audiences in the hundreds of thousands. A 2017 April Fools' Day broadcast of *Rick and Morty* pulled in nearly 11 million viewers for the channel, along with three million watching online and another 8.7 million watching via Facebook. All three figures were records for the channel, and demonstrate the popularity of [adult swim]'s often-nonsense humor among young adult audiences. The brand has parlayed this success into several college campus tours and other demographic-specific events and promotions.

[adult swim] is an example of extremely effective demographic marketing in its combination of satirical and rebellious humor, it's late-night time slot, and its blend of nontendentious humor and nostalgic references.

Psychographics
Psychological or intangible characteristics of an audience including attitudes, aspirations, and tastes

Content producers aren't just focused on demographics. **Psychographics**—that is factors that partition individuals based on psychological features such as attitudes, aspirations, and taste—are another component of marketing programming. Netflix produces a large portion of science fiction–related content, including *Stranger Things*, *Black Mirror*, *Altered Carbon*, and *The Cloverfield Paradox*. Audiences interested in science fiction are likely more accurately categorized based on their shared interests and attitudes than age, race, or sex (Chamorro-Premuzic, Kallias, & Hsu, 2013).

Taste Cultures

taste
The ability to make discriminating judgments about art and artistic matters

We can also consider audiences in terms of **taste** and **taste cultures** (Bourdieu, 1979/1984). Taste is the ability to make discriminating judgments about art and artistic matters, including entertainment and leisure activities. Developing one's taste is part of the process by which individuals construct meaning about their social world, by classifying people and things into categories of different values for them and their communities. Taste is displayed in habits, manners, style, and in the possession of consumer goods, which signal comembership into communities.

taste cultures
Groups of individuals who have similar values and aesthetic standards

Displays of taste contribute to the creation of networks and shared identities within groups, but it also allows for the identification and exclusion of outsiders whose standards of taste differ. Some cultures, such as skaters, punks, and goths, are interested not just in identifying themselves as part of the group but also identifying those "posers" who only look the part. Taste cultures are clusters of cultural forms which embody similar values and aesthetic standards. "Rich Kids of Instagram" (RKOI) provides a nice example (**Sidebar: RKOI**). RKOI is a website compiling photos that very wealthy teenagers and young adults have posted to Instagram. Although the photos themselves may vary considerably in which specific goods are displayed, the taste culture is quite clearly one in which markers of exceptional wealth, such as airplanes, champagne, and private pools and islands, are valued and heavily displayed.

Sidebar | RKOI

RKOI (now Rich Kids of the Internet) functions as both a critique of income inequality and a celebration of it. The tagline "They have more money than you and this is what they do" sums up the content of the website, which features young, usually good-looking, and always wealthy people vacationing on private islands, partying at exclusive nightclubs, and wearing designer clothes while posing on personal airplanes and fancy cars. RKOI illustrates both the tastes of these young folks, as well as the extreme privilege under which they operate. For example, a photo of a receipt shows a restaurant bill of $32,000, which is more than half the average American family's annual income as of 2017. Such wealth, however, is glorified in large swathes of youth culture, from hip-hop songs to the *Real Housewives* television franchise. (In fact, E! Online recently announced a reality show called "#Rich Kids of Beverly Hills" directly inspired by RKOI; the teaser trailer is full of Instagram references, and one of the show's stars says, "I think I'm somewhat Instafamous in the Instagram world." The show lasted four seasons.)

You try it! *RKOI demonstrates a very distinctive taste culture that features conspicuous consumption of expensive items in hard-to-access locations. What kinds of other taste cultures might you be able to identify off the top of your head? See if you can identify such a taste culture and list the markers of belonging to this culture. Is this culture more of a sociological-level phenomenon or a fandom?*

Sociologists such as Thorstein Veblen (1899/1939) and Bourdieu (mentioned earlier) have proposed notions of entertainment as a function of taste. Veblen argued that both leisure time pursuits, as well as consumption of expensive items, including entertainment, are driven by notions of honor or social status. Things that accorded more status for the consumer were considered in better "taste."

Like Veblen, Bourdieu argues that taste and status go hand in hand. But he advanced earlier understandings by positing that taste is a mark of distinction related to classifying and setting apart those who have specific tastes from one another. Bourdieu argues that taste itself is not a matter of social status, but that those who already have high social status set the taste levels. Taste, in Bourdieu's terms, is a component of cultural capital, which is a source of wealth transmitted through family and society. In other words, very few of the RKOI are self-made billionaires—rather they rely on family or cultural wealth and access to high-status consumer goods to demonstrate taste in accordance with their culture. In this way, taste serves as both an *identity* and a *status* marker.

Taste and entertainment have been linked in many observations about human cultures. Perhaps the most common distinction is between **high art** and **low art** which has guided understandings about media entertainment for over two centuries. High art (or highbrow art) is equated with elite culture, which is whatever cultural critics approve of. In general, high or elite art is nonrepresentational that is, it doesn't represent or look like something in the real world, time-intensive, and requires either education, money, or cultural capital to access. Low art (or lowbrow art) is representational (it looks like the object it represents), accessible without barrier to entry, and embraced by lower cultural classes or mass audiences. This creates a hierarchy of cultural taste which is associated with education, exposure, and social class. In this distinction, we can see how taste and preferences are not natural or biologically determined, but socially constructed. There is a high correlation between taste and education, and taste and social origin, as well as taste and geography. Interestingly, things that were once considered low art can be elevated to high art over time. Consider for example jazz, which cultural critic of the early 20th century Theodor Adorno despised as low class and simple, but which today is celebrated as high art.

The audience designation of art—lowbrow or highbrow, mass or elite—was once considered a valid and objective way to describe entertainment and entertainment audiences. However, with the application of social scientific studies in the form of communication, psychology, and sociology to understandings of entertainment, that notion is changing. As we now realize how much of "good taste" is

high art
Art that is related to an elite culture and is approved of by cultural critics

low art
Art that does not have a barrier of entry and is embraced by lower cultural classes or a broad audiences

inseparable from sociological considerations such as access, status, and class opportunities, it is difficult to talk about highbrow or low-brow entertainment as a function of the content alone.

In this vein, we now turn from considering the audience and audience tastes to understanding the marketplaces in which they operate. We now examine the creators and merchants of content, as well as the media industries which produce content that is bought and sold.

Media Entertainment Industry

In the 21st century (at least, as of the writing of this book), major media conglomerates include:

- Comcast Corporation, which owns major cable television provider Xfinity as well as NBC and Spanish-language broadcaster Telemundo

- The Walt Disney Company, which owns WarnerMedia and popular channels such as ABC and cable channels such as ESPN and A&E

- National Amusements, which controls CBS and the television and film distributor Viacom

- Sony, which produces music, television, films, and video games (such as the PlayStation console).

The four media conglomerates listed above have **assets** that total over half a trillion dollars—or about as much as the entire gross domestic product of countries such as Belgium, Singapore, Sweden, or Switzerland! This half-a-trillion-dollar figure, however, does not include revenues of many of the newer entertainment producers. For example, Alphabet, Inc., which owns Google and YouTube, and Amazon, Inc., which delivers media streaming services through its Amazon Prime subscription, both had revenues of over $100 billion in 2017. Netflix (one of the most popular media streaming companies) had over $12 billion in 2017 revenue. And still left unaccounted for are video game manufacturers such as Electronic Arts (famous for the sports games such as *Madden* and *FIFA*); Nintendo (*Mario* and *Donkey Kong* franchises); and Activision Blizzard (maker of *World of Warcraft*). These companies produce entertainment media properties that are instantly recognizable around the world, and generate a lot of revenue (and employ a lot of people) in the process.

asset
Anything that is owned by a company

vertical integration

An organizational structure in which a company controls numerous aspects of a supply chain; in entertainment media, this might refer to the same company producing, marketing, and distributing media content

consolidation

An industry structure by which several different companies within a given market are merged into a single entity

The numerous entities that are controlled by these companies produce the vast majority of your favorite television shows, movies, music, video games . . . just about all of the different types of content that you would consider when thinking about entertainment media. One reason relatively few companies control so much of the media landscape is due to **vertical integration** and **consolidation**. Prior to the Telecommunications Act of 1996 (S.652, 1996; also summarized at https://www.fcc.gov/general/telecommunications-act-1996), there were strict ownership requirements for media producers. The same company couldn't own newspapers and broadcasters in the same outlet. However, the deregulation policies included in the Telecommunications Act of 1996 allowed companies to merge and own more and more of the media landscape.

Since 1996, many independent companies have merged together through consolidation. Today, companies produce content, advertise for it on their networks, and deliver it to consumers. For example, the 2013 film *Despicable Me 3* was produced by Illumination, and distributed by Universal Pictures (both owned by Comcast). Following its production, actors Steve Carell and Kristen Wiig made the rounds going on TV shows like *Today* (aired on NBC, which is also owned by Comcast) to promote the film. This type of vertical integration, where the owner maintains control throughout the process, allows for minimizing risk and maximizing profits. The costs for production and distribution are spread out among various entities and the advertising for the content becomes cheaper as well; Comcast had a direct interest in allowing the segments aired on Today related to the movies release to be seen by as many people as possible.

Media entertainment is a large and high-stakes industry (**Sidebar: What does success mean?**), and in order to minimize the risks associated with producing content, the financiers are highly cognizant of their target markets. The remainder of the chapter examines what an entertainment market is, and describes the key elements related to the production and distribution of content.

Sidebar | What does Success Mean?

Consider the 2017 film *Star Wars: The Last Jedi* (notably, one of the many properties owned by The Walt Disney Company). The film grossed over $1.3 billion worldwide from ticket sales. With a budget of $200 million,

(Continued)

Star Wars: The Last Jedi was hugely profitable for Disney. However, with great potential rewards comes great actual risk. Disney was willing to spend $200 million financing *Star Wars: The Last Jedi* because they were confident it would make that amount back and then some. By the time the ticket sales started, Disney was $200 million dollars in the red, hoping that enough tickets would sell world-wide to bring them back into the black. In this way, every piece of entertainment media produced or distributed by a major media entertainment company is essentially a bet by the producer, and this one surely paid off.

Of course, these investments do not always work out so well. The 2018 film *Solo: A Star Wars Story* (also produced by The Walt Disney Company) had a production budget of $275 million, but its worldwide box office gross was only $392.7 million. Movies typically need to earn three to four times their production budget to break even, given all the other expenses associated with a film's release and promotion. Thus, *Solo* is considered the first box office bomb for the *Star Wars* franchise with estimated losses of up to $80 million. Again, Disney was willing to spend the $275 million producing *Solo* because they were confident that it would make that amount back and more. By all accounts it should have been financially successful. It was part of a hugely profitable franchise, and it had big-name stars (Woody Harrelson, Emilia Clarke, Donald Glover, and Paul Bettany), a fantastic writer (Lawrence Kasdan who previously wrote *Empire Strikes Back* and *Raiders of the Lost Ark*, along with his son Jonathan Kasdan), an Academy Award winning director (Ron Howard), and talented producers (which included Kathleen Kennedy who produced *E.T.: The Extra-terrestrial* and *Jurassic Park*). That *Solo* did so poorly demonstrates that there are large risks present even when projects include known commodities.

Entertainment Markets

Entertainment markets are the markets that have to do with buying and selling entertainment products. A useful place to begin a discussion of entertainment markets is by interrogating what *product* is being sold. For some entertainment content, the product being sold is the content itself, such as buying a book, a movie on Blu-ray, or a video game. In these situations, the content is the product. However, for other types of entertainment content, the product is less obvious. Some of these products, such as a movie ticket or seats at a sporting

Entertainment markets

The markets involved in buying and selling entertainment products

experience goods
An economic good that has no future value once it is consumed; examples might include a movie or concert ticket

event, are what economists call **experience goods**. Experience goods are goods where the value is simply that they provide access to something exclusive, and they can only be used once (although the memories could last a lifetime; **Sidebar: The Big Game**).

Sidebar	The Big Game

For sports fans, the thought of your favorite team winning the championship in its sport is the very pinnacle of fandom. Although you might not be on the team, research has shown that sports fans can carry very strong social identities with their favorite teams, to the extent that when those teams win, the fan themselves feels as if they've also won (see Basking in Reflected Glory from Chapter 11).

How does this social identity impact the market value of entertainment media products and events? Consider that in 1967, the most expensive tickets to the very first Super Bowl—the championship game for the National Football League—cost $12, or about $80 when adjusted for 2019. Fast-forward to 2019, and the lowest face-value tickets for Super Bowl 53 were $950, representing a nearly 1,200% price increase, even when adjusting for inflation; on the open market, the cheapest Super Bowl 53 tickets were being sold for an average of over $3,000 and the most expensive tickets were over $10,000! How could any entertainment media product be worth this much money? Likely, the answer comes down to whether or not an individual fits within the market segment for that product. Sports fans and in particular, NFL fans, are far more likely to set aside money to experience an event that will gratify their needs, whereas individuals who are not sports fans might not even attend the Super Bowl if the tickets were offered to them at no charge. In many ways, the value of an entertainment media product, while it can be expressed in terms of dollars, is probably something completely held within the user.

Other types of products are even less obvious. Consider *Brooklyn Nine-Nine*, a sitcom about a police precinct entering its sixth season of broadcast (currently on NBC, after a five-year run on Fox). Like other network television shows or radio broadcasts, the show is broadcast over the airwaves for free. Anyone with a TV set and antenna who lives near an NBC affiliate can pick it up, and the viewers seemingly pay nothing for the privilege of watching it (except perhaps for the cost of a television set, and the electricity to power it). So, if the audience isn't paying for the show, then how is NBC making any money from it? The answer is that the television show really isn't the "product" being sold. In fact, producing the show costs NBC quite a lot of money.

For broadcast programs like *Brooklyn Nine-Nine*, the product being sold is the viewer's attention, and this attention is sold to advertisers who pay a premium to ensure that as many people as possible are exposed to their advertising campaigns. It may seem strange to think of it this way, but the product for all advertisement-supported television, radio, and print is the audience's eyes and ears. The more eyes and ears watching or listening to a TV show, the more expensive the commercial breaks are for advertisers. In 2019, approximately 98.2 million people watched the Super Bowl. A 30-second advertisement during the Superbowl cost around $5.25 million (or $175,000 per second). Of course, not all TV is **advertising-supported**. For channels without advertisements like HBO and Showtime, the product is the **subscription** to the channel itself: Access to the content is what is being sold. And for services like PBS or the BBC, the government subsidizes programming for educational or informative purposes.

So far, we have discussed three different types of entertainment products: The individual content; advertisement-supported content; and subscription-based products. Although what is considered a product might differ between different types of media, the goal for producers is the same. Creators of content want viewers to enjoy and value what they see so that they buy the ticket, can't turn away from the screen during commercial breaks, or subscribe to their channel. As Ridley Scott, the director of *Alien*, *Blade Runner*, and *Gladiator*, is fond of saying, it is the job of the entertainment creator to put "**bums on seats**."

Whose bums do entertainment producers want on seats? The simple answer is as many as possible. The reason **air time** for Super Bowl commercials is so expensive is because so many people of so many different demographics are watching. On February 3, 2019, 44.9% of U.S. television owners (i.e., the **rating**) and 68% of those individuals with their TV on (i.e., the **share**) were watching Super Bowl LIII. The Super Bowl, thus, is a program with appeal that seems to cut across various groups of people. While this example isn't necessarily talking about ticket sales like Ridley Scott was (notably, Super Bowl L(III did

advertising-supported
A model of media distribution in which media content is sponsored by companies and organizations who pay to feature their brand or product in segments external to the narrative

subscription
A model of media distribution in which an individual pays directly to have access to content

bums on seats
The idea that the goal for media creators is to get as many people as possible to pay and consume their content

air time
An amount of time that companies buy for broadcasting their advertisements during a media event

rating
The percent of people who own a television that were watching a particular show

share
The percent of people who were watching television that were watching a particular show

sell out, just as every single Super Bowl has, since the first one), it does speak to the power of having lots of bums in lots of seats, so that lots of eyes and ears are all watching the same advertisements at the same time. All those eyes and ears pay off even more the next day, when colleagues are discussing their favorite commercial (see the water cooler effect from Chapter 11).

Some entertainment media is produced to be broadly appealing in hopes of getting as many people from as many different groups to watch. Such content is often referred to as **lowest common denominator (LCD)** programming. Although LCD often carries connotations of simple and of poor quality, the basis of LCD programming can be thought of in more appealing terms (**Sidebar: Let's Gather Around the LCD**). For example, LCD programming could be programming that is universally appreciated. Take for instance 1985's *Back to the Future*. It appealed to adults of the time because it was a reminder of their childhood with lots of nostalgia-inducing content. It appealed to teenagers of the time because of the young, attractive, and hip cast. In addition, it was rated PG and contained very little content that could cause social critics to get in an uproar. It was also adored by movie critics as unique and charming. All of these facts suggest that *Back to the Future* is the pinnacle of LCD content; everyone loves the movie from kids to grandparents, and the film endures even today: From a production budget of a meager $19 million, the film has nearly $381 million in revenue, with numerous re-releases on VHS, DVD, Blu-Ray, and even in other media forms, such as video game and comic book adaptations.

Of course, this isn't to say that all LCD content is critically adored. Take for instance the 1990s television show *Baywatch*. Although detested by the highbrow critic and roundly criticized for storylines with "plots as skimpy as a string bikini" (Alan Carter, of *People Magazine*), *Baywatch* is one of the most popular television shows of all time in terms of viewership, with up to 1.1 billion weekly viewers tuning in from all around the globe during its weekly broadcasts. One reason for *Baywatch*'s success was the fact that the stories were simple and the visuals drove the show. Perhaps attractive people running in bathing suits down a beach translate into every language. For many, these types of shows are **guilty pleasures** that everyone seems to deny watching yet remain remarkably popular.

lowest common denominator (LCD)
The broadest range of audience members available that entertainment can appeal to

guilty pleasure
A product (such as a entertainment media program) that one consumes even though they feel it has little or no redeeming cultural, social, or critical value

Sidebar — Let's Gather Around the LCD

It can be really easy to mock so many different types of entertainment media programs for being "trashy" or otherwise having tacky content. Most of us have that collection of songs that "we don't know how they got there" or favorited Netflix shows that we're embarrassed to tell each other that we watch. A few of us might hide our favorite band t-shirt under our jacket or maybe put away our comic books and science fiction novels when friends come over to visit.

The **reality television** show *Keeping up with the Kardashians* might serve as a good example of this. A show that is widely panned as featuring a cast of characters that are "famous for being famous." The show has a rating of 2.8 out of 10 (based on nearly 24,000 ratings) on www.imdb.com, and it is incredibly easy to find blogs or social media discussions trashing the show. Yet the show has been on the cable network *E!* for 11 seasons (with over 200 individual episodes having been produced) and heading into 2019, has audience sizes between one and 10 million people, with no signs of slowing down.

There are many reasons why the show is so popular, but one reason relates to the fact that the show provides people from any variety of backgrounds and interests with something in common to talk about. With so many people watching the show weekly and following related content online, such as through the character's social media accounts and blogs, the result is that millions of people all share a common interest in one show, and might have something to talk about the next day.

You try it! *Can you recall a time in which you talked about the content of a television show or other piece of media entertainment with somebody that you never expected to interact with? Why did you talk with, and what did you talk about? Did the conversation go as you would have expected? Did you learn anything about the person, as a result? Do you still talk to that person?*

Producing LCD programming can be a lucrative strategy, and it used to be the primary focus of electronic media producers. During most of the 20th century, electronic media production and distribution was incredibly expensive. The recording equipment was expensive, the magnetic tapes and film used to record performances were expensive, not to mention the human work hours involved. Once a film or song was recorded it then had to be mass produced onto a physical medium and physically shipped to exhibition locations. The overhead for such costs precluded mass production of **niche content**—content that appeals to a small, specialized section of the population. It simply was too cost-prohibitive to produce content for a small group of fans. As technology has advanced into the 21st century however, production and distribution has become much cheaper. Today, a band could record an album in their home studio and distribute it over the Internet for little to no cost. Thus, today more selective strategies of audience targeting have become more common.

niche content
Content that appeals to very small and specialized audiences

The Current Entertainment Marketplace: Seismic Shifts

It is an interesting time for media scholars studying entertainment markets, but a difficult time for industries. Globalization, technological convergence, and the Internet have fundamentally altered the relationship between producer and consumer. As alluded to earlier in the chapter, mass media products were once predominantly produced and distributed by large corporations with deep pockets. Today, the costs of production and distribution are minimal which has allowed "amateurs" to compete with professionals so to speak. James Rolfe, more popularly known as the Angry Video Game Nerd, started posting video game reviews on YouTube in 2007. He produced the content himself filmed on consumer grade cameras and edited the content on consumer grade computers. Yet, his top 100 videos have over half a billion views as of this writing, and his channel has nearly three million subscribers. The process of technological convergence has leveled the playing field and created large markets of **user-generated content**. Although user-generated content might seem less impressive and professional than major blockbusters, the ability to distribute media entertainment broadly has opened up the marketplace of ideas. Strange, avant-garde media entertainment producers, such as Everything is Terrible! Oney Cartoons, and Sick Animation, can air content that would have likely failed to secure an outlet for their products before the Internet.

user-generated content
Any media content that is created and/ or distributed by individual users, rather than by a media company

Other areas where the marketplace is changing can be seen in the products of major studios. China is an emerging entertainment market with a growing middle class. With a population of 1.3 billion people, producing content that appeals to the Chinese market can yield massive gains for U.S. entertainment producers. Several strategies have been employed. For example, in the 2013 film *Iron Man 3*, a special scene—only added to the Chinese release of the film—was shot featuring Chinese actors and inserted into the film in the hopes of pandering to the Chinese market (**Sidebar: "What does Iron Man rely on to revitalize his energy? Gu Li Duo"**).

Sidebar	"What does Iron Man Rely on to Revitalize His Energy? Gu Li Duo"

An article from *The Hollywood Reporter* covered the Chinese market response to the release of *Iron Man 3*. Given the popularity of Tony Stark's Iron Man character, the movie was highly anticipated worldwide. For the Chinese version of the film, four additional minutes were added to the film, including several **product placements** of Gu Li Duo (a popular milk drink) and additional lines of dialogue for Chinese actors Wang Xueqi and Fan Bingbing that were not included in U.S. releases of the film.

One reason for these alterations? The Chinese government only allows a very specific selection of foreign films to be released each year (in 2013, 14 foreign films were allowed wide release; you may recall our discussion on entertainment quotas from Chapter 4). The film also set records for is release-day box office sales, earning 13 million yuan (or $2 million) during its midnight screening along. The film would go on to earn over $120 million in the Chinese market (and over $1.2 billion worldwide).

product placement
The practice of including conspicuous real-world products and brands within the context of a media program

Other blockbusters have set portions of their plot in China—for example *The Dark Knight*—perhaps in the hope that familiar settings will make U.S. movies more interesting and appealing for international audiences. These strategies are difficult though. China features government censors which have to approve of the content of U.S.-produced films in order to release them there. Many films, such as the 2012 remake of *Red Dawn*, were heavily edited by Chinese censors before the film was released. The market pressures applied here could lead U.S. media companies to shy away from certain types of content. For example, if negative references to China are too difficult to remove, a film might be blacklisted altogether from release in China. Failing to secure a release in China for a big blockbuster could be the difference between a major money maker and a major money pit.

Conclusion

Entertainment markets are an important, but often understudied, aspect of media entertainment. What makes something entertaining and for whom is a question that other chapters of this book attempt to answer at a more individual level. The goal of this chapter was to illuminate the importance of understanding aggregate media appeal as it relates to the goal of most media producers: To generate interest and through that profit. Entertainment products can range from buying tickets and Blu-rays to the eyes and ears of consumers. Like other markets, entertainment markets present a combination of competition, taste cultures, and production cycles. Current changes to the entertainment delivery landscape suggest exciting new potentials for the future.

Key Terms

Sunk costs   The time, energy, and money already put into pursuing a goal; in media entertainment, this might refer to investment into an experience or media product

Time-shifted viewing   The ability for audiences to choose when to watch media programming that previously required life or scheduled viewing

Demographics   Objective properties of an individual, such as their age, race, and biological sex

Late-night time slot   Usually considered the time of day between 11:30 p.m. and 2 a.m., a television programming period in which stations and channels may broadcast more adult themed or mature content

Psychographics   Psychological or intangible characteristics of an audience including attitudes, aspirations, and tastes

Taste   The ability to make discriminating judgments about art and artistic matters

Taste cultures   Groups of individuals who have similar values and aesthetic standards

High art   Art that is related to an elite culture and is approved of by cultural critics

Low art   Art that does not have a barrier of entry and is embraced by lower cultural classes or a broad audiences

Asset   Anything that is owned by a company

Vertical integration   An organizational structure in which a company controls numerous aspects of a supply chain; in entertainment media, this might refer to the same company producing, marketing, and distributing media content

Consolidation   An industry structure by which several different companies within a given market are merged into a single entity

Entertainment markets   The markets involved in buying and selling entertainment products

Experience goods   An economic good that has no future value once it is consumed; examples might include a movie or concern ticket

Advertising-supported   A model of media distribution in which media content is sponsored by companies and organizations who pay to feature their brand or product in segments external to the narrative

Subscription   A model of media distribution in which an individual pays directly to have access to content

Bums on seats   The idea that the goal for media creators is to get as many people as possible to pay and consume their content

Air time   An amount of time that companies buy for broadcasting their advertisements during a media event

Rating   The percent of people who own a television that were watching a particular show

Share   The percent of people who were watching television that were watching a particular show

Lowest common denominator (LCD)   The broadest range of audience members available that entertainment can appeal to

Guilty pleasure   A product (such as a entertainment media program) that one consumes even though they feel it has little or no redeeming cultural, social, or critical value

Niche content   Content that appeals to very small and specialized audiences

User-generated content   Any media content that is created and/or distributed by individual users, rather than by a media company

Product placement   The practice of including conspicuous real-world products and brands within the context of a media program

 # References

Bourdieu, P. (1979/1984). A social critique of the judgement of taste. Routledge: London.

Chamorro-Premuzic, T., Kallias, A., & Hsu, A. (2013). Understanding individual differences in film preferences and uses: a psychographic approach. *The social science of cinema, 87.*

Krantz-Kent, R (2018). Television, capturing America's attention at prime time and beyond. *US Bureau of Labor Statistics.* Retrieved from https://www.bls.gov/opub/btn/volume-7/television-capturing-americas-attention.htm

Marwick, A. E. (2015). Instafame: Luxury selfies in the attention economy. *Public culture, 27*(1(75)), 137–160. doi: 10.1215/08992362-2798379

Telecommunications Act of 1996, S. 652, 104th Cong. (1996). Retrieved from https://www.congress.gov/bill/104th-congress/senate-bill/652

Truong, A. (2015). You're not alone: Binge watching is a solo activity for most people. *Quartz.* Retrieved from https://qz.com/460587/youre-not-alone-binge-watching-is-a-solo-activity-for-most-people/

Veblen, T. (1899/1934). *The Theory of the Leisure Class: An Economic Study of Institutions.* New York: The Modern Library.

CHAPTER 13

The Future Is Now Versus Everything Old Is New Again

"The new media are not ways of relating to us the 'real' world; they are the real world and they reshape what remains of the old world at will. All the new media are art forms which have the power of imposing, like poetry, their own assumptions."

—Marshall McLuhan

Trying to define "new media" is like trying to hit a moving target. What is new today is old tomorrow. Technological change is exponential and often transformative. Take mobile phones as an example. They started out as huge bricks that were plugged into your car or wall, and they only had one function: To make phone calls. If you wanted to listen to music on the go, you had to bring along a portable tape or CD player. If you wanted to take pictures, you had to additionally carry around a camera. So, a person wanting to stay in touch with friends, listen to music, and take pictures while walking around would have to carry at least three different devices. Now, mobile phones are essentially small and portable computers that function as phones, music players, cameras . . . and a whole host of other devices.

In the first chapters of this book, we discussed this technological convergence by which one device becomes the source for a whole host of functions and media messages. So how does entertainment theory cope with this type of dramatic change? Where do we see growth in entertainment for the future and the research that examines it? And what are commonalities across new media theories that are relevant for understanding the future of entertainment?

Objectives

➤ Be able to define and recognize unique attributes of "new media"

➤ Apply understandings of new media to virtual reality, virtual environment, and augmented reality settings

➤ Understand the potential for entertainment in these markets

Medium Theory and Marshall McLuhan

Medium theory

The idea that media technology, rather than content contained within a medium, can influence users' thoughts, feelings, and behaviors

In order to understand what new media are, let's first talk about **Medium theory** and the history of studying media in general. Marshall McLuhan was a Canadian professor of English who was posted in the United States for some of his first teaching jobs. He realized the students in the United States were very different from those in Canada based on their slang, dress style, and relevant interests, and he attributed much of those differences to media.

Rather than focus on media content—like shows or songs—as a source of the differences, as most media researchers do, McLuhan focused on the technology behind the content. McLuhan felt that the media themselves rather than their messages were the central mechanisms for societal change. McLuhan is famous for aphorisms, such as the following quote defining medium theory: "We become what we behold. We shape our tools and then our tools shape us." By this he means that the things we build and use alter us in turn, so it is not a consumption process, but a give-and-take between user and medium. However he may be better known for his more famous saying: "The medium is the message," which echoes the same sentiment.

Medium theory focuses on the effects of media technologies, rather than the effects of the content within the media. For McLuhan, a medium is any technology that extends or enhances the "biological five" senses of touch, taste, sight, smell, and hear in a way that was previously impossible. According to McLuhan, when a medium is introduced into society, humans are shaped by that new medium in unexpected ways, and society rearranges itself around the new technology. For example, when messages and people began to travel faster than horseback, time zones were created to ensure that recipients on both sides of a message were on the same clock. Before time zones, each locality set its noon by the sun, leading to cities that were close geographically to have different "noons." For example, before time zones, when it was noon in Washington, DC, it was already around 10 minutes past noon in New York City. Now, "noon" on the east coast extends halfway through Michigan, due to time zones. Although this is just one example of how society might change, McLuhan suggested that many changes went unseen.

How media technologies change humans and society is perhaps most clearly seen in McLuhan's idea of a **Media Tetrad**. According to McLuhan, media often go through changes and evolve, and the media tetrad predicts a certain series of stages. We can illustrate these changes with the radio. The first stage of the media tetrad is **enhancement**, in which a particular sense is amplified. In the case of radio, the medium amplified music and other audio signals. This amplification comes with a cost in that it often makes another medium obsolete (the second stage is **obsolescence**). Radio reduced the public's reliance on print media for news and entertainment. Mcluhan also suggests that media will bring some sense, which had been previously ignored, back to the forefront, in a process known as **retrieval**. Before radio, print had reduced the importance of oral storytelling. However, with the invention of radio, oral storytelling again became important; society began to retribalize, only instead of sitting and hearing stories around the fireside, humans sat around the ambient glow of their radio dials. The final stage of the media tetrad is **reversal**, when a medium adds another sense, and generates a new medium. In the case of radio, television utilized similar technologies for distribution but added visual to the previously audio only format.

McLuhan considered his work as a toolkit to understand media. Yet, his theories have been difficult to test quantitatively or conclusively. Because of these facts, McLuhan was embraced by pop culture creators as a prophet (he even had a cameo appearance in Woody Allen's *Annie Hall*), but his ideas were not directly adopted by the media psychologists whose work we've focused on in this book. Yet, through his work, McLuhan anticipated many changes the digital revolution has brought about, including retribalization into salient ingroups (**see Sidebar: Global Village**), reductions of privacy, and the erosion of personal identity.

Media Tetrad

A series of stages that media technologies go through, originally proposed by Marshall McLuhan. The stages are enhancement, obsolescent, retrieval, and reversal

Sidebar | Global Village

One of Marshall McLuhan's most basic concepts was the notion of a "global village." He first used the term in reference to the "new media" of his day: mainly, the electronic media of radio and television. He suggested that using electronic technology for communication would support the return of tribalism, as we replace "literate man" with "retribalized man." That is, rather than reading our information from a flat screen, we would respond like tribal units, with more diversity and less conformity than our literature, mechanical, and standardized society.

One reason for this is because of the speed and volume of information that electronic media provide. When radio and television emerged, we suddenly had two prominent forms of media that could distribute mass quantities of information from almost anywhere on Earth, and almost instantaneously. Furthermore, as the amount of information available to us increased, we were less reliant on a smaller set of uniform messages. That is, while the "literate man" (or "literate person," if we wanted to modernize the term) mostly consumed the same content, the "retribalized man" ("retribalized person") is able to be much more selective and varied in what they consume.

We can see evidence for the retribalization argument in the increasing political polarization in online discussion boards. Some scientists have even suggested that the ways in which online discussions are set up increases the likelihood of polarization, regardless of the topic at hand. The extent to which the internet has allowed diverse and isolated members of fan cultures to connect to each other and organize certainly also speaks to the movement of isolated individuals toward larger, homogenous groups.

You try it!   *What do you think? Has the Internet and other "new media" technologies facilitated you finding your "tribe?" Or has it increased the noise of the background world so much that you cannot find the signal?*

What is "new" media?

So now that we've covered medium theory, what do we mean when we say "new" media? Some people distinguish digital media (i.e., media delivered by means of a computer) as new, whereas "traditional media" are those delivered by broadcast. For example, television, print, and radio may fall into the traditional or "old" media category, whereas video games, virtual reality, websites, and smartphones would fall into "new." This categorization is a bit difficult as more and more technologies are introduced. Where would we classify, for example, old radio bits that are now digitized and available online? Is there a meaningful difference between radio and podcasts? If so, where and what distinguishes them? Finally, the labels "old" and "new" are very much relative. In 2012, a conversation between leading communication and technology scholars was published in the journal *Communication Monographs.* Most of the scholars rejected the notion of "new media." One reason is that "new media" is a temporal concept—as one of the scholars (Erich Rothenbuhler) explained, "newness is an experience in history and presumably all media have had their moments" (Baym et al., 257).

Still, scholars have attempted to define new media in other ways that captures something about them that distinguishes them from the media of the past. In *The Language of New Media* (2001), Lev Manovich suggests that new media are fundamentally different from old media in five important ways. First, new media are **numerically represented**. That means that information (here, media content) can be transmitted in numeric form, such as **binary code**. This fact allows the content of new media to be transmitted and stored more easily; it no longer needs to be recorded on a physical medium such as a book or record. Compare how music is stored in an .mp3 file as compared to a physical record. The record is the physical embodiment of the sound waves of the song, whereas the .mp3 is a digital representation. The record is limited to being played on one type of technology (a record player), but the digital file can be played on anything that can read numbers, from a desktop computer to a car stereo to a smartphone. This also allows new media to be flexible, or as Manovich describes, **modular**. This means that new media can be broken into pieces and reassembled in other ways—think of the evolution of .gifs from digitized films. Third, new media can be characterized by being **automatic**, that is, many actions can be performed without the input of the user. Think about red-eye removal from digital photos, or the Netflix "auto-advance" feature. Fourth, new media are **variable**, that is, the same content can exist across multiple versions or updates. Many people have both a record and a digital version of the same album, which they use for different purposes. Finally, new media are **transcodable**. Once a media message is in digital format it can be easily edited or altered. We can take a .mp3 file and recode it as a .mp4, a .mov, and so on.

numerically represented

When information and content is transmitted in a numeric format

binary code

When data used in computer technologies are transmitted as ones and zeros

modular

When media content can be broken into pieces and reassembled in other ways

automatic

When actions can be activated and performed without the input of a user

variable

When the same media content is accessible on multiple platforms or versions

transcodable

When media content is in digital format and thus, it can be easily edited or altered into other formats altered

Another useful way to look at the difference between old and new media may be by looking at the relationship that media users have with media content. In general, newer media can be distinguished from old media in multiple ways; see the chart below. For web developers such as Tim O'Reilly, one distinguishing characteristic of new media is that they are interactive, and that they encourage users to "create and collaborate with" content—he referred this to as a Web 2.0 architecture. Simply put, old media did not allow the consumer to create, edit, curate, distribute, and publish directly. However, new media endow their users with these options, and many others. If we think about new media compared to old media, we might say that new media offers greater interactivity, overall. Below, a few ways in which older and newer media might differ:

	Old	New
Channels	Few	Many
Audience	Unified	Diverse
Control	Sender	User
Transmission	One-way, time specific	Interactive, at convenience
Typification	Traditional broadcast	Digital
Learning	Social modeling	Experiential

Interactivity

New media is interactive, but what is interactivity? Communication and entertainment researchers define interactivity broadly as any form of interface between the end user and the medium. For Steuer (1992), a scholar who studies the intersection of humans and technology, interactivity occurs when a user can influence the form and content of what appears on-screen. Vorderer (2000) refined the definition with respect to entertainment by pointing out that there are not interactive media per se, but instead "interactive ways of using the media" (2000, p. 26). If we accept these definitions of interactivity, we must consider what additional interactivity means for selection of entertainment, responses to entertainment, and direct effects from exposure on users.

To begin this examination, we might ask if interactivity leads to enjoyment. Key ideas that are central to understanding the relationship between interactivity and enjoyment would be: How do we measure interactivity? Can we measure it by the level of control a user has over their choices in a game or movie? What about level of perceived control (i.e., feeling like you have control) versus actual control? Some, such as Stromer-Galley (2004), refer to the latter as an **interactivity-as-product** (in which interactivity is understood as the property of a given medium) and the former as **interactivity-as-process** (in which interactivity is understood as a user perception).

Video games are perhaps the pinnacle of interactivity within media entertainment. The user of a video game has a lot of control over what happens in the game and the game itself can't progress without the player. Focusing on video games, Bowman (2018) has argued that interactivity can be conceptualized in reference to the amount of input required from a user. More interactive media require or *demand* more of a user's cognitive, emotional, behavioral, and social abilities (Bowman, 2018). As users get more involved in interactive media like video games, they have to solve the cognitive challenges of the system (solving puzzles and navigating foreign spaces), cope with any emotional content involved (managing emotions like nervousness, fear, etc.), master behaviors to guide their character (learning the keystrokes and controls), and they have to negotiate all of these factors with other players and characters who are increasingly lifelike (i.e., dealing with the social aspects). Of course, it's not just video games that offer these types of challenges; newer media like Netflix's *Bandersnatch* episode of the show *Black Mirror* also make demands of viewers, as does media content that requires users to make decisions and participate in the process (**Sidebar: Interactive Cinema**).

interactivity-as-product

An understanding of interactivity as being a property of a technology

interactivity-as-process

An understanding of interactivity as being a property of the technology user

Sidebar   Interactive Cinema

Although people consider cinema to be relatively noninteractive, the notion of letting moviegoers choose the ending to a film has been around for a long time. In 1967, an interactive film experience titled *Kinoautomat* by filmmaker Raduz Cincera premiered at a Montreal Film

(Continued)

Festival. At nine times during the film, the film would pause and a moderator would appear on stage to take a vote for what should happen next. However, all choices led to the same ending, which underscored the film's overall narrative. It was a smash hit.

Since that point, interactive cinema has made a periodic emergence into mainstream film, spurred on by computational advances allowing for easier creation of interactive narrative. In the United States, in 1992 the film *I'm Your Man* aired in Lowes-branded theaters, using proprietary joy-stick like in-seat technology to allow the audience to vote for their preferred ending at six points during the film. The film tanked, perhaps in part due to the dubious quality of its script and actors, and the necessity of purchasing the hardware to interact with the film, and the effort was scrapped. More recently, voting has been streamlined and filmmakers have been able to offer more options for decisions due to technological pairing of mobile apps and cinema. *Late Shift*, a film released in 2017, allows audiences with specific app downloaded to decide what happens at 180-decision points during the film.

Why is interactive cinema a mixed bag for moviegoers? It can be jarring to be immersed in a narrative and then have to come out to vote where it goes next. If your vote is in the minority, you may feel resentment watching the story progress along lines you do not approve of. Finally, the quality of the story may change based on which version you watch, and with whom.

You try it!   *Late Shift is available via purchase in the IOS App store. Does it feel like a movie? Does it feel like a game? What are you watching and how do you interact with the content?*

Decision fatigue

Decision fatigue is a state resulting from making too many choices in a row

choice paralysis

choice paralysis is when users feel they cannot choose from options provided.

Do viewers always want more interactivity? Often the answer is no, and for good reasons. First, media can provide a feeling of belonging and relaxation, but when you must constantly engage with or respond to the media, it may no longer provide those benefits. Second, too much choice is not always a good thing. Psychologists have identified a state called **decision fatigue** which can result from having to make too many effortful choices. In extreme cases, this can lead to **choice paralysis** where the user cannot make a choice. Have you ever flipped through different television streaming channels in a fog, and found yourself 30 minutes later still on the selection menu? This is an example of this kind of paralysis that can be generated through interactive media, and choice paralysis is hardly an enjoyable state. Finally, we may select media based on our perceptions of the demands that will be placed upon us. Viewers looking to kick back and relax with a film or the latest reality show may not want to participate in order to progress the plot. They'd rather just take in the sights and sounds. Still, challenging experiences can lead to their own forms of relaxation. When the difficulty of tasks is perfectly matched to our current skill levels, we can experience a very pleasurable state called flow.

Flow

An entertainment experience that is unique to interactive media is that of **flow**. This experience was proposed by psychologist Mihaly Csikszentmihalyi (1988), who defined it as "the mental state of operation in which a person performing an activity is fully immersed in a feeling of energized focus, full involvement, and enjoyment in the process of the activity." For Csikszentmihalyi, the appeal of creative leisure activities, such as playing music and strenuous activities such as long distance running, are particularly well-suited to encourage a state of flow. This is in large part because such activities both present challenges to participants, and in turn require skills to overcome those challenges. Tasks that are too difficult (in which challenge is greater than one's skill) usually result in frustration and likewise, tasks that are too simple (in which one's skill is much greater than the challenge) result in a great deal of boredom. Likely, you can think of tasks that are either incredibly frustrating or simply too easy to be fun. Along with the balance of challenge and skill, there are numerous feelings that indicate that a person is experiencing a flow state, such as intense and focused concentration on the task at hand, a merging of action and awareness, a temporary loss of self-consciousness, a sense of control over the task, a distortion of temporal experience (i.e., feeling like no time at all has passed since the activity began), and a feeling that the experience is **autotelic** or self-rewarding.

How does this flow experience apply to entertainment media? We should say that it is probably rare to feel a sense of flow when using noninteractive media because for the most part they do not require many specialized skills to use. Conversely, interactive media require numerous skills, such as the eye-hand coordination and other cognitive skills required for playing video games. Sherry (2004) argued that video games in particular were particularly

flow
The mental state of operation in which a person is fully immersed with an activity

autotelic
Defines an activity in which a person engages without receiving any external benefit, motivation, or reward; autotelic activites are those that are done for their own sake

well-suited for encouraging flow states for these reasons. Later work by Rene Weber and colleagues suggests that flow can be neurologically defined as a state of increased synchronization between diverse brain networks, often seen when players in video games indicate they are experiencing flow. Multiple video games have been adapted to test this theory, such as *Asteroid Impact* (a video game developed by researchers to test dimensions of flow theory) and *flOw* the game. (**Sidebar: flOwing Through the Game**).

Sidebar   FlOwing Through the Game

A fish-like creature is submerged in a seemingly endless ocean, looking for organisms in order to grow and survive an increasingly hostile environment. You are in control of this creature, without any instructions for how to play or narrative to explain what is going on.

From the description, this experience hardly seems to compare with many of the blockbuster video games that are popular today, and yet Jenova Chen's *flOw* was a surprisingly popular game. It was played over 350,000 times in the first two weeks of its 2006 online release (as a free-to-play Flash-based game, one that could be played in most any computer browser window), and in 2007 it was released for Sony's PlayStation 3. The game was even showcased in the 2012 Smithsonian American Art Museum as part of an exhibit on "The Art of Video Games."

What made this game so unique was its use of **dynamic difficulty adjustment (DDA)** by which the game would automatically adjust itself based on the skill of the player. DDA is directly informed by flow theory, in that the algorithm is designed to adjust the choices that a game provides to a player based on their current pattern of play. For example, if a player is consistently struggling with a particular level of a video game, DDA systems might begin to offer the player more power-ups or slow down different obstacles and challenges in order to encourage the player to stay in a flow state (matching game challenge and player skill), rather than entering a frustration state (in which game challenges overpowers player skill and as a result, the player simply turns the game off). Likewise if a player is progressing too quickly through different levels and challenges, DDA systems might offer less power-ups or speed up obstacles in order to increase

(Continued)

dynamic difficulty adjustment

In video games, the use of algorithms that automatically adjust a video game's difficulty according to the player's past and current performance the challenge of the game as a way of matching the player's high level of skill. By dynamically adapting to the behaviors of the player, game such as *flOw* aim to maximize flow states and thus, provide for intrinsically enjoyable experiences.

You try it! *A flash version of the game, along with Chen's research, is available online at https://www.jenovachen.com/flowingames/flowing.htm. Give the game a play for yourself, and when you're done, reflect on your experiences. Did you feel a loss of awareness, or a balance of the game's challenge and your own skills at achieving in-game goals? Did you lose track of time while playing? Consider sharing your experiences with your classmates.*

Presence

Another unique aspect of interactive entertainment media is their ability to fully include the user in the on-screen experience. This might sound a bit like the discussion of flow, in which user's attention is fully absorbed in an experience. However, advancements in digital technologies have allowed users to fully immerse themselves in media content by tapping into an increasing number of human senses (Biocca, 1997). Virtual reality glasses and helmets, specially made **haptic** gloves, and camera and control systems that allow users to translate their physical motions into on-screen actions go a long way in encouraging the user to feel that they are **present** within the simulated media environment.

Although presence can be caused by different technologies, the experience itself is a psychological one more so than a feature of a given technology. For example, two people using the same technology for the same media content might feel different levels of presence—one person might feel immersed by a 3D headset while another person might feel dizzy or disoriented (**Sidebar: Is VR technology sexist?**). Presence is also something that can vary over the duration of the experience, meaning that while an individual is engaging the medium, they are constantly feeling stronger or weaker levels of presence. Notably, this last part has been debated by some people, who would argue that when a person is feeling presence, they are likely no longer pay attention to their physical surroundings and instead are fully engaged in their media content.

haptic
In technology, a reference to interface systems that receive inputs through touch or transmit information back to the user through touch

Present
Present means people have the subjective perception of being within a mediated environment

Sidebar   Is VR Technology Sexist?

"Ecstatic at seeing a real-life instantiation of the Metaverse, the virtual world imagined in Neal Stephenson's *Snow Crash*, I donned a set of goggles and jumped inside. And then I promptly vomited."

—danah boyd

Virtual reality

Virtual reality is a simulated immersive media experience

Virtual reality has been something of an aspirational goal for entertainment media. After all, nearly the entire history of media has been to try and close the perceptual gap between the audience and the content: books and films, allow stories to travel the world from one culture to the next, and television and Internet news greatly accelerate how quickly we can learn about events happening the world over, in near real-time. These examples very much line up with our opening discussions of McLuhan's "global village" in this chapter.

If media is meant to close perceptual gaps, then what better way than to actually make people feel as if they are existing in a digital world, even when they're actually sitting or standing in their own living room? As early as the 1960s, computer scientists had been working virtual reality helmets and visors that a user would wear over their eyes, and that would project three-dimensional images that the user (or wearer) could interact with. The earliest was the Sword of Damocles at MIT, which projected a wire-framed cube into the wearer's field-of-vision (technically, an **augmented reality** application). As the wearer moved their head, the wire-framed cube moved with them. Fast-forwarding to the 2000s, and there are several VR technologies that are readily available to consumers, such as the PlayStation VR (which retails for about $300 at most electronic stores) Oculus Rift ($400), and HTC Vive ($500). All three technologies offer high-resolution and full-color displays to wearers, with image quality that is remarkably life-like. Industry experts such as Gartner predict that virtual reality technology is unlikely to fade, and are likely the next "killer app" for new media.

augmented reality

The inclusion of virtual objects in a user's real-world field of view-often facilitated by a mobile phone or headset

However, the next "killer app" for new media also seems to have some sex discrimination issues, according to technology scholar and futurist danah boyd. In an essay published in 2014, boyd suggested that technologies such as the Oculus Rift were inherently sexist (the full commentary is available online at http://www.zephoria.org/thoughts/archives/2014/04/03/is-the-oculus-rift-sexist.html/comment-page-1). In her experiences, using VR headsets was nauseating experience that would often lead to disorientation and vomiting; she noticed that other females (but not males) reported similar symptoms after using VR.

(Continued)

How can a technology be sexist? Through research, boyd and her colleagues discovered that this **simulator sickness** was the result of how VR systems work with the human eyes to render the very virtual environments that make them so interesting. The problem is described in detail in the above link, but essentially VR headsets prioritize a particular type of depth cue (motion parallax) that is more dominant in males than females (who use another depth cue, called shape-to-shade parallax). Because of this, female headset wearers would often get disoriented because they were unable to pick up on depth cues and thus, would get sick. Luckily it appears that simulator sickness was a function of the technology of the time, and more recent studies have not shown the same gender differences in simulator experience with newer rendering technology.

You try it! *If you have access to a VR headset, try watching a short film or online video while wearing it, or try playing a video game in virtual reality. Do you experience any of the symptoms that boyd discusses in her essay? If so, did those symptoms prevent you from being able to understand or enjoy the experience?*

simulator sickness
A phenomenon, in which wearing virtual reality helmets can cause bouts of nausea and extreme disorientation

The feeling of presence is a very complex and multifaceted one, and can be experienced numerous ways. Media scholars Matthew Lombard and Theresa Ditton (1997) explained several different types of presence, which we summarize below.

Presence as realism can be understood as the degree to which a medium can produce seemingly accurate representations of objects, events, and people that look, sound, and/or feel like the "real" thing. For example, think about your favorite animated series for adults (*BoJack Horseman, The Simpsons, Rick and Morty*, for example). While the characters may not look like people from a live-action series, many animated shows for adults *feel* real due to the rich social interactions of the characters. This is what we would call rich social realism, but poor perceptual realism.

Not to be confused with the discussion of *narrative* transportation, **presence as transportation** is the sense that "things" on screen—the objects, the people, and other elements of the entertainment medium—are physically present in the user's environment. If you have ever jumped or ducked out of the way when watching an action movie or tried to lean left and right to control a video game character when you weren't actually playing the game with a motion controller, you have probably felt this. In these cases, the user momentarily fails to distinguish between a mediated and nonreal image and the actual

presence as transportation
The sense that things are are physically present when they are not

social presence

The sense that a person is sharing space with others that are in a remote location

presence as social richness

The sense that a medium is sociable, warm, sensitive, personal, or intimate when used to interact with other people

media richness

The extent to which a medium can transmit audio-visual information

"real-world" object being represented, and thus directly responds to everything on screen as if it were physically present.

Next, we can examine the extent to which presence encourages a feeling that "we are together" This is what we may call **social presence**, which is the degree to which you get the impression of sharing space with the entities within a mediated environment. For example, Facebook may make you feel like you have contact with a lot of people, because you feel socially present with them in the social medium. This concept relates to **presence as social richness** which is the extent to which a medium is perceived as sociable, warm, sensitive, personal, or intimate when used to interact with other people (Short, Williams & Christie, 1976). Social richness can be increased by media features such as **media richness**, or the extent to which the medium can transmit audio-visual information. Different features such as the *capacity for immediate feedback*, the *number of senses a medium engages*, the extent to which the medium is *personalized*, yet allows for *intimacy* and *immediacy*, can all affect the perception of social richness (**Sidebar: Disney, now in 4D**).

Sidebar   Disney: Now in 4D

"Disneyland will never be completed. It will continue to grow as long as there is imagination left in the world"

—Walt Disney, creator of Disneyland and founder of The Walt Disney Company

In July 1955, one of the most popular **theme parks** in the world opened in Anaheim, California, when Walt Disney opened his Disneyland. For visitors to the park, they could stroll down a recreation of an imagined early-1900s period American city ("Main Street, U.S.A.") and from there visit a land of jungle adventures ("Adventureland"), high fantasy ("Fantasyland"), a recreation of the 1800s American Westward Expansion ("Frontierland"), or a vision of a future of flying cars and space travel ("Tomorrowland"). As with most theme parks, visitors were able to immerse themselves each of these different land (themes), taking rides on different roller coasters and other attractions relevant to each land. Most all of these original rides were physical recreations—actual mine cars and car-shaped buggies were used to recreate the illusion of falling through a mine, or driving on a road. As characters from Disney cartoons and movies became popular, rides were either retrofitted or

(Continued)

specifically created to feature those characters. A good example of this is the *Pirates of the Caribbean* ride that was installed in the early 1960s. The original ride was a boat tour through the Antebellum South that ends up in a pirate-infested grotto in which animatronic pirates battle each other while singing and dancing to remarkably catchy music (you might already be humming the bars to "Yo ho, yo ho, a Pirate's life for me..." as you read this. With the world-wide success of the *Pirates of the Caribbean* movies, the ride was modernized to include movie-related characters such as a Johnny Depp-inspired rendering of Jack Sparrow.

Of course, as entertainment media technologies evolve, theme park rides have also begun integrating new media into the experience. One of the most dramatic examples of this can be find in Shanghai Disneyland version of the Pirates ride, called *Pirates of the Caribbean: Battle for the Sunken Treasure* ("加勒比海盗: 沉落宝藏之战"). Unlike the U.S.-based rides that rely on physical objects and animatronics to make riders feel as if they are in a pirate grotto, the Chinese version uses 4D technologies that fully immerse the rider with a blend of physical and digital means. For example, much of the ride is really nothing more than a floating boat in front of six massive curved cinema screens that completely surround riders. The actions on the screens are synced up with minor movements of the boat itself, which can trick riders into feeling as if they are being chased by a giant kraken or pulled from the bottom of the sea and dropped into the heat of a massive battle between pirate ships ... even the air temperature is heated with a furnace, during the battle). Here, a clever mix of physical movements and motions along with high-resolution and carefully-timed mediated portrayals give riders the sensation of a dramatic journey, and hide the fact that in the end, the ride is little more than a floating ship on a nonimpressive set of steel rails (as can be seen in fan recreations of the ride, such as https://www.coaster101.com/2016/05/17/secrets-behind-shanghai-disneylands-pirates-caribbean/).

The next categories of presence focus on how we interact with technology. For example, **presence as social actor within a medium** is the extent to which we treat mediated entities as social actors. This can relate to parasocial interaction, but also can cover how we treat nonplayer characters in video games, and other members of chat rooms. If we flip to talking about presence as **medium as social actor,** however, we mean the social responses of media users to cues provided by the medium itself. In their book *The Media Equation* (Reeves & Nass, 1996), Byron Reeves and Cliff Nass covered how people use social rules based

presences as social actor within a medium
The sense that entities with a mediated experience can be treated as a real people

medium as social actor
The sense that the medium itself can be treated as a real social actor

on interpersonal interaction to deal with media and technology. In short, Reeves and Nass suggest media users are prone to treat computers as other people. Have you ever yelled at your computer, or said "thank you" to your printer? Then you are familiar with this experience.

Key ideas in the area of presence include questions about *how real is real enough?* What features of immersive environments are critical to people feeling present, and what sensations can interrupt presence (known as **breaks-in-presence**, or BIP). When we think particularly of new media entertainment such as immersive virtual reality (or simply, VR), we need to consider the experience/value trade off in experiencing presence. While VR field trips, public speaking environments, and medical and military simulations can dramatically aid learning and training capabilities for users who cannot participate in the real experience, the true boom for VR may come from users judging the entertainment experience to be worth the time and expense of setting up and learning a new system.

breaks-in-presence
Anything that interrupts feelings of presence

Conclusion

Media technologies are always changing, and with them, entertainment research will change as well. The question as to how "new media" will be harnessed for entertainment purposes will always be a relevant one, given that what makes a medium "new" or not is more of a temporal concern than a functional one. It seems more important to instead focus on the unique qualities of and user experiences with emerging media, such as the interactive components of modern digital media. As audiences shift from being more passive consumers to more active cocreators of entertainment media, the uses and gratifications of entertainment will become increasingly complex, for better or worse. At the same time, this increased interactivity is also more demanding and possibly even strenuous than ever before, and we might question the extent to which audiences always wish to be so immersed in entertainment environments.

We can see researchers using new technology such as immersive games, virtual reality, and social media to both ask and answer new questions about entertainment. We can use these technologies to generate and understand more individual determinants and effects. Within social context we can study games and virtual experiences while taking into account technological affordances and what actions users can perform in the environment. On the other hand, we are still answering the same fundamental questions (to paraphrase Lazarsfeld), Who creates which type of entertainment that appeals to whom under which conditions, and with what effects?

Key Terms

Medium theory   The idea that media technology, rather than content contained within a medium, can influence users' thoughts, feelings, and behaviors

Media Tetrad   A series of stages that media technologies go through, originally proposed by Marshall McLuhan. The stages are enhancement, obsolescent, retrieval, and reversal

Numerically represented   When information and content is transmitted in a numeric format

Binary code   When data used in computer technologies are transmitted as ones and zeros

Modular   When media content can be broken into pieces and reassembled in other ways

Automatic   When actions can be activated and performed without the input of a user

Variable   When the same media content is accessible on multiple platforms or versions

Transcodable   When media content is in digital format and thus, it can be easily edited or altered into other formats altered

Interactivity-as-product   An understanding of interactivity as being a property of a technology

Interactivity-as-process   An understanding of interactivity as being a property of the technology user

Decision fatigue   Decision fatigue is a state resulting from making too many choices in a row

choice paralysis   choice paralysis is when users feel they cannot choose from options provided.

flow   The mental state of operation in which a person is fully immersed with an activity

autotelic   Defines an activity in which a person engages without receiving any external benefit, motivation, or reward; autotelic activites are those that are done for their own sake

Dynamic difficulty adjustment   In video games, the use of algorithms that automatically adjust a video game's difficulty according to the player's past and current performance

Haptic   In technology, a reference to interface systems that receive inputs through touch or transmit information back to the user through touch

Present   Present means people have the subjective perception of being within a mediated environment

Virtual reality   Virtual reality is a simulated immersive media experience

Augmented reality   The inclusion of virtual objects in a user's real-world field of view-often facilitated by a mobile phone or headset

Simulator sickness   A phenomenon, in which wearing virtual reality helmets can cause bouts of nausea and extreme disorientation

Presence as transportation   The sense that things are are physically present when they are not

Social presence   The sense that a person is sharing space with others that are in a remote location

Presence as social richness   The sense that a medium is sociable, warm, sensitive, personal, or intimate when used to interact with other people

Media richness   The extent to which a medium can transmit audio-visual information

Medium as social actor   The sense that the medium itself can be treated as a real social actor

Presences as social actor within a medium   The sense that entities with a mediated experience can be treated as a real people

Breaks-in-presence   Anything that interrupts feelings of presence

 # References

Baym, N., Campbell, S. W., Horst, H., Kalyanaraman, S., Oliver, M. B., Rothenbuhler, E., et al. (2012). Communication theory and research in the age of new media: A conversation from the CM *Cafe. Communication Monographs, 79*(2), 256–267. doi: 10.1080/03637751.2012.673753

Biocca, F. (1997). The cyborg's dilemma: Progressive embodiment in virtual environments. *Journal of Computer-Mediated Communication, 3*(2). doi: 10.1111/j.1083.6101.1997.tb00070.x

Bowman, N. D. (2018). *Video games: A medium that demands our attention.* New York: Routledge.

Csikszentmihalyi, M. (1988). The flow experience and its significance for human psychology. In M. Csikszentmihalyi & I. S. Csikszentmihalyi (Eds.), *Optimal experience: Psychological studies of flow in consciousness* (pp. 15–35). New York, US: Cambridge University Press.

Lombard, M., & Ditton, T. (1997). At the heart of it all: The concept of presence. *Journal of Computer-Mediated Communication, 3.* doi:10.1111/j.1083-6101.1997.tb00072.x

Manovich, L. (2001). *The language of new media.* Cambridge, MA: MIT Press.

Reeves, B., & Nass, C. (1996). *The media equation: How people treat computers, television, and new media.* Cambridge University Press.

Sherry, J. (2004). Flow and media enjoyment. *Communication Theory, 14*(4), 328–347. doi: 10.1111/j.1468-2885.2004.tb00318.x

Short, J., Williams, E., & Christie, B. (1976). *The Social Psychology of Telecommunications.* London: John Wiley.

Steuer, J. (1992). Defining virtual reality: Dimensions determining telepresence. *Journal of Communication, 42*(4), 73–93. doi: 10.1111/j.1460.2466.1992.tb00812.x

Stromer-Galley, J. (2004). Interactivity-as-product and interactivity-as-process. *The Information Society, 20*(5). 391–394.

Vorderer, P. (2000). Interactive entertainment and beyond. In D. Zillmann & P. Vorderer (Eds.), *Media entertainment: The psychology of its appeal* (pp. 21–36). Mahwah, NJ: LEA.

 # Suggested Readings

Csikszentmihalyi, M. (1990). *Flow.* New York: Harper and Row

McLuhan, M. (1994). *Understanding media: The extensions of man.* Cambridge, MA: MIT Press.

Stephenson, N. (1993). *Snow crash.* New York: Bantam Books.

GLOSSARY

Chapter 1

Technological convergence   The combining of various communication and technology media into a single medium or device

Media psychology   The study of how media content is related to human thoughts, feelings, and behaviors

Hedonic Response   The basic positive feeling when consuming entertaining media

Play   A pleasurable activity where individuals change their perceived reality into an imaginative reality

Eudaimonic Response   A more complex feeling focused on righteousness, well-being, and meaning in life

Functional perspective   The idea that outcomes, such as enjoyment, are derived from the fulfillment of individual needs and wants

Intrinsic motivation   Any motivation to perform and action that is driven by one's internal desires rather than external forces

Self-Determination Theory   A theory that argues that psychological well-being is derived from the fulfillment of three intrinsic motivations: autonomy, relatedness, and competence

Multiplayer online battle arena (MOBA)   A video game genre in which players work in teams to battle each other in a confined environment

Quantitative research   Scientific research that uses numbers to describe and measure phenomena

Social science   The study of human behavior using the scientific method

Scale(s)   An instrument used to quantify a phenomenon

Conceptual scheme   The different components that represent various dimensions of a theoretical construct

Construct   A phenomenon that is theoretically understood but may not be directly observable

Likert scale   A measurement that asks individuals to rate how much they agree or disagree with a statement

Psychophysiology   The study of a person's mental processes through observation of physical responses, such as pulse, sweat, and eye movement

Functional magnetic resonance imaging (fMRI)   A method for measuring the amount of activity in different brain regions by scanning the amount of oxygen-rich blood in parts of the brain; often used in psychophysiology approaches to research

Flow   An intrinsically rewarding experience that occurs when the challenge of an activity is equally matched by a person's skill at performing the activity

Chapter 2

Functional approach A school of thought that argues that media use serves as a gratification of one's needs or wants

Mood management theory (MMT) An entertainment selection theory which predicts that people will select media content to maximize positive feelings and minimize negative feelings

Selective exposure (SE) A process of choosing what media content you will watch or listen to

Mood(s) (A) persistent emotional state

Pleasure principle The notion that people are motivated to maximize pleasure and to minimize pain; central to MMT

Excitatory homeostasis The process of maintaining an optimal (i.e., not too high or too low) level of arousal

Excitatory potential The ability of a media message to increase or decrease arousal

Intervention potential The ability of a media message to distract one's attention and intervene in an existing mood state

Hedonic affinity The extent to which a message matches the user's current mood state

Media habits Automaticity in media selection that persists over time given stable circumstances

Audience flow When audiences for one show continue to watch another, different show because the shows are broadcast in a sequential manner

Unbounded rationality The idea that humans will choose the most logical and rational option when provided with infinite resources, time, and/or information

Bounded rationality The idea that humans will use mental shortcuts in decision making when resources, time, and/or information are limited

Heuristics Mental shortcuts used to process information quickly

Recognition heuristic When people judge an object or event simply based on whether or not they recognize it or not

Fluency heuristic When people judge an object simply based on how quickly it is remembered

Take-the-best approach A selection strategy in which a person compares two choices based on corresponding features until a decision is made

Chapter 3

American Time Use Survey A US government-sponsored survey that measures the different patterns by which Americans use their time for work, leisure, and self-preservation

Autotelic or **intrinsic motivation** When a person is self-motivated to perform a task

Extrinsic motivation When a person is motivated by external reward or benefit to perform a task

Normative debate   An value-based argument about how something should or ought to be

Displacement hypothesis   The idea that the time a person uses media takes up time for other activities

Nostalgia   An emotional and cognitive process where one feels bittersweet about specific past events

Multitasking   The execution of two or more processing activities at the same time

Simultaneous cognitive processing   The act of engaging with and perceiving two different stimuli at the same time

Task switching   The act of switching, usually quickly, between two tasks

Switch cost   The delay it takes for our attention and processing to catch up to the new task when we engage in task switching

Escapism   The desire to leave "real world" problems and disappear into another world, such as those provided in an entertainment media product

Frankfurt School   A scholarly tradition and perspective that originated from the Institute for Social Research at the University of Frankfurt in the early 20th Century

Soap opera   A televised drama that is traditionally aired midday; its name comes from the first programs being sponsored by soap companies

Thought-blocker   The act of using media to remove a person's unpleasant thoughts

Coping   Any psychological or behavioral process used to deal with a stressor

Approach-oriented coping   A way to cope with stressors by confronting them either directly or indirectly

Avoidance-based coping   A way to cope with stressors by staying away from them

Psychological dependence   A craving for a behavior or substance

Over-pathologize   The trend to diagnose otherwise normal or common behaviors as medical conditions

Self-regulation   The ability to control one's behavior

Problematic   When a given behavior interferes with normal human functioning

Fear of Missing Out (FOMO)   The anxiety that comes when a person feels excluded from their social group; often discussed in relation to social media usage

World Health Organization (WHO)   A United Nations agency that monitors and addresses public health concerns

International Classification of Diseases   A reference text to diagnose human diseases; maintained and published by the WHO

Recovery experience   The experience of restoring psychological and physiological resources

Resource-providing activity   Any activity which facilitates recovery from fatigue and stress

Resource-consuming activity   Any activity which prevents recovery from, or prolongs, fatigue and stress

Chapter 4

Pseudo-environment   The constructed environment in one's mind that is derived from nonphysical observations, such as mediated observations

Mediated experience   Any experience derived from media content; usually contrasted with a lived or real world experience

Stalagmite theories   A family of media theories that predict that perception effects such as attitude change are small or undetectable in the immediate term yet cumulative and large over time

Cultural Indicators Project   A research project focused on quantifying the content and effects of television on the general population

Content analysis   A social scientific method in which researchers systematically quantify and describe properties of media content

Cultivation differential   The difference in beliefs and attitudes between heavy and light television viewers; thought to result from the prevalence of beliefs and attitudes presented on television

Mean World Index   A self-report measurement that asks people how dangerous they believe the world to be

Mainstreaming   A phenomenon by which individual differences in beliefs and attitudes more closely resemble the world on television than would otherwise be expected

First-order cultivation effects   Cultivation effects on general beliefs about the world; usually related to factual or statistical information

Second-order cultivation effects   Cultivation effects on specific beliefs about the world; usually about an individual's own environment or situation

Vicarious learning   Learning a behavior by watching another person engage in it, rather through experiencing directly-direct experience

Model attractiveness   The extent to which a person performing a behavior is perceived positively or negatively by observers

Didactic   Of or pertaining to teaching

Ecological rationality   An argument that states that rationality comes from weighing the amount of information one knows and does not know in a given situation

Exemplar   An instance of an event population that shares essential features with all other instances from the group of events

Base-rate information   The probability of an event actually occurring

Model of intuitive morality and exemplars (MIME)   A theory that proposes media exemplars can prime short-term morality accessibility and shape individual chronic morality accessibility over multiple media exposures

Moral foundations theory (MFT)   A theory that suggests individuals have variable accessibility to different types of preconscious moral intuitions; this accessibility to some over other intuitions influences how individuals process media content

Chapter 5

Moral panic   When one part of society considers another part of society or a specific behavior to be a threat or risk to society as a whole, based on little or contradictory evidence

Sexual content   Media content that includes any type of sexual intimacy

Pornography   Media content that includes graphic and explicit depictions of sexual activity

The aesthetic theory of destruction   The idea that people may be attracted to and enjoy watching the destruction of objects

Virtual violence   Violence that occurs in a virtual environment, such as virtual reality or a video game

Racialized pedagogical zones   The idea that interactive media (such as video games)s allow players to practice enacting racial and ethnic stereotypes that could transfer to the real world

Public service announcement (PSA)   A message that is design to promote a social good; central to the concept of social marketing

Network models of memory   A theory that argues that memories are organized and connected to each other in the brain

Spreading activation   The notion that when one concept is accessed in memory, related concepts will also be activated. The closer the concepts are to each other in either conceptual or semantic terms, the more quickly concepts will be activated

Priming   A short-term effect that activates associations and relations in the brain

Intensity   The frequency and duration of a prime

Recency   The amount of time since a person was exposed to a prime

Neo-associationistic model of aggression   A model that predicts that people will have more aggressive thoughts and behaviors after consuming violent media

General aggression model   A model that predicts how violent media in conjunction with personality, cultural, and social variables may lead to aggressive thoughts and behaviors

Affect or **emotion**   A concept used in psychology to describe the experience of feeling

Behavior   The way in which a person or animal acts in response to a situation or stimulus

Cognition   A concept used to describe the process of thinking, perception, or learning

Disinhibition   The weakening of a person's inhibitions

Desensitization   The process of feeling a weaker emotional reaction toward media content the more a person consumes or is exposed to the same type of content

Habituation   The lessened response to the same stimulus (in this case, media content) after multiple viewings

Generalization   The ability of habituation to transfer between similar media content

Excitation transfer   When arousal created by one event can be transferred to and added upon another event even if the two events differ in cause or result in different feelings (e.g., positive vs. negative)

Imitation   When a person copies a behavior seen on screen

Catharsis   The argument that one can purge negative feelings and behaviors by watching entertainment content directly related to those behaviors

Eye-hand coordination   The ability to react to visual inputs with bodily responses

Naturally mapped   Any interface that is designed for the five human senses: touch, taste, sight, smell, and sound

Observational or **vicarious learning**   Learning a behavior by watching another person instead of trial and error

Associative learning   Learning about a connection between two things by repeatedly observing them together

Meta-analysis   A type of study that gathers multiple previous studies together about the same topic and compare the effect sizes of each

Limited effects paradigm   A paradigm in media studies in which it is assumed that media has little effect on thoughts and behaviors

Publication bias   In media psychology research, studies that detect media effects are more likely to be published that studies that do not

File-Drawer Effect   The problem in which studies that do not detect media effects are usually never submitted for publications; related to publication bias

Chapter 6

Paradox of fiction   The idea that feeling emotions in response to fictional narratives is irrational because the events and characters are not real

Dimensional model (of emotion)   An argument proposing that emotions can be defined through a combinations of psychological factors, namely arousal and valence

Discrete model (of emotion)   An argument proposing that discrete emotional states can be identified by independent appraisals and neural architecture underlying these basic emotions

Circumplex model of affect   A dimensional model of emotion that understand emotions as a combination of positive or negative affect and high or low arousal

Discrete emotion(s)   A small group of unique, distinct, and universally felt emotions (based on a discrete model of emotions) that include including anger, disgust, fear, happiness, sadness, and surprise

Conative   Dealing with behavior

Physiological   Dealing with bodily reactions that are usually involuntary (heart rate, skin conductance, respiration, pupil dilation)

Motivational   Dealing with psychological forces that lead to behavior

Empathy   The act of understanding and "feeling with" another person

Emotional contagion   A phenomenon by which one person's emotions are experienced by others, even if those others did not experience the root cause of the original person's emotional state

Experience proper   The perception and interpretation of a witnessed event

Counter-empathic   When a person feels good about another person's suffering or feels bad about another person's happiness

Correction and redirection of affect   The ability to shift one's feelings of empathy from one character to another

Generation of affect   When a person anticipates or imagines the hypothetical emotions of another person and feels empathy toward that person as a result

Anticipatory emotions   The emotions that people predict they will feel before actually feeling any emotions at all

Showrunner   The person in charge of the creative and management aspects of a television show

Meta-emotions   Emotions that we feel about our own felt emotions, as well as the emotions of others

Empathy paradox   A problem in media theory that asks how can audiences enjoy sad or scary movies if the movie makes them feel negative instead of positive

Arousal boost and **arousal jag hypothesis**   An argument that proposes that both sudden bursts of arousal (arousal boost) and relief of arousal (arousal jag) can be pleasant experiences

Excitation transfer theory   A theory that argues that arousal created by one stimulus can be carried over to another event, which can result in higher-than-expected levels of arousal

Moral emotions   Emotions that are activated when witnessing violation or reinforcement of an individual's own moral concerns, such as guilt or elevation

Mixed affect   An emotional state brought about when an individual experiences more than one conflicting emotions at the same time

Chapter 7

Plot   The major events within a story

Characters   The person, animals, or entities within a story, play, novel, or movie

Events   Associated occurrences within a story

Temporal progression   The time-ordering of associated events in a story

Telling   The way and manner in which the events of a story are communicated to the audience

Narrator   A character who tells the story to the audience

Transportation   The feeling of "being there" in a story, that is, attentionally and emotionally absorbed into a narrative world

Presence and/or **Telepresence**   A psychological perception in which a technologically mediated interaction is experienced as being nonmediated, i.e., "being there" even when one is seeing an environment on a computer monitor

Immersion   The feeling of being perceptually absorbed into a mediated experience

Parasocial interaction   The perceived interpersonal interaction between a media user and a mediated character or persona

Consistency (behavior)   When a character acts in a manner that is expected based on previous knowledge of the character

Direct involvement   When character addresses the audience members as if they were actually present

Fourth wall   A hypothetical boundary between the fictional narrative and the audience; the fourth wall is often considered the television screen or other screen through which the characters are observed

Eye contact   When a character looks directly at the audience

Spontaneous (behavior)   When a character acts unexpectedly within the frame of a larger story

Indirect involvement   When character addresses other characters within a story, without acknowledging the audience's presence as witnesses to the events

Overhears   A storytelling convention by which audiences are able to observed characters interacting without those characters being aware of the audience's presence

Audience acceptance   Relevant to programs that use direct address, brief pauses in storytelling that provide time for the audience to process and understand events within a narrative

Parasocial relationship (PSR)   The perceived relationship between an individual and media characters, usually a consequence of parasocial interactions with that character

Relational schema   The internalized mental model of how a person experiencing a parasocial relationship understands that they would interact with the mediated character

Attachment styles   Refer to the different types of interpersonal relationships that an individual is most comfortable forming, based on how they view themselves and other people.

Parasocial contact hypothesis (PSC)   A hypothesis that predicts parasocial interactions with minority characters through media exposure can reduce prejudices that an individual holds toward the social groups that those characters represent

Surrogate   A media character that acts as a representative of a larger social group; a stand in for a particular viewpoint or group of people

Identify/Identification   A process by which one sees oneself as similar to or like a media character

Ego-confusion   When someone confuses himself or herself as the character within a story

Affective disposition theory   A theory that predicts that audiences will enjoy stories in which liked characters triumph and disliked characters are foiled

Untiring moral monitors   The notion that entertainment media audiences are constantly making moral judgments about events, characters, and narratives

Micro-plots   Smaller plots within a larger narrative that are resolved within the scope of the larger narrative

Macro-plot   The overall plot of a narrative

Moral sanctioning   Judging a character's action as morally acceptable

Antiheroes   A protagonist who engages in morally questionable behavior

Schema   A mental network of related concepts

Chapter 8

Genre   A group of conventions or styles that categorize an entertainment product

Cross genre or **hybrid genre**   When an entertainment product mixes two or more genre conventions together

Protagonist   The main character of a narrative

Antagonist   The character that works against the protagonist in a narrative

Play face joke telling   When a comedian uses exaggerated expressions or funny faces to indicate a joke is being told

Deadpan   When a comedian says or does something humorous, but without showing any reaction to the joke work

Canned laughter or laugh track   An audio recording of laughter that is played during an entertaining media program to signal a funny moment or joke in a program

Situation comedies (sitcoms)   Comedy programs that have a set of recurring characters from one episode to the next

Sweetening   An industry term for the use of canned laughter or laugh tracks when broadcasting or producing comedy programs

Copresence   The feeling that a person is using entertainment media at the same time as others or with others

Mere presence   The phenomenon when an individual feels an increased sense of arousal when in the presence of other people

Social presence   The degree to which a person feels that they are in the presence of other people, even when no other people are physically present

Disparagement humor   Humor that puts down or demeans another character or person

Schadenfreude   A German word meaning the pleasure one feels from observing others' suffering

Tendentious humor   Humor in which there is a purpose, such as disparaging a person/group or in which a taboo opinion/topic is described; disparagement humor would be a form of tendentious humor

Nontendentious humor   Humor in which there is no target being disparaged or mocked

Joke work   Any cue that tells the audience that something is not meant to be taken seriously

Buffoon   A character who is the victim of another's jokes; key to tendentious humor

Nonsense humor   Humor that presents a puzzle or incongruous situation and then refuses to solve it; a form of nontendentious humor

Supernatural horror or **Horror of the demonic**   Horror that deals with supernatural forces that disrupts the natural world

Science-fiction horror/ Horror of the Armageddon   Horror that deals with supernatural forces that threaten life and existence

Psychological horror or **Horror of the personality**   Horror that deals with threats from a nonsupernatural person or thing that results in terrible consequences

Morbid curiosity   Fascination with death and destruction

Mastery of affective disturbances   The ability to control one's emotions during a tragic, horrific, or dangerous event

Sanctioning the ultimate outcome   The idea that people enjoy horror because the threat will be stopped and the lead character will be safe at the end

Mystery   A genre in which something has happened and the plot is focused on solving a puzzle

Uncertainty model of mystery enjoyment   An explanation of the appeal of mystery genre suggesting that enjoyment is highest when the mystery resolves following complete uncertainty regarding the narrative outcome

Surprise model of mystery enjoyment   An explanation of the appeal of mystery genre suggesting that enjoyment is highest when the mystery resolves in an unexpected manner usually due to misdirection built into the narrative

Confirmation model of mystery enjoyment   An explanation of the appeal of mystery genre suggesting that enjoyment is highest when the mystery resolves in a way that the viewer expected it to

Suspense   An affective response to narrative that results from the perceived likelihood that something bad will happen to a liked character

Chapter 9

Developmentally appropriate   Media content that matches the mental and emotional competencies of (usually, younger) audiences

Payne Fund Studies   A series of privately funded studies in the early 20th century that investigated how cinema affected children and adolescents

Social scientist   Someone who studies human behavior using the scientific method

Golden age   In reference to film history, The period in cinema history after the invention of synchronized sound that lasted to the 1960s

Magic bullet theory   A paradigm in media psychology research in which it was assumed that media had a direct, powerful, and uniform effects on audiences thoughts, actions, and behaviors

Will Hays   The president of the The Motion Picture Producers and Distributors of America (MPPDA) between 1922 and 1945 who created the Hays Code

Hays Code   A set of rules used by the MPPDA to restrict certain content in films that was deemed inappropriate

The "Don'ts" and "Be Carefuls"   A list of behaviors and features from the Hays Code that were not allowed (the "Don'ts") or should rarely occur ("Be Carefuls") in movies

Ratings system   In reference to entertainment media, a set of labels sanctioned by a given media industry designed to inform audiences about specific types of content such as sexual or violent behavior or language

Comics Code Authority   A ratings system used by the Association of Comics Magazine Publishers

National Association of Broadcasters (NAB)   An industry organization that represents television and radio broadcasters in the United States

Code of Practices for Television Content or **Television Code**   A set of rules used by the NAB to restrict certain content in television

TV Parental Guidelines   A rating system used in broadcast television to inform audiences about specific types of sexual and violent content in a television show

Adolescence   The stage in development between childhood and adulthood

Symbolic thinking   The ability to understand abstract concepts, such as language, math, and social relationships

Intangible   Something that is not physically represented or able to be sensed

Moral reasoning   The ability to rationalize why a behavior in a particular context is right or wrong

Theory of mind   The ability to infer what other people are thinking

Sally-Anne Test   A psychological test of the theory of mind, often used to test theory of mind development in young children

Equilibrium   A period in child development where a child is typically calm and predictable and practices mastery over known skills

Disequilibrium   A period in child development where a child is quickly developing new skills and is uneasy and unpredictable

Neurons   Cells in the brain that transmit information to other cells

Stimulus   In media psychology, the content that one is exposed to such as a specific image or piece of content

Moderate discrepancy hypothesis   A prediction of human learning that suggests individuals need to be exposed to a challenge that is slightly more difficult than their current skill set; challenges that are too difficult will not be effective in increasing learning

Curvilinear   A relationship between two variables in which an effect increases before decreasing; also called a "U-shaped" curve. Curvilinear effects can also work in reverse, in which an effect decreases before increasing (a "reverse U-shaped" curve)

Channel-surfing   When a viewer browses through different television shows in order to select one to watch, usually spending very little time on any given show (or channel)

Saturday morning cartoons   For most of the middle to late 20th Century, US television networks would broadcast cartoons from early morning until early afternoon, referred to colloquially as "Saturday morning cartoons"

Centration   Paying attention to one particularly unique or striking feature of a media character

Sense of self   One's self-awareness that they are a unique individual

Self-report   In media psychology, measuring a person's attitude or belief by using survey questions, usually without researcher involvement

Draw-a-scientist-test (DAST)   A method of measuring an individual's cognitive biases associated with how they view scientists, such as the age, gender, ethnicity, and other personal attributes associated with the profession

Children's Television Workshop (CTW)   A nonprofit organization that created several children educational television shows. Today, the organization is called Sesame Workshop

Sesame Street   A television show created by CTW to teach children basic educational lessons and social skills

Socioeconomic status (SES)   An estimation of an individual's social standing based on a number of factors such as income or occupation

"Rich-get-richer" hypothesis   An argument that predicts individuals who already have a fair number of resources tend to acquire more resources more easily than individuals without resources

Psychological well-being   A family of individual states that relate to one's quality of life apart from physical well-being. States that lead to high levels of psychological well-being include feelings of self-worth, connection with others, capability, and mastery

Emotional intelligence   A person's ability to understand his or her emotions and the emotions of others and to express their emotions during the appropriate settings

Common Sense Media   A nonprofit organization based in the United States that rates media products for their age-appropriateness, and supports research and education into media's impact on children

Screen media   Media that involve visual information, such as televisions and computers

Stereotypes   An generalized belief about a particular group of people

Effect sizes   A standardized measure of how much one variable affects another

Motion Picture Association of America (MPAA)   An industry organization that represents film studios in the United States

Entertainment Software Ratings Board (ESRB)   An industry organization that rates video games for age-appropriateness in the United States

Pan-European Game Information (PEGI)   An industry organization that rates video games for age-appropriateness in Europe

Forbidden fruit hypothesis   Predicts that people will desire more those things that are deemed inappropriate for them by others

Gatekeepers   An individual who has the ability to either block or allow others to consume a media product

Chapter 10

Infotainment or **soft news**   News coverage of information that is primarily focused on entertainment or leisure, or stories of personal interest without major consequences

Hard news   News that cover stories related to current events and issues of great consequence

American Broadcasting Company (ABC)   A major television network established in the 1940s and currently owned by the Walt Disney Company

Columbia Broadcasting System (CBS)   A television network established in the 1940s and owned by the CBS Corporation

National Broadcasting Company (NBC)   A television network established in the late 1930s; currently owned by Comcast

Cable news   News that is produced and distributed by cable stations that is usually delivered on a 24-hour rotation; this contrasts with network news, which is usually only shown at specific times in the morning, afternoon, and evening

High-choice media environment   A media marketplace that is characterized by numerous options and channels available to consumers

American Cool   A vocal tone of news made popular in the middle 20th Century by American news anchors in which the news was delivered in a serious and emotionally neutral style

National Public Radio (NPR)   A nonprofit radio membership organization that provides news and cultural content to radio stations across the United States

Partisan   A type of bias which favors one particular cause or one particular political party over another

News aggregators   Organizations or automated programs that gather news stories from multiple sources into one place for a person to read

Echo chambers   A colloquial term used to critique news organizations for only exposing audiences to partisan news content that fits the audience's currently held political beliefs

Syndicated column   Written content, such as a regularly scheduled newspaper editorial, that is distributed to multiple news outlet

No Spin Zone   A well-known syndicated column written by conservative commentator Bill O' Reilly

Fox News Channel   A cable news station established in 1996 and owned by the Fox Entertainment Group

Poynter Institute   A nonprofit institution for journalism research and professional education in the United States

Associated Press (AP)   A syndication agency based in the United States that is used by multiple newspapers and news stations to report national and international news

Public Broadcasting System (PBS)   A nonprofit television organization in the United States, founded in the mid-20th Century

Morality plays   Used in reference to news coverage that is written to incorporate a conflict between different moral perspectives; for example, stories take on many of the conventions of traditional entertainment storytelling like having heroes versus villains

Problem frames   News stories that emphasize public risks or dangers

The Los Angeles Times   A newspaper founded in 1881 based in southern California but focused on coverage of national and international news; it is routinely one of the largest newspapers in the United States by circulation

Horse race journalism   When news coverage of political elections resemble coverage of a sport competition

Debates   Formal and organized discussions and arguments about topics between candidates for political office, usually held for public benefit

Confirmation bias   The tendency for a person to seek out and pay attention to information that is consistent with their pre-existing beliefs

Political ideology   An individual's own beliefs about social and ethical issues related to law and government

Selective perception bias   The tendency for a person to pay attention to information he or she agrees with while ignoring information they disagree with or even reinterpreting it to support their beliefs

Fake news   News articles that are intentionally misleading and verifiably false

Clickbait   A thumbnail or social media post that entices users with extravagant claims or images, but offers little to no substantive content

Annenberg School for Communication   A school at the University of Pennsylvania, founded in 1958, where the Cultural Indicators Project was conducted

Centralized mass media system   A media system in which a handful of media companies create content for the majority of the available audience

5 o'clock news   A colloquial name for news broadcast in the United States that took place when most adults were arriving home from work, but before a traditional family dinnertime

Web 2.0   An Internet architecture marked by audience participation, such as the ability to create content and directly share that content with others

Chapter 11

The storytelling animal   The idea that humans can be distinguished from other animals by their ability to think and communicate through the use of narratives

Social skill hypothesis or **Entertainment as play**   An argument that narratives are useful as "safe spaces" for audiences to vicariously experience and learn practical social skills, and that individuals use entertainment as a form of simulation

Morality sandbox   The ability for narratives to allow audience to play with what is right and what is wrong, safe from real-world consequences of those decisions

Social Identity Theory (SIT)   A theory that predicts how people identify with and function as members of various social groups

Social categorization   The tendency for people to categorize themselves and others into social groups

Social comparison   The tendency for people to compare and compete themselves with their social groups or their social groups against other social groups

Social identity   The tendency for a people to create a self-identity based on the social groups that they see themselves as part of

Self-esteem   How a person feels about their self-worth

Narrative collective-assimilation hypothesis   Argues that people become more similar to the groups that they read about by adopting the psychological aspects of the characters in those groups

Social surrogacy hypothesis   Argues that characters in entertainment media programming can serve as substitutes for a person's peers or friends

Watercooler effect   The time people spend talking about popular media entertainment in their break time from nonleisure activities, such as work or school; named after an observation that most office employees tend to socialize in break rooms where a watercooler is present

Social capital   The benefits that social networks may offer among people in society

Social desirability   The tendency for a person to behavior in ways that make themselves attractive to others

Geek culture   The community and culture of fans of geek products or material

Cosplay   The act of dressing up as a character from a media entertainment product

Participatory cultures   When fans of an intellectual property both consume and produce media content

Wikis   An online site where individuals can contribute information about a particular topic to build an online encyclopedia; based on the Hawaiian word for "fast" or "quick"

Intra-audience effect   A phenomenon by which individual people in a larger audience are influenced by the emotions and behaviors of the other audience members

Field experiments   Experiments that occur in a real-world setting instead of in a laboratory

Transmission   The purpose of music to communicate some message using lyrics, emotion, beat, or content

Ritual use   A purpose of entertainment media to serve as a form of signaling and a form for social gathering

Black Lives Matter   An activist movement in the early 21st century protesting against police brutality and systemic racism toward African Americans in the US.

Adolescent role moratorium   A period when adolescent break away from existing social structure of the family to form their own social groups

Artificial intelligence   The capacity for machines to possess and display original thoughts and decisions without input from a human operator or programmer

Motion sensor controllers   Any sort of video game controller that uses body movement as inputs

Tandem play   A form of coplaying video games in which one person is in direct control of on-screen action and others are watching and providing input to the player controlling the game

Game streaming   Playing video games while broadcasting or recording the gameplay for online audiences to watch

Basking in reflected glory (BIRG)   When fans increase expressions of their fandom after a win

Cut off reflected failure (CORF)   When fans decrease expressions of their fandom after a loss

Blast   To verbally or physically fight against an opposing fan group

Hierarchy of needs   A theory that argues that humans have to fulfil fundamental needs like food and shelter before they can satisfy higher order needs and wants such as inclusion and self-actualization

Chapter 12

Sunk costs   The time, energy, and money already put into pursuing a goal; in media entertainment, this might refer to investment into an experience or media product

Time-shifted viewing   The ability for audiences to choose when to watch media programming that previously required life or scheduled viewing

Demographics   Objective properties of an individual, such as their age, race, and biological sex

Late-night time slot   Usually considered the time of day between 11:30 p.m. and 2 a.m., a television programming period in which stations and channels may broadcast more adult themed or mature content

Psychographics   Psychological or intangible characteristics of an audience including attitudes, aspirations, and tastes

Taste   The ability to make discriminating judgments about art and artistic matters

Taste cultures   Groups of individuals who have similar values and aesthetic standards

High art   Art that is related to an elite culture and is approved of by cultural critics

Low art   Art that does not have a barrier of entry and is embraced by lower cultural classes or a broad audiences

Asset   Anything that is owned by a company

Vertical integration   An organizational structure in which a company controls numerous aspects of a supply chain; in entertainment media, this might refer to the same company producing, marketing, and distributing media content

Consolidation   An industry structure by which several different companies within a given market are merged into a single entity

Entertainment markets   The markets involved in buying and selling entertainment products

Experience goods   An economic good that has no future value once it is consumed; examples might include a movie or concern ticket

Advertising-supported   A model of media distribution in which media content is sponsored by companies and organizations who pay to feature their brand or product in segments external to the narrative

Subscription   A model of media distribution in which an individual pays directly to have access to content

Bums on seats   The idea that the goal for media creators is to get as many people as possible to pay and consume their content

Air time   An amount of time that companies buy for broadcasting their advertisements during a media event

Rating   The percent of people who own a television that were watching a particular show

Share   The percent of people who were watching television that were watching a particular show

Lowest common denominator (LCD)   The broadest range of audience members available that entertainment can appeal to

Guilty pleasure   A product (such as a entertainment media program) that one consumes even though they feel it has little or no redeeming cultural, social, or critical value

Niche content   Content that appeals to very small and specialized audiences

User-generated content   Any media content that is created and/or distributed by individual users, rather than by a media company

Product placement   The practice of including conspicuous real-world products and brands within the context of a media program

Chapter 13

Medium theory   The idea that media technology, rather than content contained within a medium, can influence users' thoughts, feelings, and behaviors

Media Tetrad   A series of stages that media technologies go through, originally proposed by Marshall McLuhan. The stages are enhancement, obsolescent, retrieval, and reversal

Numerically represented   When information and content is transmitted in a numeric format

Binary code   When data used in computer technologies are transmitted as ones and zeros

Modular   When media content can be broken into pieces and reassembled in other ways

Automatic   When actions can be activated and performed without the input of a user

Variable   When the same media content is accessible on multiple platforms or versions

Transcodable   When media content is in digital format and thus, it can be easily edited or altered into other formats altered

Interactivity-as-product   An understanding of interactivity as being a property of a technology

Interactivity-as-process   An understanding of interactivity as being a property of the technology user

Decision fatigue   Decision fatigue is a state resulting from making too many choices in a row

choice paralysis   choice paralysis is when users feel they cannot choose from options provided.

flow   The mental state of operation in which a person is fully immersed with an activity

autotelic   Defines an activity in which a person engages without receiving any external benefit, motivation, or reward; autotelic activites are those that are done for their own sake

Dynamic difficulty adjustment   In video games, the use of algorithms that automatically adjust a video game's difficulty according to the player's past and current performance

Haptic   In technology, a reference to interface systems that receive inputs through touch or transmit information back to the user through touch

Present   Present means people have the subjective perception of being within a mediated environment

Virtual reality   Virtual reality is a simulated immersive media experience

Augmented reality   The inclusion of virtual objects in a user's real-world field of view-often facilitated by a mobile phone or headset

Simulator sickness   A phenomenon, in which wearing virtual reality helmets can cause bouts of nausea and extreme disorientation

Presence as transportation   The sense that things are are physically present when they are not

Social presence   The sense that a person is sharing space with others that are in a remote location

Presence as social richness   The sense that a medium is sociable, warm, sensitive, personal, or intimate when used to interact with other people

Media richness   The extent to which a medium can transmit audio-visual information

Presences as social actor within a medium   The sense that entities with a mediated experience can be treated as a real people

Medium as social actor   The sense that the medium itself can be treated as a real social actor

Breaks-in-presence   Anything that interrupts feelings of presence

CPSIA information can be obtained
at www.ICGtesting.com
Printed in the USA
LVHW062016110819
627247LV00001B/1/P

9 781524 962739